HOLOCAUST MEMORY IN THE DIGITAL AGE

STANFORD STUDIES IN JEWISH HISTORY AND CULTURE

Edited by David Biale and Sarah Abrevaya Stein

HOLOCAUST MEMORY IN THE DIGITAL AGE

Survivors' Stories and New Media Practices
JEFFREY SHANDLER

Stanford University Press ▐ Stanford, California

Stanford University Press
Stanford, California

Printed in the United States of America on acid-free, archival-quality paper

Library of Congress Cataloging-in-Publication Data

Names: Shandler, Jeffrey, author.
Title: Holocaust memory in the digital age : survivors' stories and new media
    practices / Jeffrey Shandler.
Other titles: Stanford studies in Jewish history and culture.
Description: Stanford, California : Stanford University Press, 2017. |
    Series: Stanford studies in Jewish history and culture | Includes
    bibliographical references and index.
Identifiers: LCCN 2016052823 (print) | LCCN 2016053579 (ebook) |
    ISBN 9781503601956 (cloth : alk. paper) | ISBN 9781503602892 (pbk. : alk. paper) |
    ISBN 9781503602960 (e-book)
Subjects: LCSH: USC Shoah Foundation Institute for Visual History and
    Education—Archives. | Holocaust, Jewish (1939–1945)—Historiography. |
    Holocaust survivors—Interviews. | Collective memory. | Digital media.
Classification: LCC D804.348 .S45 2017 (print) | LCC D804.348 (ebook) |
    DDC 940.53/18072—dc23
LC record available at https://lccn.loc.gov/2016052823

Typeset by Bruce Lundquist in 10/15 Minion

CONTENTS

ACKNOWLEDGMENTS

I began exploring the Visual History Archive (VHA) at Rutgers in 2010, when, thanks to the initiative of Douglas Greenberg, the university first gained online access to the Archive. I am indebted to Doug not only for his sparking of my interest in the VHA but also for his continued encouragement of my work. Conversations with Rutgers colleagues Ethel Brooks, Michael Levine, Karen Small, and Yael Zerubavel have also stimulated my thinking about the VHA, and I am particularly grateful to Yael for prompting me to write my first paper on the topic for a conference at Rutgers in 2011. In addition, I thank the School of Arts and Sciences at Rutgers for providing me with a sabbatical and a fellowship leave, which were essential to the research and writing of this book, and Department of Jewish Studies staff members Sherry Endick and Arlene Goldstein for their help in bringing this book to fruition. During the final year of work on the manuscript, I benefited greatly from the assistance of Valerie Mayzelshteyn, my Aresty Research Assistant at Rutgers, who diligently and thoughtfully examined dozens of segments of VHA interviews and compiled the information in the appendix.

The USC Shoah Foundation provided invaluable assistance to my research, including the opportunity to spend several months in 2013 at the University of Southern California as a visiting fellow. This visit enabled me to learn about the workings of the VHA from its dedicated staff and to discuss my work in progress with them. I am deeply grateful for the generosity with which the Foundation's staff—especially Douglas Ballman, Crispin Brooks, Renée Firestone, Georgiana Gomez, Ita Gordon, Kia Hayes, Karen Jungblut, Dan Leshem, Kim Simon, Stephen Smith, Anne-Marie Stein, Kori Street, and Ari Zev—shared their advice and expertise. During my stay at USC, I also benefited from the counsel of faculty members Wolf Gruner, Tara McPherson, and Michael Renov, and I am particularly grateful to Tara for inviting me to write an essay on some of this research for a special issue of *American Literature*, which she edited, on new media. Part of this essay, "Holocaust Survivors on *Schindler's List*; or, Reading a Digital Archive against the Grain," originally published in the journal's December 2013 issue (vol. 85, no. 4), appears in chapter 2 of this book and is reproduced with permission of Duke University Press.

For their kind assistance during the writing and research of this book, I also thank Rachel Baum, Sarah Bunin Benor, Esther Brumberg, Hinde Burstin, Elizabeth Castelli, Alexandra Garbarini, Bonnie Gurewitsch, Louis Kaplan, Marjorie Kaplan, Judith Keilbach, Todd Presner, Alasdair Richardson, and Melissa Shiff, as well as all the participants in the seminar on Video Interviews of Holocaust Survivors: Intersecting Approaches, convened at the annual Association for Jewish Studies conference in 2013. I am especially indebted to Ayala Fader and Diane Wolf for their insightful comments on drafts of the manuscript. Opportunities to present lectures on aspects of my research at Vassar College, the YIVO Institute for Jewish Research, Humboldt-Universität, the American University of Paris, and Universität Wien afforded me invaluable occasions to learn from audience comments and questions. At Stanford University Press, David Biale, Margo Irvin, Nora Spiegel, Sarah Abrevaya Stein, and Kate Wahl provided vital support and guidance for the development of this publication.

Last, but foremost, I thank Stuart Schear, my partner in life, who has been this book's first reader, sharpest editor, and greatest enthusiast.

AUTHOR'S NOTE

All transcriptions from VHA interviews are mine, except where indicated. Transcriptions of English-language interviews preserve speakers' grammatical irregularities. Ellipses indicate abridgements made by me. Translations from interviews in languages other than English, except where indicated, are mine as well. Names of people are spelled per the listing in the VHA, except where indicated.

I I I

Bracketed additions to transcriptions include the following.

Definitions and translations: *goyim* [**Yiddish: "gentiles"**]. The name of the language is omitted when it is clear. In interview transcriptions, Yiddish is romanized according to the speaker's dialect: *a yid a seykher* [**a Jew (who was) a merchant**].

Referents, added to disambiguate pronouns and other references: **he [i.e., Spielberg]**.

Insertions and clarifications, added when the meaning of the cited text is not readily apparent: **he came . . . to us [in the factory in 19]44, [he was there for] just a few months.**

Descriptions of interviewee's gestures and camera movements: **I start to run, and I feel the first bullet here. (*He points to his left wrist.*) See? The marks are still here. (*The camera pushes in on his forearm, then pulls out again.*)**

HOLOCAUST MEMORY IN THE DIGITAL AGE

INTRODUCTION

On any given day, individuals around the world sit before computer screens to watch and listen to videotaped interviews with Holocaust survivors. More than seven decades after the end of World War II, many people approach this resource with some expectation of what they will encounter, reflecting their various intents: Descendants of deceased Holocaust survivors view these recordings to learn about their ancestors' prewar lives and wartime experiences as well as about relatives killed during the war. High school students are exhorted to listen to survivors' narratives as morally galvanizing exemplars. Historians screen these videos to research instances of Nazi persecution that are otherwise undocumented. Psychologists scrutinize survivors' storytelling for insights into how people cope with trauma. Victims of more recent genocides listen to these recordings to discover how, decades after the Holocaust, its survivors articulate their memories.

At the same time that screening these videos addresses an array of established objectives, the accounts survivors offer are full of surprises. For as much as these interviews are shaped by the protocols of the projects that produced them and by decades of accumulating tropes of Holocaust remembrance, each video documents a singular encounter with an individual who takes a distinct approach to the task of recalling the past. What, then, are viewers of these videos to make of moments when, in the course of describing his or her experience of the genocide, a survivor bursts into song, starts speaking in another language, or exposes bodily scars of wartime injuries? What is the significance of survivors' comparing their own experiences during the war to how the Holocaust is portrayed in a novel or feature film? What might be the value of videos in which interviewers prompt survivors' answers or argue with interviewees? How should one understand those moments when survivors can't recall the past or resist doing so? Moreover, what do these moments reveal about the potential significance of the videos generally, above and beyond the value invested in them by their creators and advocates? And how do these moments elucidate the efforts to record, preserve, and share these memories with this choice of medium?

▌ ▌ ▌

Video recordings of Holocaust survivors recounting their wartime experiences have become a mainstay of how the most notorious genocide of the modern age is documented, studied, and memorialized. There are now tens of thousands of these recordings in archives and libraries around the world. Museum exhibitions dedicated to commemorating the Holocaust show excerpts of these interviews, filmmakers include them in documentaries, and, thanks to the availability of these recordings on videotapes, then on DVDs, and, most recently, through online streaming, students around the world examine them in classrooms or access them on laptops and tablets.

The practice of videotaping survivors arose at a strategic convergence of the dynamics of Holocaust memory practices and innovations in communications technology. During the 1970s, the Holocaust became an increasingly prominent fixture of public culture in the Western world. Holocaust survivors were elevated to a new stature, hailed both as witnesses of unrivaled authenticity to a defining event of modern times and as models of tenacity in the wake of unspeakable persecution. This rise in survivors' prestige correlated with their aging. A growing attention to their mortality heightened the sense of survivors' importance and prompted concerns to preserve survivors' memories in the face of their imminent passing. Though Holocaust survivors had been relating their personal histories since the war's end, the increased sense of urgency to document these recollections prompted the search for new means to do so.

Concurrently, video cameras and videotape players, previously an expensive technology used mostly by professionals in the broadcasting industry, became readily available to middle-class consumers. Video quickly replaced

Super 8 mm film as the preference for making home movies, given the newer medium's increased flexibility for recording and facility of viewing. The ease with which videos could be taped and watched greatly expanded amateur film-making, especially in the "home mode" of recording family life[1]—only to be surpassed in the early twenty-first century by the advent of digital video cameras and smart phones, which have made recording, viewing, and especially disseminating moving pictures even easier. In addition to individual recordings of survivors' memories, typically made by their family members for private use, a number of organized efforts were undertaken to record collections of videotaped interviews with Holocaust survivors. From the mid-1970s to the mid-1990s, more than a score of these archives were established in the Americas, Europe, Israel, and Australia; some recording continues to this day.[2]

In 1994 the project that would come to be known as the USC Shoah Foundation's Visual History Archive (VHA) was initiated. Within a few years, it became the largest and most widely available collection of video recordings of Holocaust survivors' life stories. The beginning of the VHA coincided with an unprecedented level of attention to Holocaust remembrance in the American public sphere, in the form of official days of remembrance, widely seen feature and documentary films, the inauguration of high-profile museums and memorials, a proliferation of education programs, and increased scholarly attention to memory practices centered on the Holocaust. At the same time, the Holocaust loomed large as a paradigm for other genocides as well as an array of large-scale atrocities, even as some works of Holocaust remembrance provoked public controversy.

Though the VHA set out to use state-of-the-art technology to preserve the memories of survivors as this cohort's passing approached, the Archive is itself evidence of how mutable memory practices are and how quickly the media they employ have changed. The VHA was initiated shortly before analog videotape yielded to digital media as the choice for recording moving pictures. The Archive's goal of preserving memories was also challenged by the growing realization that newer media are less stable than older ones. At the same time, the advent of the Internet marked the start of a new era in media practices, transforming the ways in which information could be stored, inventoried, disseminated, and engaged. Digital and online technologies soon became central to the Archive's agenda, facilitating the preservation, indexing, and access of its collection of videos. Thus, as it straddles the temporal boundary marked by the loss of living witnesses to the Holocaust, the VHA also bestrides the transition from the "video age" to the "digital age."

The VHA's conjoining of new media and Holocaust memory practices at this convergence of threshold moments exemplifies the new possibilities and challenges now being addressed in the digital humanities, even as the issues at hand are often specific to the concerns of Holocaust remembrance. Examining the Archive as a subject of interest in its own right engages multiple, interconnected issues: What are the implications of using video to document someone's life history? What impact does using digital media to catalog, index, and disseminate these videos have on the ways they can be engaged? From watching and listening to Holocaust survivors tell their life stories, what can be learned about memory practices, both old (telling stories) and new (screening videos, searching digital databases), as well as their interrelation? How is each video simultaneously a singular account of an individual's personal history and part of a large-scale effort to preserve Holocaust memory? What are the implications of recording these life histories at the turn of the millennium, centered on an event that took place a half century earlier and that has been extensively documented in a variety of media for decades?

❚ ❚ ❚

Holocaust Memory in the Digital Age addresses these and other questions by exploring the VHA's holdings and scrutinizing the Archive as itself a work of Holocaust remembrance. The first chapter, "An Archive in Contexts," provides an overview of the VHA's conceptualization and situates the Archive within a set of historical trajectories and contemporary contexts that inform its content, form, and agenda: Jewish ethnographic projects, dating from the late nineteenth century; the efflorescence in the final years of the twentieth century of public memory projects and new thinking about memory practices, especially those concerning the Holocaust; and the interrelation of media and memory, as shaped by the cascade of new communications technologies of the post–World War II era.

The subsequent chapters present a series of case studies that read the Archive "against the grain"—that is, they use the VHA's rubrics for searching its holdings to examine issues of Holocaust remembrance other than those that are central to the Shoah Foundation's mission. Doing so reveals the Archive's potential as a

resource for subjects beyond the vision of its creators, offering insights into Holocaust remembrance and personal narratives more generally, and revealing how
the apparatus of this resource is an exemplar of digital humanities. These case
studies examine selected interviews to understand how Holocaust survivors relate their life stories within—and sometimes against—the Archive's parameters.
This approach demonstrates how the VHA's indexing and search functions both
facilitate and constrain researchers' inquiries into its holdings and thereby inform the meaning of individual interviews.

The case studies in *Holocaust Memory in the Digital Age* approach these
interviews as cultural works that are complex in form. They are simultaneously
autobiographical narratives, collaborative performances, works of video, and
archival documents. To analyze their multiple aspects, each case study addresses a different key issue for understanding the VHA and its holdings. By
no means do these case studies strive to offer a comprehensive approach to
the VHA; rather, the approach is meant to suggest additional possibilities for
further study of this and similar collections. Nor are the interviews selected for
examination meant to be viewed as representative of the Archive as a whole—
an impossible prospect, given the wide-ranging diversity to be found within
the VHA's extensive holdings. In fact, many of these interviews were chosen
because they are in some way exceptional, and they offer insights into the larger
subject at hand by virtue of their distinctions.

The case studies are grouped according to three basic elements of these
videos: narrative, language, and spectacle. As three of the six elements of drama
enumerated in Aristotle's *Poetics*—*mythos*, *lexis*, and *opsis*—they are venerable
categories of formal analysis. This approach situates VHA interviews within the
extensive history of performed narrative works, rather than confining them to
a particular genre (such as oral history or wartime memoir) or treating them
as exceptional phenomena. In addition, these categories invite analyses of the
VHA that look beyond established notions of the interviews' value or of how
they should be studied, in particular challenging methodologies that neglect
the interviews' mediated nature. Each case study within these categories takes
a distinct approach to its subject of inquiry, defined by the scope of material
selected from the VHA, which varies from a single interview to selections from
among thousands of possible segments, and by analytic approaches apposite to
the particular topic.

Chapter 2, "Narrative: Tales Retold," challenges the widely held notion that video interviews with Holocaust survivors provide eyewitness accounts of unrivaled immediacy by analyzing how these life histories are informed by other narratives, whether storytelling encountered in the mass media or a survivor's own prior accounts. In addition, this chapter examines how survivors incorporate reflections on the practice of recalling the past within the telling of their personal histories. Though speech is fundamental to these videos' creation and reception, their analysis often disregards survivors' choice of language as a topic in its own right. Chapter 3, "Language: In Other Words," considers distinctive examples of survivors' engagement with language that reveal their investments in its symbolic value, focusing on the role of Yiddish in hundreds of these videos. Chapter 4, "Spectacle: Seeing as Believing," probes the visual aspect of video interviews with Holocaust survivors, which, though much acclaimed, has received relatively little scholarly discussion. To ascertain how spectacle informs the videos' creation and reception, this chapter examines exceptional moments in VHA interviews that disrupt the Archive's austere visual aesthetic of "talking heads," including survivors' display of wartime injuries, prisoner tattoos, and religious artifacts.

Together, these case studies address tensions central to the VHA. Though each recording is a singular work, all these interviews are shaped by the larger project of the Shoah Foundation, which enabled their creation, provided guidelines for their recording, and facilitates their preservation, storage, cataloging, dissemination, and access. As extensive as the Archive is, its interviews present the recollections, thoughts, material relics, and performances of only those survivors willing and able to offer their personal histories, each related on a certain day to a particular interviewer. These tensions do not diminish the value of the VHA's videos but inform their significance and are emblematic of memory practices in the digital age.

As is true of any archive, a test of the VHA's value lies in what can be found within its holdings above and beyond what its creators envisioned. By probing the Archive in this manner, *Holocaust Memory in the Digital Age* explores the possibilities of working both with and against the matrices that structure digital humanities resources. Thus, as this book addresses issues that are particular to recalling the Holocaust, it considers larger questions about the interrelation of media practices and memory practices at this threshold moment in their respective histories. Indeed, the VHA's conjoining of new media and memory, at a time of heightened concern about both the transformative potential of digital humanities and the future of Holocaust remembrance, exemplifies the new cultural possibilities and challenges now being addressed in digital humanities.

1

AN ARCHIVE IN CONTEXTS

The Visual History Archive: An Overview

The USC Shoah Foundation's Visual History Archive—the largest and most widely available collection of videotaped interviews with survivors and other witnesses of the Holocaust—began, we are told, serendipitously, in the wake of creating another work of Holocaust media. While making the 1993 feature film *Schindler's List*, director Steven Spielberg talked with a number of Jewish Holocaust survivors who are referred to in German as *Schindlerjuden* (Schindler Jews). During World War II they had been imprisoned in the Cracow ghetto and the Płaszów concentration camp when they were conscripted by the film's protagonist, Oskar Schindler, an ethnic German businessman and Nazi Party member, to work in his factories in Cracow and, later, Brünnlitz. Schindler's efforts saved these Jews from harsher treatment—and the possibility of death— during the war. In addition to some of the *Schindlerjuden* whose stories figure in the book by Thomas Keneally on which *Schindler's List* is based, Spielberg met other survivors who sought him out at their own initiative in Poland, where most of the film was shot.[1] Unlike most people who might show up uninvited at the set of a Hollywood feature, these men and women were not turned away. Rather, the makers of *Schindler's List* reported that speaking with survivors helped the film's storytelling to "be more authentic." Over a hundred *Schindlerjuden* also appeared in the film's epilogue, a tribute to Schindler filmed at his gravesite in Jerusalem.

Spielberg's encounters with survivors while directing *Schindler's List* prompted him to envision a follow-up project to the film. After considering the possibility of a documentary on the *Schindlerjuden* he had met, Spielberg eventually proposed interviewing "as many Holocaust survivors as possible."[2] By April 1994, a plan to establish what was first known as the Survivors of the Shoah Visual History Foundation (referred to hereafter as the Shoah Foundation) was under way, with the initial goal of interviewing fifty thousand survivors within three years. Eventually, the Foundation recorded over fifty-one thousand interviews with survivors and other eyewitnesses to the Holocaust, conducted in fifty-six countries and in thirty-two languages, between 1994 and 2000.[3] Profits from *Schindler's List*—unanticipated by either the director or the film's producers, who did not expect it to be a commercial success—provided initial financial support for creating what is now known as the Visual History Archive (VHA).

The VHA is far from the first effort to record and collect videos of Holocaust survivors' personal narratives. Yet from the start, the Archive was conceived on a grander scale than all previous projects, most of which had been undertaken by preexisting institutions dedicated either to research on the Holocaust or to some related topic, such as local Jewish history or World War II remembrance. By contrast, the Shoah Foundation was established for the specific purpose of creating the VHA. The Archive was envisioned as a stand-alone resource, international in its reach, surpassing other similar projects in range, quantity, and prominence. Inaugurated in the mid-1990s, when most Holocaust survivors were senior citizens, the VHA was also driven by a sense of urgency, "a race against the clock" of an aging cohort of interviewees.[4] In contrast to other oral history collections, assembled for research purposes with more constrained and selective inventories of interviews, the VHA's scope is manifestly monumental, similar to other memorial impulses that strive to demonstrate the Holocaust's enormity and to recall as many names of the genocide's victims as possible.

Despite the project's envisioned vast scale, and energized by the acute time pressure, the VHA came together swiftly, involving many hundreds of people as coordinators, advisers, videographers, interviewers, technicians, indexers, and educators. To recruit interviewees, the Shoah Foundation publicized its mission in mainstream media as well as through survivor communities' social networks. Seeking a diversity of interviewees, the Foundation made special efforts to include Jewish survivors living in eastern Europe and those who are *haredim* (Hebrew: "God-fearing," referring to those Jews who are most stringently observant of traditional religious practices and, at the same time, most resistant to integration into a cultural mainstream), populations largely absent from older videotaping collections.[5] Though the project centered on Jewish survivors, members of other groups persecuted by the Nazis—Sinti and Roma, political prisoners, Jehovah's Witnesses, homosexuals, survivors of eugenics policies and of forced labor—were also interviewed, as were various eyewitnesses to the Holocaust: rescuers, aid providers, liberators, and participants in war crimes trials.[6] The Shoah Foundation recruited a wide variety of people to conduct the interviews.[7] Rather than employing only scholars of the Holocaust, psychotherapists, or experts in documenting oral histories, as some other videotaping projects have done, the Archive's creators have argued that the interviewers' "diversity of backgrounds and experience . . . made the archive richer." At the same time, the Foundation ran training programs for its interviewers in order to establish a "consistent methodology" for their work by providing background information on Holocaust history and guidance on interviewing practices.[8] Even though interviewers sought to conform to the Foundation's standards, the interviews vary considerably in approach, reflecting the diversity of both interviewers and interviewees.

The Shoah Foundation also established protocols to standardize the project's recruiting, record keeping, videotaping, and inventorying. After contacting the Foundation and providing basic information about his or her wartime experience, each survivor was assigned to an interviewer. Several days before the taping session, the interviewer spoke with the survivor to collect answers to an extensive preinterview questionnaire, which asked for detailed information about the survivor's family background and wartime experiences, as well as the particulars of prewar and postwar life. Gathering this information was primarily intended "to serve as a guide for the interviewer." In addition, this task provided the survivor and interviewer with an opportunity to establish a rapport with each other, and, perhaps most importantly, it enabled survivors to reflect on the impending task of relating their life histories.[9]

Both interviewers and videographers were given detailed guidelines regarding the form of the interview and its documentation.[10] Interviewers were instructed to begin and end with specified questions and to progress chronologically though the survivor's life story, devoting proportionally more attention

to the Holocaust period than to the prewar or postwar era. While advising interviewers that "preparation and research are vital" to the task, the Foundation
also instructed them to avoid turning the interview into "a 'question and answer'
session" and counseled that an "ideal interview consists of open-ended questions that allow the interviewee's testimony to flow."[11] The tension between these
divergent goals is resolved differently in each recording, reflecting how each interviewer and survivor approached the task at hand as well as the nature of their
relationship with each other. Following the interview proper, videographers were
to film a separate sequence documenting the survivor's photographs and other
memorabilia and to record a group interview with members of the survivor's
family. For each of these sequences the Shoah Foundation's guidelines specify
the composition of shots, lighting, and camera movement.

Standardization of the VHA is perhaps most readily evident—and most
consequential—not in the interviews themselves but in their inventorying and
indexing, as these are the rubrics through which users access the Archive's
holdings. The act of searching the Archive's online databases precedes the
users' screening of survivor interview videos, becoming not merely the instrument of access but the primary activity for engaging this repository of memory.
While the videotaping of interviews was under way, the Shoah Foundation
began the task of developing a computerized system for searching and access-
ing interviews, creating a customized matrix of search terms specific to the Archive. The decision had been made to index the videos, rather than transcribe
them, as both a more expedient undertaking and a more useful aid to researchers.[12] The VHA's vast size can make the prospect of searching among its many
thousands of hours of video seem daunting. The Archive's creators realized
that addressing this challenge was essential to its use, even if doing so would
complicate the integrity of individual recordings as discrete narratives. "Each
of the nearly 52,000 testimonies of survivors and other witnesses of the Holocaust, preserved for all time, is invaluable," the Shoah Foundation explained on
its website in 2007. "However, the full social and educational potential of the
Foundation's archive cannot be realized without creating an effective means for
future viewers to search through the tens of thousands of hours of testimony."[13]

Like the VHA itself, the index is vast, consisting of over fifty thousand "experiential" and "geographic" search terms. It is structured as a taxonomy, with
search terms nested within a graduated series of broader topics. For example,

one of the index's twenty-two main headings is "daily life," within which are seven subheadings, including "family life." This term is divided into more than a dozen categories, among them "childbearing," which is, in turn, subdivided into "camp childbearing," "forced march childbearing," "ghetto childbearing," and five other search terms. Search terms are keyed to particular interview segments during which interviewees discuss these topics.[14] The experiential search terms are generalized, enabling users to cross-reference interviews tagged with the same term, including interviews in various locations and languages.

In addition, each search of the VHA using an index term can be "filtered"— that is, the list of interviews tagged with a given term can be narrowed by the criteria of interview language, gender of interviewee, and "experience group" (e.g., Jewish survivor or liberator). Searches can also be conducted for the names of particular people, places, events, or institutions. Searching multiple terms (e.g., finding interviews in which both "early personal aspirations" and "school antisemitism" are discussed) can further winnow interview selections.[15] Even when one narrows the scope of interviews by a particular search term, language, location, and type of interviewee, the search can yield dozens, even hundreds, of segments.

As is true of archives generally, access to the VHA is not simply facilitated but structured by its index and search functions. As philosopher Jacques Derrida observes, an archive's "technical structure . . . determines the *archivable* content . . . and its relationship to the future. The archivization produces as much as it records."[16] As with other large-scale indexed works, much of what one might find in the VHA, except by chance, is determined by what is itemized in the index. Its terms and structure reflect core goals of the Shoah Foundation for the Archive's use: As a memorial project, it endeavors to list the name of every person mentioned during the interviews, including survivors' family members and other acquaintances, many of whom died during the war. As a documentation of Holocaust history, the VHA's index references locations, events, and core experiences of the genocide; the indexing of interviewees' prewar and postwar experiences is both less extensive and less specific than the wartime portions of their narratives. As an instrument of moral edification, the Archive indexes terms that tag interview segments in which survivors reflect on ethical issues or on lessons of the Holocaust (e.g., "future message," "Holocaust education," "Holocaust testimony sharing willingness").

Implementation of the index relies on the properties of video and digital technologies. Video both enables continuous recording for an extended period of time (tapes used for VHA interviews run thirty minutes each) and facilitates the articulation of the interview into discrete segments, measured by the recording's time code, to which index terms can be tagged. The Archive atomizes and reconfigures the running flow of video through its digitization: first, by means of the VHA's index, which isolates segments of interviews according to its taxonomy; second, through the VHA's search function, which culls segments from multiple interviews, according to a user's choice of criteria, and aggregates these segments into pools of information. This property of the VHA, in effect, enables survivor interviews to tell different stories, which are engendered neither by the interviewees nor by the Shoah Foundation, but by users of its Archive.

The Foundation's protocols, the videotaped interviews created according to these guidelines, and the archival structure that inventories and indexes these recordings to facilitate their access are more closely interrelated than is generally the case in archives, including digital collections. The VHA's holdings were recorded expressly for this collection, which distinguishes them from many, if not most, documents in paper archives as well as media archives, whose holdings were originally created for other purposes and users. Moreover, the VHA's digitized interviews are connected online with their cataloging and indexing as part of an integrated database and retrieval system. When summoned through the Archive's search mechanisms, videos appear on computer screens alongside the display of information that inventories the recordings and identifies particular segments. For users, the videos do not exist as works independent of the Archive's digital framework.

Even as digitization transforms how these recordings are stored and searched, the original thirty-minute videotapes on which the interviews were recorded remain a vestigial presence and structure the interviews' flow. Interviewers can be heard informing interviewees that they are near the end of a tape, and subsequent tapes typically begin with the interviewer iterating the identifying information stated at the beginning of the first tape or providing some narrative transition from the previous tape. Thus the constitution of the VHA is manifest not only in its index and databases but also in the individual video recordings within the Archive, each of which bears the imprint of the Shoah Foundation's protocols and, in turn, exemplifies the VHA in miniature.

The VHA's online viewing screen surrounds the video of the survivor interview (center) with links to metadata and indexing information (lower left), a scrolling display of indexing terms for the video segment as it plays (lower center), and a world map identifying locations mentioned in the interview (right). Provided by the USC Shoah Foundation.

The digitization of the Archive's holdings poses distinct opportunities and challenges for their storage, dissemination, and preservation. On one hand, digital media are well suited to the duplication of information, enabling the production of a potentially infinite number of copies that replicate the original perfectly, and to its dissemination among multiple users in widely dispersed locations. The Shoah Foundation's planners envisioned making its collection of videos available through an online data retrieval system early in the institution's history, at a time when the Internet was just becoming widely used as a tool for sending and receiving text messages. As a result of its pioneering work on indexing and cataloging videos, as well as creating a digital platform for their viewing online, the Foundation holds patents on eleven technological innovations.[17]

On the other hand, digital video recordings are unstable—in some respects, more mutable than, say, celluloid films or paper transcripts. The binary code that is the foundation of all digital materials is stored on a substrate— whether a compact disc, a hard drive, or the remote server of a computer "cloud"—that can easily be corrupted. Preservation of the VHA's holdings became "another race against time," echoing the initial urgency with which these interviews had been recorded. Given that one of the VHA's primary goals is sustaining Holocaust memories "in perpetuity," the task of maintaining the Archive's recordings is doubly onerous, as it ties the upholding of remembrance to the conserving of media.[18]

The VHA's duplication of its interviews in different media and formats is central to the Archive's preservation efforts and demonstrates the rapid changes in technologies that have taken place since its initiation. Videographers recorded the interviews on Betacam SP format videotapes, the broadcast industry standard in the mid-1990s. Once delivered to the Shoah Foundation, these analog tapes were duplicated and coded for entry into the Archive's master database. One copy of the interview was digitized for storage in a 150-terabyte robotic retrieval system, which enables users to access and navigate the entire collection. In 2009, the Shoah Foundation began saving its original master tapes as Motion JPEG 2000 files, the format that "the Library of Congress has decided to use . . . to archive its video collections." To do this, the Foundation "utilizes advanced dual robot technology to digitize, preserve, and access the testimony in the archive. One robot digitizes the Institute's original testimonies into various file formats for preservation and access. Once digitized, the nearly 52,000 testimonies are transferred to a second robot, which serves as an online storage system for the Institute's archive."[19]

Disseminating the VHA's holdings has followed a similar dynamic of shifting media and formats, reflecting technological developments as well as the Shoah Foundation's evolving mission. The Foundation first presented excerpts of its interviews to the public in compilation documentaries, beginning with *Survivors of the Holocaust* (1996), and eventually produced eleven documentary films. In 1999 the Foundation issued *Survivors: Testimonies of the Holocaust*, the first of its educational CD-ROMs, which use the medium's capacity to hyperlink materials in multiple formats (video, audio, still images, text) to enable users to explore connections between survivor interviews and a selection of supporting materials, such as time lines, archival photographs, maps, and reference materials.[20] These CD-ROMs all pursue specific pedagogical goals that determine which interviews or parts of interviews are presented and how they should be studied.[21]

Concurrently, the Shoah Foundation explored the possibility of making its collection available online to researchers and teachers to enable them to undertake their own studies of the Archive's holdings. Doing so entailed developing new technology as well as addressing concerns specific to the material at hand, especially fears among interviewees that "the detailed personal information they'd provided could find its way into the wrong hands," including those of Holocaust deniers. Unlike the more restrictive policies of other collections of Holocaust survivor interviews, the VHA elected to pursue means to "provide the broadest possible access" to its holdings, while also caring for them "ethically and responsibly," by taking what the Shoah Foundation characterizes as a "techno-optimist line that the information revolution was a good thing."[22]

The Foundation initiated a series of projects that follow the rapid development of digital and online technologies to make its archival holdings available. Beginning in 1999, the Foundation established access to collections of VHA interviews at museums and research institutions, including the Simon Wiesenthal Center in Los Angeles, the Joods Historisch Museum in Amsterdam, and the Jüdisches Museum Berlin. In 2012, the VHA was installed in the Los Angeles Museum of the Holocaust in an exhibition called *Tree of Testimony*. "Part monument and part informational presentation," the installation takes the form of "a 70-screen video sculpture displaying all of the [Shoah Foundation's] nearly 51,000 video testimonies over the course of a single year." Visitors can access the sound track of an individual interview, as it plays on one of the screens, using the museum's audio guides.[23] While the visual display is monumental in scope, the visitor's audial encounter with the exhibition is more intimate. Each museumgoer listens on headphones to one selected interview at a time, while simultaneously seeing—but not hearing—dozens of other interviewees talking.

Following the advent of the computer networking consortium Internet2, the Shoah Foundation began to offer universities and research institutions an online subscription service to the full VHA in 2002. Online platforms that facilitate use of a more limited, but still sizable, collection of complete interviews followed.[24] IWitness, a website launched in 2009, was designed primarily for use in American secondary schools. The site provides a "guided exploration" of over 1,500 VHA videos, which combines learning "first hand from survivors and witnesses of the Holocaust" with "participatory" use of

Tree of Testimony exhibition, designed by E. Randol Schoenberg and Hagy Belzberg, installed in 2012 at the Los Angeles Museum of the Holocaust. Courtesy of Los Angeles Museum of the Holocaust.

the collection through a "built-in online video editor" that enables students to "build [their] own video projects." IWitness explains to students that the site offers "the opportunity to enrich your understanding of how this historical event had an impact on individual lives" while learning "important digital media skills, including searching and ethical remixing, that will prepare you for becoming a digital citizen in the 21st century."[25] Through this site, the Foundation situates its videos as moral touchstones by virtue of both content and form, while inviting students to sample the VHA for cinematic narratives of the users' creating. IWitness proffers the exercise of making one's own compilation video as an opportunity for ethical instruction in its own right, extending the Foundation's conviction that viewing the Archive's interviews has a morally galvanizing power.

The Shoah Foundation's mission evolved considerably over the first two decades of its existence, expanding in several capacities. First, the Foundation broadened the scope of its collection by taking a wide-ranging approach to Holocaust remembrance, most recently extended to include interviews of Jews who lived in North Africa and the Middle East during World War II and who "witnessed the destruction created there by Nazi occupiers or governments that were Nazi sympathizers."[26] In recent years, the VHA has integrated into its holdings video interviews with Holocaust survivors conducted by other institutions.[27] Moreover, the Foundation has undertaken the recording or preserving of audiovisual interviews with survivors of mass murders in Armenia, Guatemala, Nanjing, and Rwanda.[28] Some of these interviews have also been integrated into the VHA and its index, enabling researchers to examine common topics among survivors of different atrocities. Second, the scope of the Shoah Foundation's efforts to present its holdings to the public developed through a variety of media as well as through training programs, colloquia, and other events for teachers and researchers. In 2001, the Foundation redefined its mission, stressing a focus on educational use of the VHA "to overcome prejudice, intolerance, and bigotry—and the suffering they cause."[29] Besides creating pedagogical materials and hosting teachers' workshops on its own, the Foundation has collaborated on Holocaust education with other organizations, including the Anti-Defamation League and Yad Vashem, Israel's Holocaust memorial and research center.[30]

In 2006 the Shoah Foundation affiliated with the University of Southern California and is now known as the USC Shoah Foundation: The Institute for Visual History and Education. This relationship has enabled the Foundation to expand scholarly work on the Archive through teaching, research fellowships, and academic conferences. Its presence at USC also provides the Foundation with opportunities to explore new technologies for preserving and providing access to interviews with survivors of mass atrocities. Among these endeavors is New Dimensions in Testimony, developed in concert with the USC Institute for Creative Technologies, which will enable audiences "to interact personally with testimony through true holographic display" of a Holocaust survivor. Audience members' questions, asked of an animate, three-dimensional image of the interviewee, will trigger apposite prerecorded responses, stored in a database, by means of a "technology called Natural Language Understanding."[31] While this project continues the Shoah Foundation's mission to use state-of-the-art technology to record and disseminate survivors' memories, the interactive holograph shifts the mode of engaging survivors' memories from searching and utilizing the extensive amount of information to be found in the VHA to interacting with a simulation of a living survivor. At the same time, the Foundation continues to develop the VHA, initiating in 2016 a multiyear

plan "to design and implement a new Visual History Archive platform and interface that will offer enhanced functionality and better search results, improve
access by building new pathways across a variety of devices for audiences to
view and utilize testimony, and develop multi-modal support resources."[32]

I I I

The VHA is an exceptional resource: daunting in its scope, elaborate in its
structure, dynamic in its sense of mission, vigorous in its engagement of the
public. The Archive not only is widely used but also has been the subject of
extensive attention, both positive and negative. Before we examine the VHA as
a major artifact of Holocaust memory and a notable work of digital humanities
by probing the Archive's holdings, a manifold understanding of the project in
context is called for. Given the complexity of the VHA, this entails examining
its place within multiple frames of reference, defined by its subject, historical
moment, and medium.

Jewish Ethnographic Projects

The VHA's reach extends beyond Jewish experiences to include interviews with
other survivors of Nazi persecution and witnesses to the Holocaust as well as
survivors of other mass murders. Nevertheless, the motive for creating this archive originated with Steven Spielberg's desire to document the life histories
of Jewish Holocaust survivors. They constitute by far the largest group interviewed for the VHA (49,871 individuals), and, as the institute's name manifests,
they remain fundamental to the Shoah Foundation's definition of its mission,
even as it extends to addressing other atrocities. Moreover, the project's origins
and its core subjects situate the VHA within the annals of Jewish ethnographic
projects, especially those that study East European Jewry, dating back more
than a century before the Shoah Foundation was initiated. Though the VHA is
in some respects a singular undertaking, its similarities with these earlier endeavors in form, content, and agenda indicate the considerable extent to which
the work of the Shoah Foundation rests on previous investments in the value
of ethnographic work for understanding Jews' past and informing their future.

The first efforts to use modern research methods to document Jewish life
in eastern Europe took place in the late nineteenth century. Among these was

an 1890 expedition to collect demographic and ethnographic statistics on Jews living in provincial towns in Congress Poland. This endeavor—underwritten by Jan Bloch, a financier and economist who, though a convert to Catholicism, remained dedicated to Jewish philanthropy—was intended to refute accusations that Jews were economic parasites and draft evaders. One of the people collecting statistics was Yitskhok Leybush Peretz, who would soon become a leading figure in modern Jewish letters. Then a young, budding writer, Peretz described his experiences on this mission in a narrative published in 1891.[33] As all other records of Bloch's expedition were lost, Peretz's account, a landmark work of Yiddish literature, remains its sole legacy.

Amid growing interest in the practice of ethnography in the early twentieth century, East European Jews established a number of projects to collect Jewish folklore. The most ambitious and extensive of these efforts were expeditions organized by the writer and activist S. An-sky (the pen name of Shloyme-Zanvl Rappoport) during the years 1912–14. In addition to playing a pioneering role in the field of Jewish folkloristics, An-sky's career embraced literature (he is best known for his drama *The Dybbuk*) and political and social activism. An-sky's expeditions, underwritten by the Günzburgs, a family of Jewish philanthropists in St. Petersburg, were not the first efforts to collect folklore among East European Jews but at the time were the most extensive and elaborately planned undertakings of this sort. An-sky had prepared an extensive questionnaire in advance of the expedition, so as to gather information on folk beliefs and practices systematically. Though this project centered on "salvage" ethnography— using modern methods of documentation to preserve a record of cultural practices understood as being in danger of disappearing—An-sky was equally invested in future possibilities for Jewish folkways. His vision for the outcomes of these expeditions was expansive, including scholarly publications, creative works of music, theater, and visual art based on folk materials, and a network of museums to exhibit artifacts gathered by this project. The expedition made use of what was then state-of-the-art technology: photographing people, buildings, and other subjects and recording folk music on wax cylinders. Given the newness of the enterprise, An-sky's team of researchers was diverse, including young scholars, students, artists, and musicians with an interest in Jewish folkways.[34] An-sky intended to make a comprehensive survey of provincial Jewish communities throughout the Russian Empire's western provinces. But two

Zusman Kiselgof, a member of S. An-sky's ethnographic expedition, making a field recording in Kremenets, Russia, in 1912. Courtesy of Archives of the YIVO Institute for Jewish Research.

years into the project, the outbreak of World War I brought these expeditions to an abrupt end.

The new nations established in eastern Europe after the war offered unprecedented opportunities for their citizens, including Jews. Of particular note for Jewish ethnography was the work of the YIVO Institute, established in 1925 in Vilna, then part of Poland. YIVO (a Yiddish acronym for *Yidisher visnshaftlekher institut*, "Institute for Jewish Research") was an independent scholarly institution dedicated to the study of East European Jewry and Yiddish culture, subjects that then received scant attention in universities. The institute collected a variety of materials, initially focusing on documenting waning traditional folkways and then expanding to include contemporary ethnography. To carry out these projects, YIVO established a network of amateur collectors. The institute's mission was complex, committed to conducting dispassionate scholarship while also demonstrating the value of East European Jewish culture. YIVO saw its scholarly work not merely as documentary but also as engendering resources for the future; it characterized *visnshaft* (research) as *visn vos shaft* (knowledge that creates).[35]

During the years that YIVO began its work, scholars in state-run research academies in the Ukrainian and Belorussian Soviet Socialist Republics undertook ethnographic studies of Jewish life in the USSR. This research was part of a larger flourishing of Yiddish culture in the Soviet Union during its first decades, unprecedented in both state support and governmental oversight, working within the mandate that all national minority cultures conform to Marxist scholarly principles and advance the establishment of a socialist state. Soviet researchers produced pioneering works of scholarship on Jewish language, folk music, and the economy of provincial towns. Here, too, amateurs were enlisted in the task of collecting ethnographic information for scholars.[36] Concurrently, American Jewish philanthropies, notably the Joint Distribution Committee, engaged social scientists to study Jewish life in eastern Europe, in order to assess how best to provide financial aid to communities suffering from impoverishment and discrimination and how to campaign effectively on their behalf in the public sphere.[37] The commitment to Jewish ethnography continued even during World War II. In the ghettos established under German occupation in Łódź and Warsaw, groups of volunteer researchers documented the devastating impact of imprisonment on the Jewish population, creating secret archives of material at great risk to their lives. These materials, recovered after the war, became essential resources for scholarship on the Holocaust.[38]

For decades after the war it was all but impossible to undertake ethnographic studies of East European Jews in situ, given the political regimes under which they lived, yet efforts to document their prewar culture flourished elsewhere, especially in the United States and Israel. Whereas Israeli scholarship on prewar European Jewish life was centered in state-run universities and research institutes (especially Yad Vashem), postwar American scholars of this subject were based in private universities as well as independent research centers, notably the Leo Baeck Institute and the YIVO Institute, both headquartered in New York. Among the most influential early postwar efforts was the 1952 anthropological study *Life Is with People: The Jewish Little-Town of Eastern Europe*, by Mark Zborowski and Elizabeth Herzog. Their book evolved from a wartime scholarly project, pioneered by anthropologist Ruth Benedict, of conducting fieldwork "at a distance"—that is, interviewing immigrants and refugees living in America about their cultures of origin.[39] At the same time that scholars were researching and writing *Life Is with People*, Jews who had lived in communities throughout eastern Europe—both those who had immigrated before World War II and Holocaust survivors—began to produce *yizker-bikher* (Yiddish: "memorial books"), anthologies of recollections of prewar life in individual Jewish communities and accounts of their destruction during the Holocaust. Eventually numbering in the hundreds, these self-published books provide local history as recalled by eyewitnesses together with their memorialization of murdered relatives and neighbors.[40]

Perhaps the most elaborately structured scholarly effort to collect information on the prewar culture of East European Jews is the *Language and Culture Atlas of Ashkenazic Jewry* (*LCAAJ*), initiated by linguist Uriel Weinreich at Columbia University in the late 1950s. The *LCAAJ* charts the configuration of Yiddish dialects of the immediate prewar period across northern Europe, using responses from over six hundred native informants to a 220-page questionnaire. Like earlier ethnographic projects, the *LCAAJ* made use of new technology as well as more vestigial media. Its interviews were recorded on reel-to-reel tape and then transcribed; computers were used to compile some data, but maps delineating the project's findings were hand-drawn. Decades later, the *LCAAJ*'s recordings were digitized and its maps computerized, and this material has been made available online.[41] Anthropologist Barbara Myerhoff initiated a pioneering work of American Jewish ethnography in the mid-1970s, when she studied a community of elderly Jews, working-class immigrants from eastern Europe who had retired to Venice, California. This study, published as *Number Our Days* in 1978, championed the value of life review as an essential component of the task of growing old. Myerhoff's work played a leading role in promoting the documentation of life histories among the elderly. While she primarily used established methods of anthropological fieldwork (participant observation, interviewing), Myerhoff also collaborated with filmmaker Lynn Littman to make a documentary about this community of elderly Jews, and her work inspired a play and a traveling exhibition.[42]

The VHA resembles these and other Jewish ethnographic projects in several noteworthy respects. Like the mission to collect statistics in which Peretz took part, An-sky's folklore expeditions, and the compiling of *yizker-bikher*, the VHA began as a privately funded project, operating independently of academic and governmental agencies. As is true of most of these earlier undertakings, the Archive centers on salvage, striving to preserve information understood as being in danger of disappearing. Like An-sky's expeditions, the wartime ghetto archives, *Life Is with People*, and the *LCAAJ*, the VHA is an undertaking on a grand scale, collecting large amounts of information so as to offer a comprehensive vision of its subject. To fulfill a mission of this scope, the VHA enlisted a wide range of participants to help interview Holocaust survivors, much as YIVO and Soviet researchers recruited amateur folklore collectors during the interwar years and former members of Jewish communities in eastern Europe collaborated to compile *yizker-bikher*. As is true of several of these undertakings, the VHA has employed state-of-the-art technologies for documenting its subjects. Like An-sky and Myerhoff, the VHA has pursued multiple formats for sharing its resources with the public—in this case, documentary films, pedagogical materials, online access, and museum display. Like Soviet scholarship and *Number Our Days*, the VHA is understood to have value for others beyond the community being researched, offering insight into the human condition generally and providing inspiration for a better future for humankind. As is true for most of these projects, the investment in collecting information according to methodical protocols is tied to—and is in tension with—a deeply felt commitment to the people being studied. And though these projects span more than a century, they share a sense of urgency—a conviction that their work must proceed swiftly, whether because of pressing, sometimes life-threatening circumstances or because of the passing of an aging generation and, with it, information of historical value on a unique way of life.

The connection of the VHA to Jews' ongoing investment in undertaking self-reflexive ethnographic studies may be obscured by the Shoah Foundation's expansion beyond interviewing Jewish survivors to include other survivors and witnesses of the Holocaust and of different atrocities altogether. This development reflects larger trends in Holocaust scholarship and pedagogy that situate the Holocaust within the comparative study of genocide and other human rights violations. Nevertheless, key characteristics of the VHA—and, moreover, its very existence—are indebted, if obliquely, to these earlier Jewish ethnographic projects and to a widely shared conviction among Jews that such initiatives are worthwhile. Though it predates the Holocaust, this conviction deepened considerably in the postwar era, as scholars of Jewish life and Jewish community leaders alike turned to ethnographic research in order to address contemporary concerns. Beyond the dedication of academics, writers, filmmakers, philanthropists, and activists, these projects have enjoyed support from members of the Jewish public, whether as participants in the research, funders of the organizations undertaking this work, or audiences for these projects' outcomes. A similar commitment has been instrumental to the realization of the VHA from its origins to the present.

Memory at the Turn of the Millennium

In addition to situating the VHA diachronically, in the history of Jewish ethnographic projects, we can contextualize the Archive synchronically, among a remarkable range of political events and cultural endeavors relating to memory in the public sphere that flourished during the final years of the twentieth century. This proved to be a watershed period for projects and discussions of public memory practices, especially in Europe and the United States. These undertakings include films, telecasts, museum exhibitions, memorials, public art works, and pedagogical and scholarly initiatives. Though not all of these phenomena address Holocaust memory, the subject looms large in this new attention to memory practices and serves as a paradigm in many late twentieth-century discussions of public memory generally.

This threshold moment engaged events that were both long anticipated—notably, the fiftieth anniversary of World War II—and unexpected, especially the collapse of communist rule in eastern Europe, interethnic warfare in the Balkans, the Rwandan genocide, and the end of apartheid in South Africa. Both kinds of events proved to have a strong resonance with the Holocaust, including those connected with this genocide's paradigmatic status, rather than its history. The period's anniversaries and political events inspired a wide array of public culture endeavors as well as scholarship devoted to examining recollections of the past as a subject of interest in its own right. Initiated at this time, the VHA echoes some of these undertakings' key concerns and agendas, and it engages similar larger questions about memory practices.

World War II was by far the most anticipated event memorialized in the 1990s, with fiftieth-anniversary commemorations marking key dates from Germany's invasion of Poland on September 1, 1939, through Japan's surrender to the Allies on August 15, 1945. These anniversaries called attention to the aging of combat veterans and others who had lived through the war, including

Holocaust survivors. In the United States, this cohort was hailed as the "Great-est Generation," a term made popular by journalist Tom Brokaw's eponymous book of 1998.[43]

The salience of World War II remembrance in the 1990s was heightened by end-of-century retrospectives. Consider, for example, the choice of Albert Einstein as the "Person of the Century" by *Time* magazine, an extension of its practice of honoring a Man (later, Person) of the Year on its cover since 1927. When *Time* announced that it would name a Person of the Century at the end of 1999, the selection of this individual prompted extensive public discussion in the American media. As *Time* eventually reported, its readers submitted many letters nominating someone for the honor, a selection of which appeared in the issue honoring Einstein.[44] Prominent among the nominees were figures whose renown (or infamy) was tied, at least in part, to World War II, including Frank-lin Delano Roosevelt, Winston Churchill, Adolf Hitler, and "the American GI," as well as Einstein. To many people drawn to this topic, it seemed self-evident that the war was the central event of the twentieth century and that its history might be conceptualized as leading up to, and then away from, the war years.

Key dates in the history of the Holocaust were marked amid the fiftieth-anniversary commemorations of World War II. In fact, these memorial events began beforehand, notably remembrances of Kristallnacht, the state-mandated violent attacks on Jews and their property that took place on November 9–10, 1938, throughout Germany and Nazi-controlled territories in Austria and Czechoslovakia. Some public events recalling events of the Holocaust also looked forward, such as the official opening of the US Holocaust Memorial Museum in Washington, D.C., on April 22, 1993, timed to coincide with the fif-tieth anniversary of the Warsaw Ghetto Uprising. The same year also witnessed the opening of Beit Hashoah—Museum of Tolerance in Los Angeles, as well as the premiere of *Schindler's List*, prompting *ABC News Nightline* to proclaim 1993 the "year of the Holocaust" in a late December telecast.[45]

Concomitant with the long-anticipated anniversaries of World War II were several large-scale, transformative events that took many people by surprise: the reunification of Germany (1990), following the fall of the Berlin Wall the previ-ous year; the demise of communist regimes in eastern Europe, the undoing of the Warsaw Pact, and the end of the Soviet Union (1989–91); the end of apart-heid in South Africa (1990–96); the murderous "ethnic cleansing" operations

in the Balkans, following the collapse of Yugoslavia (1991–95); and the genocide of the Tutsi in Rwanda (1994). These events came to be implicated in the
decade's recollections of World War II and of the Holocaust, either because of
their political resonance—notably, the reunification of Germany and the fall
of communism in eastern Europe, marking the end of the Cold War that had
begun in the aftermath of World War II—or because of their significance for
human rights, whether positive (the end of apartheid) or negative (genocides
in the Balkans and Rwanda). In particular, public discussion of these outbreaks
of mass murder often characterized them as "another Holocaust."

These anticipated memorial occasions and unforeseen events sometimes in-
tersected in provocative ways—for example, the coincidence of East Germany's
opening of the Berlin Wall with the fifty-first anniversary of Kristallnacht on
November 10, 1989. At the inaugural ceremonies of the US Holocaust Memorial
Museum, Holocaust survivor Elie Wiesel, who had chaired the commission that
led to the museum's creation, appealed to President Clinton, as he sat among
the world leaders attending the event, to "do something to stop the bloodshed"
in the Balkans. Clinton also addressed ethnic cleansing in the former Yugoslavia in his remarks at the ceremony, stating that "we are reminded again and
again how fragile are the safeguards of civilization."[46] The readiness with which
observers continued to draw parallels between the Holocaust and genocidal
attacks in the Balkans provoked outcries in North America and Europe, which
eventually prompted NATO's military intervention in the conflict.[47]

This surge of anticipated and unanticipated events at the end of the twentieth century helped inspire a proliferation of works that interrogated the nature of Holocaust remembrance, and of memory practices generally, in the
public sphere. Created in different countries in Europe, the United States, and
Israel, these works reflect local responses to recalling the Holocaust. Germany
witnessed a spate of memorial projects and artworks centered on the Nazi era,
the Holocaust, and the Cold War, especially in Berlin, a city transformed by the
reunification of its eastern and western sectors. Among these efforts are what
came to be known as "countermonuments" to Holocaust remembrance. As these
works recall the genocide perpetrated by Nazi Germany, they offer a critique of
established memory practices through aesthetic strategies that flout the conventions of public memorials, especially the monumentalism associated with fas-
cism, by creating memorial works that are, for example, small, underfoot, or

empty, or that disappear. Countermonuments demand a different kind of engagement with both the Holocaust and the implications of recalling this abject moment in Germany's history within the country's contemporary landscape.[48]

After the fall of communism in eastern Europe, travel to places in Poland associated with the Holocaust burgeoned. In addition to the sites of former death camps or ghettos, visitors have flocked to Cracow and environs for "Schindler's List" tours, which take participants both to locations where Spielberg's film was made and to places where some of the wartime actions depicted on screen actually took place (the two are not always identical). The slippage in these tours between sites of World War II history and those of film history elides the border between the Holocaust and its representation and thereby "opens up new possibilities for the subjunctive experience of entering a film's virtual world" as a form of Holocaust remembrance.[49]

With the passing of time, the significance of recalling the Holocaust in the public sphere evolved, reflecting the dynamic concerns of various rememberers as well as developing knowledge of the genocide itself. As a result, some of the earliest works of Holocaust remembrance were reworked or replaced, reflecting changes in sensibility as to how this episode of history should be recalled. In Israel, plans to replace the history museum at Yad Vashem with a new building and core exhibition began in 1993. (The new museum eventually opened in 2005, replacing the previous one, which, when it had opened in 1973, was hailed for its innovative approach to exhibiting a historical narrative.)[50] The three most popular representations of Anne Frank, perhaps the best-known victim of Nazi persecution, were reconfigured during this decade: the Anne Frank Fonds in Basel issued a new, "definitive" redaction of her diary in 1991; in the mid-1990s the Anne Frank House in Amsterdam underwent extensive renovations that reconfigured how visitors tour the building where the Frank family had hid during the war; *The Diary of Anne Frank*, the diary's only authorized dramatization, first staged in 1955, was substantially revised for its first Broadway revival in 1997.[51] These efforts reflect changes in public knowledge about Anne Frank's years in hiding and her death as well as new valuations of her life and work.

The revival of *The Diary of Anne Frank* was but one of a series of high-profile works of Holocaust remembrance realized during the 1990s in the United States, where the genocide had come to loom large in the nation's public culture as a moral exemplar. Prominent among these undertakings were the opening of three major museums dedicated in whole or in part to the Holocaust in Washington, D.C. (the US Holocaust Memorial Museum), Los Angeles (the Museum of Tolerance), and New York (the Museum of Jewish Heritage— A Living Memorial to the Holocaust, in 1997) and the presentation of Academy Awards to six feature and documentary films dealing with the Holocaust (*Schindler's List*, 1993; *Anne Frank Remembered*, 1995; *One Survivor Remembers*, 1995; *La vita è bella (Life Is Beautiful)*, 1998; *The Last Days*, 1998; and *Into the Arms of Strangers: Stories of the Kindertransport*, 2000). In addition, the prominence of the Holocaust in the American moral landscape was affirmed and increased at local levels, notably through the expansion of Holocaust education. To cite but one example, in 1994 the New Jersey State Legislature passed a resolution requiring all public school students to learn about the Holocaust not only as a subject of interest in its own right but also as a means to "emphasize the personal responsibility that each citizen bears to fight racism and hatred whenever and wherever it happens."[52]

The study of cultural memory practices emerged as a fixture of the academy in the final years of the twentieth century, involving scholars of anthropology, history, literature, and sociology, among other fields, based in Europe and America. Landmark works include French historian Pierre Nora's essay on what he termed "les lieux de mémoire," translated into English in 1989; his longer work on this subject, published in several volumes in French in 1984–92, appeared in English translation (as *Realms of Memory*) in 1996–98.[53] The year 1989 also witnessed the publication of anthropologist Paul Connerton's *Bodily Practices: How Societies Remember* and the debut of the journal *History and Memory*, devoted to "Studies in Representation of the Past," founded by Holocaust scholars Saul Friedländer and Dan Diner.[54] Holocaust remembrance figured prominently in the conceptualization of memory studies as a field. Indeed, scholars posthumously situate one of its major founding figures—the Belgian sociologist Maurice Halbwachs, who inaugurated study of what he termed "collective memory" in 1925—within the penumbra of the Holocaust. Halbwachs was arrested by the Gestapo for anti-Nazi activity and was imprisoned in Buchenwald concentration camp, where he died in 1945.[55]

During the 1990s, scholars published key works on Holocaust remembrance, including pioneering studies of monuments (James Young) and photography (Marianne Hirsch) as works of cultural memory.[56] Several scholars addressed the interrelation of history and memory in studies centered on the Holocaust (Saul Friedländer, Berel Lang) or on Jewish history writ large, culminating in the Holocaust (Pierre Vidal-Naquet).[57] Other scholars analyzed Holocaust remembrance in particular countries, notably Germany (Dan Diner, Andreas Huyssen), Israel (Tom Segev, Yael Zerubavel), Poland (Iwona Irwin-Zarecka, Michael Steinlauf), and the United States (Peter Novick).[58] Following scholarship on Holocaust literature, art, and film published in earlier decades, the 1990s witnessed studies of the Holocaust in other media, including the first books on videotaped interviews with Holocaust survivors (Geoffrey Hartman, Lawrence Langer).[59] The Holocaust proved so central to the field of memory studies that in 1998 historian Dominick LaCapra characterized this area of scholarly inquiry as standing "in the shadow of the Holocaust."[60]

The heightened attention to memory practices during this period extended beyond the academy to the public sphere, where a number of works of Holocaust remembrance engendered highly publicized controversies. The issues raised in these debates are not all of a kind; rather, they evince a range of concerns about the aesthetics, ethics, and politics of remembering the past. The controversies around Holocaust remembrance demonstrate the extent to which it had come to attract regular scrutiny by the final years of the twentieth century, so much so that debating the appropriateness or legitimacy of these representations has, in itself, become part of remembering the Holocaust.

As the genocide came to be widely considered an extreme event that, according to Friedländer, tests the "limits of representation," questions frequently arose as to what aesthetic was appropriate for Holocaust remembrance.[61] Prompting the debates on this issue were works about the Holocaust that made pointed use of media or genres generally considered inimical to the subject's gravitas and enormity. The publication of Art Spiegelman's *Maus* (1986, 1991) prompted considerable critical opprobrium both for his use of comics (or "comix," Spiegelman's preferred term) to relate the story of a Holocaust survivor's wartime experience and for the artist's depiction of Jews as mice, even as many readers admired *Maus* for its self-reflexive engagement with the challenge of representing the Holocaust.[62] In the late 1990s a spate of comedic films set during the Holocaust—Radu Mihaileanu's *Train de vie* (*The Train of Life*, 1998), Peter Kassovitz's *Jakob the Liar* (1999), and especially Roberto Benigni's *La vita è bella* (*Life Is Beautiful*, 1997)—raised questions about the appropriateness of comedy as a genre for recalling so powerfully tragic an episode of history.[63]

The extensive epiphenomena surrounding *Schindler's List* included controversies over the propriety of Holocaust representation, ranging from the film's depiction of violence to the choice of music for its epilogue.[64] In addition, the growing investment in Holocaust remembrance as a moral paradigm engendered another set of controversies tied to the film, concerning proprietary rights to the topic. Among these were contentious incidents that took place at special screenings of *Schindler's List* for American high school students, at which the film's paradigmatic value collided with challenging analogies to the Holocaust, including the abortion rights debate and the civil rights movement. These controversies raised larger questions about Americans' use of the Holocaust as a paradigm for a wide array of social concerns, a practice consistent with Spielberg's explanation of his film as being "about human suffering. About the Jews, yes, because they were the ones Hitler wanted to annihilate. But it's [also] about AIDS, the Armenians, the Bosnians. It's a part of all of us."[65] Common to these and other controversies over Holocaust remembrance were the conversations they prompted in the press, schools, houses of worship, and other forums. Even as these discussions sometimes assailed the memory project in question, they furthered the value of Holocaust remembrance by reinforcing its significance as a locus of reflection about the implications of recalling the past generally.

Some Holocaust memory practices attracted extensive attention at the end of the twentieth century, involving artists, scholars, critics, politicians, as well as members of the public. At times, especially in instances of controversy, the discussion of memory practices reached larger audiences than the practices themselves. Occurring at an especially momentous time, this engagement with remembrance in the public sphere responded both to anniversaries that marked the aging of a generation of witnesses to World War II, widely considered the defining event of the century, and to concomitant major shifts in world politics. That these manifold changes coincided with the turn of the millennium no doubt heightened public attention to what was "ending" or "disappearing." The notion that public memory stood at a threshold in the 1990s was especially acute with regard to the Holocaust. The imminent passing of Jewish survivors constituted a loss not only of eyewitnesses to the genocide but also of the last generation to recall life in Europe when the continent had been a major center of Jewish religious, political, and cultural activity.

During the half century following World War II, the Holocaust emerged as a subject of importance in world culture both in its own right and as a paradigmatic event. For example, UNESCO promotes Holocaust education internationally, in order "to better understand the causes of Europe's descent into genocide; the subsequent development of international law and institutions designed to prevent and punish genocide; and that the careful comparison with other examples of mass violence may contribute to the prevention of future genocides and mass atrocities."[66] Increasingly, the Holocaust figures as a paradigm for discussing other events, including large-scale persecutions, both older (massacres of Native American peoples, slavery in the Americas) and more recent (mass murders in Indonesia, Cambodia, Guatemala, Yugoslavia, Rwanda, Chechnya, Sudan), as well as political conflicts (notably in the Middle East) and an array of social issues: the AIDS pandemic, animal rights, the nuclear arms race, and world hunger, among others. The paradigmatic value of the Holocaust has proved especially powerful in the United States, where few people have lived who were directly implicated in this event, and where the public has always encountered this subject at a distance, through some form of mediation. By the last years of the twentieth century the Holocaust was established as a mainstay of American public education and the nation's civil religion, realized in memorial programs, monuments, and institutions on a grand scale.[67]

As one of the many works of Holocaust remembrance realized in the 1990s, the VHA engages several issues that figure in the decade's discussions of memory in the public sphere. The Shoah Foundation's intensive efforts to videotape survivors in "a race against the clock" reflects larger concerns of the imminent passing of a singular generation, as the motive to record these interviews responds to mounting questions of how Holocaust remembrance will change when there are no longer any living eyewitnesses. Discussions of the interrelation of history and memory informed the VHA's interviewing protocols regarding scholarly notions of historical accuracy, authority, and reliability vis-à-vis survivors' recollections and their authenticity. The paradigmatic value widely ascribed to the Holocaust informs the Shoah Foundation's motive for recording and disseminating survivor interviews as a morally galvanizing resource that will help "overcome prejudice, intolerance, and bigotry," extended to addressing other genocides. At the same time, the Foundation's vision of the VHA as a memorial endeavor suggests that the Archive is a kind of countermonument. As a work of public memory vast in scope, yet made not of stone but of digital media, the VHA is, in effect, a monument experienced not in space but in time. In this respect, the VHA also figures within the long-standing discussion of the interrelation of media and memory.

Memory, Media, Technology

The VHA connects communications technology with Holocaust remembrance as each phenomenon stands at a threshold of major change. As a consequence, the Archive raises larger questions about the interrelation of media and memory that are both very timely and resonant with long-standing concerns dating back to ancient times. In the fourth century BCE, Socrates famously cautioned against the consequences of relying on writing as a memory aid, arguing that it "will introduce forgetfulness into the soul of those who learn it: they will not practice using their memory because they will put their trust in writing, which is external and depends on signs that belong to others, instead of trying to remember from the inside, completely on their own."[68] Not only did writing become a fixture of memory practices, while transforming the way that people remember, but almost two millennia after Socrates the advent of print in the West engendered unprecedented consequences for remembering by means of the written word. The rapid pace with which new communications technologies have appeared since the Industrial Revolution has engendered a cascade of innovative uses of media, especially still photography and motion pictures, as means of remembrance. These developments have prompted an extended discussion of the interrelation of photography and memory, in which this medium is often seen as inimical to remembering. Thus, in *Camera Lucida: Reflections on Photography*, critic Roland Barthes insisted that "not only is the Photograph never, in essence, a memory . . . , but it actually blocks memory."[69]

Today scholars ponder the impact of the Internet, with its "sophisticated algorithmic search engines," on how people remember. As a consequence of ready access to an unrivaled wealth of information online, psychologists Betsy Sparrow, Jenny Liu, and Daniel M. Wegner argue, people "have lower rates of recall of the information itself and enhanced recall instead for where to access it. The

Internet has become a primary form of external or transactive memory, where information is stored collectively outside ourselves." Echoing concerns voiced by Socrates some twenty-five centuries earlier, these authors posit that "processes of human memory are adapting to the advent of new computing and communication technology. . . . We are becoming symbiotic with our computer tools."[70]

Work began on the VHA as this latest watershed development in communications technologies was under way. The Shoah Foundation used analog-format videotapes to record its interviews and, in its first years, relied on the telephone, fax, mail, and print media to communicate with the many people involved in the project. Concurrently, digital media and the Internet were coming into widespread use, fostering expansive new possibilities for creating, copying, integrating, disseminating, and engaging with information. Since its inception, the VHA has grappled with the possibilities and challenges that new media offer for memory practices. In doing so, the Archive stands as a landmark in the annals of Holocaust remembrance, which, literature scholar Alan Rosen notes, has from the start "been bound up . . . with technological advance and obsolescence."[71]

Jews in Europe began to document their personal experiences of Nazi persecution during the war. In addition to group documentary projects, such as those undertaken in the ghettos of Łódź and Warsaw, many individuals kept diaries, wrote narratives, or created artworks. From 1941 through the end of the war, Soviet filmmakers recorded evidence of the mass murder of East European Jews at numerous locations, including death camps and sites of executions by German mobile killing units. Some of this footage was used in propaganda films shown within the USSR or was screened as evidence at war crimes trials.[72]

Following the end of World War II, new efforts were initiated to document what survivors of the genocide had witnessed. Individual survivors began to write memoirs chronicling their wartime experiences. Over time, many of these texts have been published, and some widely read, while others remain private manuscripts. Institutional efforts to collect eyewitness accounts of Nazi atrocities also began in the war's immediate aftermath. These undertakings include the work of Jewish organizations in Europe, Israel, and the United States as well as government officials in Germany and Poland tasked with gathering evidence for war crimes trials or restitution claims.[73] These documentary efforts were primarily in written form, whether penned by the survivors themselves or by interviewers.

Among these early efforts to document the genocide, one seldom hears recordings of survivors speaking about their own experiences. Radio news reports on the liberation of concentration camps were narrated by journalists, most famously Edward R. Murrow's broadcast of April 15, 1945, about Buchenwald.[74] Though the US Army Signal Corps and the British Ministry of Information made extensive film records of conditions in liberated concentration camps in April and May 1945, almost all the footage is silent.[75] In these films, as well as those made during the war by Soviet filmmakers, survivors of the genocide are seen but seldom heard.

An outstanding exception amid these early documentations is the work of American psychologist David Boder, who traveled on his own to displaced persons camps and other sites in western Europe in the summer of 1946 to interview Holocaust survivors, documenting them on what was then state-

American psychologist David Boder, documenting interviews with Holocaust survivors on a wire recorder in Europe, 1946. Courtesy of University Archives & Special Collections, Paul V. Galvin Library, Illinois Institute of Technology.

of-the-art equipment: a wire recorder. Boder conducted 119 interviews, which provide the earliest substantial opportunity to hear survivors speak at length about the war. His audio recordings also reveal the challenges Boder faced in ascertaining how to interview survivors about their wartime ordeals, as the wide-ranging scope of the genocide was still becoming known.[76]

Though Boder published transcripts of his interviews, translated into English for an American readership, the recordings themselves were not widely heard until they were transferred to digital files and posted on the Internet in 2000.[77] Many Americans first listened to accounts of Jewish persecution during World War II enacted in radio dramas (notably *The Battle of the Warsaw Ghetto*, first aired on NBC in the fall of 1943).[78] In the early postwar years, American radio and television broadcasts occasionally offered dramatic portrayals of the Holocaust and provided a few opportunities to hear from survivors themselves. *Reunion*, a radio program produced by the Jewish philanthropic organization United Service for New Americans, broadcast an episode in 1947 in which Siegbert Freiberg, a Holocaust survivor, was reunited on air with his father.[79] In 1953, the popular television program *This Is Your Life* honored Hanna Bloch Kohner on the first of several episodes that the series aired devoted to a Holocaust survivor. These early broadcasts relate survivors' stories within the strictures of the programs' rubrics. On *This Is Your Life*, for example, Kohner's story is told to her by others, following the conventions of the series, while she says relatively little herself.[80]

As scholars have often noted, the value accorded to Holocaust survivors and their personal histories in the public sphere increased substantially over the half century following the war.[81] The media involved in disseminating these stories both enabled and informed this development. For example, the war crimes trial of Adolf Eichmann, held in Jerusalem in 1961, is regularly cited as a threshold event in public attention to Holocaust survivors and their stories. The trial not only placed the eyewitness accounts of dozens of survivors of Nazi persecution at the center of attention (unlike the Nuremberg war crimes trials, which focused on perpetrators and documentary evidence) but did so on television, where parts of the proceedings were seen by millions of viewers in thirty-eight countries.[82] As the first court case of any kind to be televised internationally, the Eichmann trial provided an audience of unprecedented scope with opportunities to hear and watch Holocaust survivors testify about the ordeals they had endured under Nazi persecution.

The wide availability of audiotape recorders, beginning in the 1950s, and videotape recorders, starting in the 1970s, enabled a new kind of documentation of survivor narratives. Once again, these efforts included both personal recordings, typically made by a survivor's family members, and institutional projects. Some organizations that had collected written accounts of survivors' wartime experiences began recording them with these new technologies. For example, Yad Vashem started archiving written accounts of survivors' experiences in the late 1940s, shortly after it had been established; it began recording survivors on audiotape in 1954 and on videotape in 1989.[83] The Center for Holocaust Studies, Documentation, and Research in Brooklyn, New York, one of the first institutions in the United States dedicated to this subject, recorded 2,747 oral history interviews with survivors and other witnesses to the Holocaust between 1974 and 1989; almost all of these were audio recordings.[84] The Jewish Holocaust Museum and Research Centre in Melbourne, Australia, began taping audio interviews with survivors in 1987 and then switched to video in 1992, eventually conducting some 1,400 interviews in both media.[85] Beyond expanding the inventories of Holocaust survivors' personal histories, these recordings have transformed the way that survivors' recollections are documented, stored, accessed, and studied. For example, communications scholar Amit Pinchevski argues that the turn to videography to record Holocaust survivor narratives in the 1970s, especially at the Fortunoff Video Archive for Holocaust Testimonies, facilitated the advent of a scholarly "discourse of trauma and testimony," for which the medium of videotape served as "the technological unconscious" by enabling closer scrutiny of survivors' oral accounts than had previously been possible.[86]

In the United States, early efforts to videotape interviews with Holocaust survivors emerged in the late 1970s in relation to televised commemorations of the Holocaust. The project that eventually became the Fortunoff Archive began in 1979 with an impromptu spate of interviews for a local television documentary on the dedication in New Haven, Connecticut, of a monument to victims of the Holocaust.[87] Journalist Judith Miller situates the ensuing videotaping project as a riposte to the 1978 NBC miniseries *Holocaust*:

> Though the program scored record ratings and was widely credited with having
> prompted interest in the Holocaust among young Americans and Europeans,

survivors in Connecticut and elsewhere were angered by what they saw as the program's trivialization of the searing experiences. "Everything had been taken from them. Now television was trying to take away their stories too," said [Fortunoff project manager Joanne] Rudof.[88]

The first videotaped interviews of Holocaust survivors were recorded as they attracted increased public attention. In the United States, this included extensive media coverage of events in which survivors were central figures: a legal dispute in the late 1970s over an American neo-Nazi group's bid to march through the Chicago suburb of Skokie, home to a large number of Jewish survivors, and an international gathering of Jewish survivors convened in Jerusalem in June 1981, the largest such event held until then. During the 1980s, a spate of documentary films about the Holocaust was produced, either for theatrical release or for television broadcast, in which survivors' voices predominate.[89] In addition, the plans of large-scale exhibitions on the Holocaust in major museums in Washington, D.C., Los Angeles, and New York all involved projects to videotape survivor interviews, so as to incorporate excerpts of these recordings into exhibitions.

At the start of the twenty-first century, fewer survivors' life stories are being recorded on video, and the preservation and dissemination of these recordings rely increasingly on digital technologies. They pose new challenges to the interrelation of media and memory, even as these technologies are widely used to remediate earlier forms of communication, including films, videos, photographs, visual artworks, sound recordings, maps, tables, print materials, and manuscripts. The impact of digital technology on older media can destabilize their communicative powers—or, at least, trouble long-held assumptions about their value as media—in ways that suggest an undoing of media as memory aids. Film critic J. Hoberman notes that digital technology "broke the special relationship between photography and the world" by disrupting the notion that a photographed image was "a form of evidence."[90] Photography scholar Fred Ritchin argues that the photograph's "perceived credibility has also been purposely misused to manipulate the public since the medium's inception." Therefore, he posits that the advent of digital photography, "noted for its nearly effortless malleability, provides a propitious moment to ask whether this evidentiary role can and should be retained, or even expanded."[91]

The advent of the Internet promised to transform not only the sharing of information in a virtual public space of unprecedented reach but also the very nature of how the public might be constituted. The implications of this new medium for memory practices are unresolved: On one hand, the anarchic, utopian potential ascribed to the Internet in the 1990s might seem inimical to works of remembrance, given that so much of the attention to memory practices has focused on established, venerable media, such as monuments, memoirs, and photographs. On the other hand, as "a medium that collects and stores, that forgets nothing,"[92] the Internet might seem to offer the potential to stabilize and preserve memories on an unprecedented scale. Yet this is a misleading promise, as it assumes a conceptualization of how the human brain remembers that neuroscientists were challenging as use of the Internet was becoming more widespread and diversified. "Cognitive scientists commonly speak of human memory as a kind of information-processing device—a computer that stories, retains, and retrieves information," psychologist Daniel Schacter observed in 1996. "Although this sort of analogy does capture some of memory's important properties, it leaves no room for the subjective experience of remembering incidents and episodes from our pasts." Thus, Schacter asks, "Could a computer ever feel that a memory belongs to it?" Similarly, he argues, "The brain does not operate like a camera," nor does memory work "like a video recorder, allowing us to replay the past in exact detail." Rather, he argues, "Memories are built from fragments of experience" in what psychologists term "an encoding process—a procedure for transforming something a person sees, hears, thinks, or feels, into a memory."[93]

The VHA proffers a resource that strives to transcend the mutability of human remembrance by preserving survivors' recorded memories "in perpetuity." But this promise is complicated by the dynamics of the Archive's creation and operation: its scope and mission continually expand and shift, the technologies it uses are regularly outmoded and superseded, and the Shoah Foundation's commitment to provide public access to the VHA's holdings fosters manifold new understandings of these recordings' significance, extending beyond the original vision of the Archive's purpose. The Foundation's protean character might seem to be inimical to remembrance, but this quality is in fact emblematic of the inherent instability of memory. The desire to arrest the past in unwavering recollections has powerful appeal, but this notion controverts the nature of memory as subjective, relational, and contingent. The VHA embodies this tension both in the interviews housed within the Archive and in the way that it guides users to search for memories. In this respect, the VHA is an exemplary subject for the study of memory practices and new media in their manifold complexity.

NARRATIVE
Tales Retold

The various projects undertaken to videotape Holocaust survivors' life histories rest on the conviction that these narratives constitute unrivaled resources about the genocide, whether for the eyewitness information they provide or for the morally galvanizing impact the narratives can have on others, especially through the medium of video. These projects vaunt their recordings as "raw documents" with an unrivaled immediacy and authority,[1] surpassing the abundance of other narrative sources on the same events, including official reports, journalistic accounts, wartime diaries or letters, memoirs, literary works, and analyses by historians or other scholars. Thus the videotaping project of the Holocaust Education Foundation, established in Chicago in 1983, hailed its recordings as "authentic, first-hand testimonials" that were "unrehearsed, unedited, and often never before told." The project's creators championed video for its ability to bridge the past and present: not only in making "history come alive" but also in redressing wrongs of the past by enabling survivors to say what "they could have spoken at an earlier time if only there had been listeners" and even by "giv[ing] voice to the thousands who were killed and were unable to speak."[2] Video, in effect, was envisioned as undoing past injustices, such as ignoring survivors, as well as reanimating the past and even the dead.

The salience accorded to survivors' eyewitness accounts of the Holocaust does not rest on a long historical precedent. Historian Alexandra Garbarini notes that the extensive reports from victims of anti-Jewish violence in Ukraine during the Bolshevik Revolution and Russian Civil War generally met with public incredulity. This response necessitated "establishing a credible account of the pogroms," because

> the evidence did not speak for itself. Experts reading documents, not documents on their own, established the truth about these pogroms. . . . The victims of the Ukrainian pogroms could not speak, either in person or in writing, in an unmediated fashion by dint of having simply "been there." Their accounts were crucial evidence, but they needed to be vouched for and presented by "experts" recognized as having authority to speak on behalf of the victims.[3]

Following this precedent of collecting evidence to be scrutinized by dispassionate professionals, intensive efforts to collect eyewitness accounts from Holocaust survivors began in the immediate aftermath of World War II.[4] However, the high regard now publicly accorded their recollections emerged later. As historian Annette Wieviorka observes, these early projects were largely "closed to the outside"—that is, they were undertaken not to be presented to a general public but to provide resources for scholars and jurists. Similarly, the early postwar publications of individual or collective memoirs of prewar life and wartime experiences addressed an audience that primarily consisted of the authors' cohort of fellow survivors and refugees. Wieviorka postulates that the widely followed war crimes trial of Adolf Eichmann in 1961 marked the "advent of the witness" by situating survivor testimony at the center of the prosecution's case against Eichmann.[5] This strategy was intended as much to instruct an international public about the Holocaust as to provide evidence against the defendant, if not more so. The Eichmann case is now widely cited as a threshold event in public consciousness of the Holocaust, significant not simply for increasing awareness of the genocide but for shaping how it has come to be conceptualized as a discrete episode of history, distinct from narratives of Nazism or World War II, and one in which Jews both figure centrally as subjects and play a leading role in its narration.

The Eichmann trial marks a shift more in the reception of Holocaust narratives than in their production, which by 1961 had established their own repertoire of topics and conventions of storytelling. These tropes were reinforced by the considerable extent to which survivors' narratives were created for an audience largely composed of other tellers of similar stories and often were the product of collective memory projects. Moreover, the narratives that Jewish Holocaust survivors produced during the first postwar decades draw on precedent narrative practices, ranging from liturgical and literary works and scholarly studies to autobiography, diary keeping, and oral storytelling.[6] These models continued to inform the narratives offered in survivor videotaping projects. Nevertheless, the life stories that survivors relate on video differ substantially from earlier narratives in several key respects, even though interviewees often iterate certain Jewish storytelling conventions and address similar topics, such as observing religious traditions or establishing a new life after moving to another country.

Social contexts play defining roles in determining which stories people choose to tell and how they relate their stories. In her analysis of East European Jews' narrative traditions, folklorist Barbara Kirshenblatt-Gimblett characterizes their storytelling—whether a Hasidic rebbe's spiritually charged relating of tales to his followers, a parent's parable offering moral instruction to a child, or a group of adults trading stories on related topics during casual conversation—as a practice that "always seems to occur as part of another activity."[7] The narratives that Holocaust survivors offer in these collections of videos, by contrast, do not emerge from within other activities but rather are initiated as entities unto themselves and as singular occasions for storytelling, undertaken for the express purpose of being recorded. As literature scholar Aleida Assmann notes, "In the case of video testimony . . . the purpose of preserving and storing a narrative is inscribed into the very genre. From the start, its function is to transform the ephemeral constellation of an individual voice and an individual face into storable information and to ensure its communicative potential for further use in an indefinite future."[8]

Similarly, there are noteworthy distinctions between survivor narratives and those offered by elderly Jewish immigrants, such as the community studied by Barbara Myerhoff in the 1970s. She characterized her subjects, who had immigrated to the United States from eastern Europe at the turn of the twentieth century, as "an invisible people, marginal to mainstream American society, an impotent group—economically, physically, and politically."[9] Their personal histories, told largely to one another, Myerhoff argued, constituted a self-reflexive act of validating their lives in response to being largely ignored or held in low regard. The videotaping of Holocaust survivors' stories took place under quite dif-

ferent circumstances, as their collective public stature was rising in renown and
esteem, defined in large measure by their ability to offer eyewitness accounts of
extreme experiences. Indeed, widespread use of the term *survivors*, which con-
notes tenacity, to identify this cohort epitomizes the transformation of its stature by the end of the 1970s. In the immediate aftermath of World War II, these
people were typically referred to in language that signaled their deprivation and
liminal status: refugees, Europe's homeless, displaced persons, and, within the
Yiddish-speaking community, *sheyres hapleyte* (rescued remnants).

A series of other interrelated factors distinguish these survivors' videotaped
life stories from earlier works of Jewish autobiography as well as from other
Holocaust accounts. To begin with, the videos offer narratives within the rubric
of the interview—that is, a unilateral dialogue, with one person asking questions, the other providing answers. The protocols for interviewing Holocaust
survivors in these videos typically strive to "give the initiative to the witness.
The witnesses are the experts in their own life story, and the interviewers are
there to listen, to learn, and to clarify."[10] Yet even as interviewers are instructed
to be "unobtrusive" enablers of narrative "flow,"[11] their questions—and their
very presence—shape survivors' storytelling.

Similarly, the use of video to document these interviews informs what survivors tell their interviewers and how they do so. As literature scholar James
Young notes, video foregrounds the process of remembrance by recording "both
the witness as he makes his testimony and the understanding and meaning of
events generated in the activity of testimony itself." Consequently, observers of
these videotapes "become witness not to the survivors' experiences but to the
making of testimony."[12] Video's ongoing documentation of survivors' every utterance foregrounds attention to the act of narration for interviewees as well.
The presence of the camera, microphone, and lights, in addition to the videographer and other technicians, reminds survivors that they address their narratives
beyond the immediate audience of the interviewer to unseen future listeners.

The film equipment and crew also serve as a tacit reminder that the survivor's interview is not an isolated undertaking but part of a collective project, to be housed and cataloged alongside the accounts of other survivors and
eyewitnesses to the Holocaust. The larger project further shapes survivors'
storytelling, whether explicitly or obliquely, through its protocols, which
may impose certain standards on the narrative, such as asking all survivors

to answer the same questions or to tell their life story in chronological order. Moreover, as surviving the Holocaust is the reason for being interviewed, it becomes the center of the life history, which survivors as well as interviewers generally periodize into sections "before," "during," and "after" the genocide.

Both survivors and interviewers may also assume that the personal narrative, as part of a collective undertaking, bears the onus of offering more than an account of the interviewee's own life and therefore should include recollections of a sizable number of people (members of extended families and acquaintances from prewar communities, especially those who did not survive the war) and discussions of events beyond the survivor's direct experience, including the Holocaust writ large. Similarly, the various parties involved in documenting survivor narratives may regard them as having a value beyond what this undertaking provides to the survivors themselves, whether validation, catharsis, or satisfaction in knowing that their stories will be preserved for posterity. Because these narratives are esteemed as providing information to historians, moral guidance to the young, and retorts to Holocaust deniers, survivor videos are often referred to as "testimonies," invoking this term's implication of bearing witness in a legal proceeding or making a religious avowal.

In the United States, the first efforts to videotape Holocaust survivors' life histories were part of a larger turn in the American public sphere toward privileging the accounts of eyewitnesses to history, as opposed to the analyses of experts, in works of social history and public culture. The popularity of documentary films composed largely of eyewitness interviews and eschewing scholarly experts or omniscient narrators, notably the Academy Award-winning *Harlan County USA* (1976), exemplifies this turn. Anthropologists and gerontologists advocated for the value of life review among the aged, especially Myerhoff's influential study *Number Our Days*, which promoted the universal value of telling one's personal history as "equipment for living."[13] The advent of amateur videotaping equipment in the mid-1970s enhanced the democratizing of both telling and documenting life histories through a medium that was closely, if sometimes contentiously, associated with television, then the mass medium with the largest audience in America and elsewhere in the West.[14]

Initiatives to document survivors' life histories also reflected a growing public interest in the Holocaust, especially in North America and western Europe, driven by widely seen films and telecasts; a growing inventory of published works of history, memoir, and fiction; and the expansion of Holocaust education in secondary and higher education. Even though many thousands of survivor narratives had already been collected, in one form or another, since the war's end, support nonetheless grew for new projects to record survivors' stories on videotape. These efforts were motivated in part by desires to gather additional information about the Holocaust from sources esteemed as unrivaled, including survivors who might have never before told their story publicly. Intensifying this desire were mounting concerns that the time remaining for documenting the stories of the aging population of survivors was limited. Supporters of these projects championed the medium of video as offering new possibilities for engaging the public, especially younger generations, in recognizing the importance of the Holocaust. Thus the Fortunoff Archive validated the choice of video as "crucial . . . for the education of students and community groups in an increasingly media-centered era."[15]

Even as opportunities for survivor storytelling in the public sphere continued to proliferate—in public education and memorial programs, documentary films, museum installations, and guided trips to sites in Europe associated with the Holocaust—the special value accorded to these videos as providing survivors' "first-hand" narratives, often told "for the first time," endured. Yet the high regard for survivor interviews as exceptional resources has overlooked the extent to which these life histories are informed by other narratives. Over the decades, many survivors have encountered other accounts of the Holocaust in works of history, memoir, fiction, and drama, as well as in museums, films, telecasts, courses, and lectures. As is true of all storytellers, the ability of these men and women to tell stories of their wartime experiences has been shaped in large measure by exposure to earlier narratives. And as eyewitness accounts of the Holocaust have become increasingly sought after, many survivors have had ample opportunities to tell their personal histories, sometimes doing so in multiple forms: writing memoirs, giving interviews to print or broadcast journalists, and speaking in classrooms, houses of worship, or other public forums, as well as participating in these video projects. This is especially the case for survivors interviewed for the VHA, which was inaugurated almost fifty years after the end of the war.

Though survivors who have never told their stories before garner special recognition, attention should be paid to the value of interviewees who have related their life histories repeatedly. Scholars of these interviews might fret that, in such instances, "too often . . . the survivor delivers 'the usual spiel,'"[16] but multiple opportunities to relate stories enable tellers to refine and enrich their narratives, incorporate insights gained over years of reflection, and establish their reputation as skilled storytellers. Disciplinary differences may inform scholarly predilections. The story never before told may attract greater attention from a historian or psychologist, who is interested in heretofore undisclosed information or the possible cathartic value of its revelation. By contrast, the story told repeatedly can have special appeal for an anthropologist, folklorist, or literature scholar, for whom the craft of storytelling is of interest in its own right.

The following case studies examine VHA recordings in which survivors' life histories are informed by other narratives. First, interviews in which survivors discuss the 1993 feature film *Schindler's List* offer personal histories that engage an established Holocaust narrative of wide renown at the time these interviews were recorded (and which is also a work with a special connection to the establishment of the VHA). Second, interviews with famous survivors entail relating an oft-told personal narrative; moreover, as celebrities, they offer metadiscussions of telling one's life story as part of the narrative. These case studies challenge assumptions that the interviews' value lies primarily in the uniqueness of their content or the spontaneity of their telling. Rather, the interviews examined here are noteworthy for what they reveal about the telling of one's life history as a deliberate and multivalent enterprise, responsive to other narratives.

Survivors on *Schindler's List*

Listening to others' stories about the Holocaust has been a fixture of survivors' lives from the war years onward. During the war Jews suffering under Nazi persecution anxiously sought out information from others while they struggled to understand what was happening to them as members of a people targeted for annihilation. In the war's aftermath, survivors listened to each other's stories in order to learn the fate of family members and acquaintances, to grasp the scope of the genocide, and to grapple with the challenge of making new lives for themselves. Giving evidence to researchers or collaborating on *yizker-bikher* helped forge a sense of communion among the cohort of survivors during the early postwar years, even as they dispersed to new homes around the world. Survivors who related their wartime experiences in public—whether through printed memoirs, press interviews, court testimonies, or commemorative events—had often read or heard other survivors' stories. As works about the Holocaust grew in number and variety over the years—autobiographies, histories, novels, films, broadcasts, museum installations, courses of study, and so on—survivors could attend to an ever-widening array of narratives on the subject. Some survivors devoted much effort to following this burgeoning phenomenon and engaged new works on the Holocaust critically. In fact, Holocaust survivors' negative responses to public works on the topic have sometimes become newsworthy events in their own right.[17] By the time survivors were interviewed for the VHA in the 1990s, they were likely to have incorporated other accounts of the Holocaust in some way—including critical reactions to them—into an understanding of their own wartime experience. Even survivors who had never before told their life story had had decades to contemplate how they might do so.

In a singular way, the VHA makes it possible to consider how survivors' personal histories are shaped by other Holocaust narratives: the Archive indexes those moments when interviewees discuss films in general and one film in particular, *Schindler's List*. (Although this is the only individual film about the Holocaust that the VHA indexes, it is not the only film referenced in interviews.)[18] The VHA database lists 118 interviews during which interviewees mention *Schindler's List*; all but three are videos of Jewish Holocaust survivors.[19] Most of these survivors (77) are interviewed in English, and of these, 23 are *Schindlerjuden*.[20] This set of interviews provides an unusual opportunity to examine how a considerable number of survivors directly reference the same Holocaust narrative, within five years of its initial presentation to the public, in the course of telling their personal histories, all recorded according to the protocols of the same project. Examining this body of material thereby contributes to a more general understanding of how individuals, caught up in epochal events that have become the subject of extensive public attention, engage this history and its mediation in the course of relating their personal narratives.

I I I

The unique place of *Schindler's List* in the VHA's index exemplifies the film's special relationship with the Archive. Because Steven Spielberg was inspired to establish the VHA as a result of talking with Holocaust survivors while making *Schindler's List*, the Archive is part of the film's extensive epiphenomena. During the months following its premiere in December 1993, *Schindler's List* engendered an array of responses unusual in their scope, even for a film by a major director that had achieved critical as well as financial success. Early on, *Schindler's List* received considerable attention in the United States as something more than a feature film, marking a watershed event in Holocaust remembrance and in Spielberg's career.[21] To some extent, the film's creators invited this response by conceiving and presenting *Schindler's List* as a cinematic work of exceptional stature that, unlike what its producers characterized as "your average feel-good 'date' movie," would deliver viewers a morally charged, galvanizing experience.[22] To that end, in 1994 Spielberg's production company, Amblin Entertainment, offered free theatrical screenings of *Schindler's List* to American high school students, planned in conjunction with Facing History and Ourselves, a Holocaust education organization.[23]

However, some responses to *Schindler's List* were clearly not sought by its creators. Members of the anti–abortion rights group Massachusetts Citizens for Life provoked controversy when they attempted to exploit a screening of the film for students in Great Barrington by distributing literature to them about what the organization denounced as "America's Holocaust."[24] More notorious was a public screening of *Schindler's List* in Oakland, California, on Martin Luther King Jr.'s birthday in 1994, during which a group of students, most of them African Americans, were asked to leave the movie theater after laughing during a scene in the film in which a German officer shoots a Jewish prisoner. The students' behavior and their ejection from the cinema quickly became the subject of debate in national media.[25]

Schindler's List was implicated in American politics, including the controversial use of a clip from the film in a campaign advertisement by a candidate for sheriff in Virginia, and US Representative Tom Coburn's protest, in 1997, against airing the film on broadcast television because of its disturbing content.[26] Even the announcement that Ford Motor Company would sponsor this telecast proved somewhat provocative.[27] As *Schindler's List* was distributed internationally, its reception prompted more debate, notably in Germany and Poland.[28] In the Middle East, the film's first Israeli audiences objected to the use of the modern Hebrew song "Yerushelayim shel zahav" (Jerusalem of gold) in the opening of the film's epilogue (another musical selection was substituted for subsequent screenings in Israel),[29] and several countries in the region with majority Muslim populations refused to show *Schindler's List* altogether.[30]

The most elaborate responses to *Schindler's List* were realized in other cultural works. Some of them capitalize on the film's acclaim, notably "Schindler's List" tours of Cracow and environs, in which participants visit sites where the wartime events depicted in the film took place as well as locations where the film was shot, thereby obscuring the distinction between actual events and their reenactment.[31] Other works interrogate *Schindler's List* as a work of Holocaust remembrance. A 1994 episode of the American sitcom *Seinfeld* both lampoons the outsized heroism of the film's protagonist and flouts its stature as a moral touchstone in public culture, as Jerry Seinfeld's friends and family are shocked to discover that he and his girlfriend were necking during a screening of *Schindler's List*—that is, behaving as if it were "your average feel-good 'date' movie."[32] In the mid-1990s the Israeli sketch comedy program *Ha-hamishia ha-kamerit* (Hebrew: "The chamber quintet") featured a skit that mocked the much-vaunted verisimilitude of *Schindler's List* while parodying Claude Lanzmann's 1985 documentary *Shoah*. In this skit an interviewer, similar to Lanzmann, speaks with an interviewee, who relates a narrative that "sounds like a stereotypical 'Holocaust' story" of standing in line with others on a cold night, waiting, surrounded by "barbed-wire, dogs, guards." Then, the interviewee explains, a car pulled up and a man emerged and began shouting. When the interviewer asks if that was Schindler, the other replies, "What Schindler? Spielberg!" and thereby reveals that the "interview" is with an actor describing the ordeal of making *Schindler's List* and not with a survivor recalling actual wartime experience.[33]

French filmmaker Jean-Luc Godard assails *Schindler's List* in his 2001 film *Éloge de l'amour* (*In Praise of Love*) as his "prime negative object," according to J. Hoberman, by dint of the "totalizing re-creation of World War II and the Holocaust" in Spielberg's film, epitomizing American misappropriations of the European past.[34] For his 2003 video piece titled *Spielberg's List*, media artist Omer Fast interviewed Poles who had played Jews as extras in *Schindler's List*. Interview segments are shown simultaneously on two adjacent screens, each with English-language subtitles offering slightly different renderings of what the Polish interviewees are saying. Their recollections of filming scenes set in the Cracow ghetto and the Płaszów labor camp seem to resemble survivors' recollections of actual wartime experiences—as in the aforementioned *Ha-hamishia ha-kamerit* skit—and thereby destabilize the viewer's understanding of what is actually being remembered. Amid this complex intersection of public debates and cultural phenomena concerning *Schindler's List* and its implications for remembering the Holocaust, survivors of this genocide faced the VHA's cameras in the mid-1990s to relate their personal histories.

The English-speaking survivors who discuss *Schindler's List* during their interviews for the VHA generally do so at one of two different points: either in accounts of the war years (this is especially true of *Schindlerjuden*) or toward the end of the interviews, when, according to VHA protocols, survivors are asked general, "reflective questions" about their lives, including "questions concerning faith and meaning, dreams, and messages to future generations."[35] Several survivors with no direct connection to Oskar Schindler refer to Spielberg's film while recounting wartime events in order to compare their own experience with a scene in the film, citing it as an analogue they assume is familiar to the interviewer. Sia Hertsberg describes witnessing deportations of children in

Photograph of survivor Celina Biniaz, a *Schindlerjude*, at a preview screening of the film *Schindler's List*. Biniaz's VHA interview concludes with her discussion of this photograph. Provided by the USC Shoah Foundation.

Riga: "When they were taking the children, I remember in *Schindler's List* he showed that the children were taken by a truck, but an open truck, and ours was a closed one."[36] Ritta Silberstein, a native of Romania, who was interned in Auschwitz as well as in a concentration camp in Czechoslovakia, says of watching *Schindler's List*, "This is my life. I worked in the factory, like Schindler, thanks to him, they are alive, and the same was with me, thanks to my *Meister* [i.e., foreman], I am alive. . . . This is exactly—you saw the movie? Then you know how the life was."[37] Other survivors also ask their interviewers whether they have seen the film, not only establishing this as a shared experience but also reversing, if briefly, the role of interviewer and interviewee.

Survivors who were rescued by Schindler reference *Schindler's List* in their wartime narratives for reasons that are both more specific and more complex. These *Schindlerjuden* variously validate, enhance, or challenge the film as a widely familiar chronicle of events in which they participated. Whereas the film has an acknowledged authority, so do these survivors, though of a different kind, and in the course of their interviews the two are juxtaposed. So, too, if implicitly, are the limits of each source's authority.

Some *Schindlerjuden* readily identify their own experience with scenes in the film. When asked to recount her arrival in Auschwitz, Marianne Rosner explains:

> We had to go to the gas chamber, not the gas chamber, to the shower—Matter of fact, when I saw *Schindler's List*, the movie, and I saw . . . the scene in the shower, with the women—you remember, did you see the film?—I was looking for myself. Because we went through exactly the same thing. We were standing there in the shower, and we were looking is there going to come water or is there going to come gas. We didn't know. Exactly the same. When I was looking, I was thinking—Oh, that must be me![38]

Rosner's initial confusing of the gas chamber with the shower in her narrative recalls the film's suspenseful juxtaposition of these two sites and the respective fates that awaited prisoners in each location. Her account of "looking for myself" in the film extends this conflation of remembering her own experience in Auschwitz with what she saw enacted on screen. Even as she acknowledges the distinction between the two, Rosner seeks her "self," transformed into a dramatic character, in *Schindler's List*. The survivor's subjectivity, a much-vaunted attribute of these interviews generally, seems to be in limbo, searching for re-alization in a virtual simulation of her "self." Similarly, the distinction between the actuality of being a prisoner at Auschwitz and its reenactment is obscured; rather, they are "exactly the same thing."

Later in the interview, Rosner explains how she and her husband, Henry, were involved in the making of *Schindler's List*. In addition to appearing with other *Schindlerjuden* in the film's epilogue, both were portrayed as characters in the wartime drama:

> We were played by Polish actors, Henry as the musician—a matter of a fact, Mr. Spielberg was so nice, he cut out a scene from the film where Henry played [at] a party by [Amon] Göth, [commandant of Płaszów labor camp,] where one German officer committed suicide. Henry played a song, "Sad Sunday." . . . This was a song where people used to commit suicide. . . . And Henry claims . . . that he had . . . some kind of a suggestive power that, when . . . he played this song for the . . . German [officer], maybe ten times or twelve times in a row, over and over again, . . . until this guy, he [i.e., Henry] hypnotized him. He [i.e., the German officer] went out on the patio and he took out his revolver and he shot him[self]. And they had filmed that. But somehow they cut it out. But they sent me this cutout. I have it.[39]

As she recounts an episode of her husband's past, narrated in Keneally's book and evidently included in the original shooting script of *Schindler's List*, Rosner merges this incident and its mediation.[40] Indeed, she mentions the epi-sode's staging for the film before relating the incident itself. Similarly, Rosner's championing of her husband's purported powers to drive one of their captors to commit suicide merges with her pride in the privileged relationship that the couple enjoys with Spielberg. Not only does she have insider information on the making of *Schindler's List*; she has an outtake from the film unseen by the public. Rosner, in effect as an auteur, offers her own alternate "cut" of *Schindler's List*, restoring her husband's heroic act to the film's narrative.

When *Schindlerjuden* discuss *Schindler's List*, they more often focus on differences between the film and their recollection—even when they identify themselves as portrayed in a scene. Roman Ferber claims he was the boy shown hiding in the sewer during the liquidation of the Cracow ghetto ("You're looking at him right now") and then promptly critiques its depiction in the film: "There

were two of us [boys] and three girls. But we didn't ever jump in, that was . . .
commercialized in the movie, we just hid in the toilet . . . , and we standed on
poles on the side. The stench was terrible. But had we jumped in, like it's shown
in the movie . . . I would have been dead today, because it was about sixteen,
eighteen feet deep."[41] When John Armer is asked his impression of the film, he
characterizes it as "90, 95 percent correct" and then enumerates its flaws:

> I can't see [Abraham] Bankier [i.e., the office manager of Schindler's factory,] in
> it; . . . he wasn't mentioned at all. Maybe . . . he didn't want to be mentioned. . . .
> I don't know why he was not mentioned at all. Must be some purpose in it. . . .
> I don't remember the incident with the man with the one arm. . . . There was
> no such a man in Emalia [i.e., Schindler's factory in Cracow], otherwise I would
> know it. . . . I think they made it up to make him [i.e., Schindler?] even better.[42]

As Armer lists these discrepancies, he offers possible rationales for them. Like
other survivors, Armer has to reconcile *Schindler's List* with his own recollections, and in the course of the interview this reckoning becomes part of his
personal narrative.

The discussion of *Schindler's List* between a survivor and an interviewer sometimes reveals their different understandings of the film in relation to its historical
subject, as when Stella Eliezrie interviews Leon Leyson, another *Schindlerjude*:

> Eliezrie: Without getting you in too much trouble, was there anything bla-
>   tantly incorrect?
> Leyson: In the movie?
> Eliezrie: Yes.
> Leyson: . . . In my opinion, those who were depicted as camp or ghetto police,
>   Jewish ghetto police, were glossed over too lightly.
> Eliezrie: What should have been said?
> Leyson: Well, a little bit should have been put in that these were not your ca-
>   sual friends, your next-door neighbors, . . . but, . . . in some cases, they
>   were vicious people.
> Eliezrie: Were these Jews?
> Leyson: Yes. . . .
> Eliezrie: Were they forced to be vicious?
> Leyson: Well, not really. . . . That's the sad part of it, of course.[43]

The interviewer is both interested in the survivor's critiques of *Schindler's List* and anxious about their implications. One is left to wonder what kind of trouble Eliezrie thought might be visited upon Leyson for discussing the film's inaccuracies.

Schindlerjuden demonstrate a need to reckon not only with the film's narrative but also with its origin. Several discuss what they know about how Spielberg's film or Keneally's book was realized, explaining their participation in the process or absence from the results. Helena Jonas Rosenzweig, who was one of two Jewish maids working in Göth's villa at Płaszów, reports that her family and friends were upset that she was not mentioned in Keneally's book. Rosenzweig rationalizes that everyone involved in the actual events could not be included as a character, "otherwise the book would never end and the stories would never end." Of her absence from both the book and the film, she remarks, "It doesn't matter; the story is there."[44] In her account, Rosenzweig's actual experiences vie with fiction's parameters of character and plot, ultimately yielding to them. At the same time, Rosenzweig affirms her place in "the story," an implicit master narrative.

Several survivors discuss the politics of creating both Keneally's book and Spielberg's film, explaining, for example, how Keneally first learned about Schindler from Poldek Pfefferberg, a *Schindlerjude* whom the writer met in 1980 at Pfefferberg's leather goods store in Los Angeles. (Keneally dedicated the book both to Schindler's memory and to Pfefferberg, "who by zeal and persistence, caused this book to be written"; Spielberg also thanked Pfefferberg upon accepting an Academy Award for the film.)[45] When an interviewer asks Victor Dortheimer, another *Schindlerjude*, how true *Schindler's List* is to actual events, he discusses omissions and disparities at length, including the number of people originally on the list and how they got on it, the more limited role that Schindler's bookkeeper, Itzhak Stern (portrayed by Ben Kingsley in the film), actually played during the war, and, to Dortheimer's mind, Pfefferberg's self-serving involvement in the creation of *Schindler's List*: "This film is made under the influence of . . . Pfefferberg. . . . The film is from his point of view, and he came . . . to us [in the factory in 19]44, [he was there for] just a few months, which is nothing. . . . He wanted to be most important. . . . I met Pfefferberg . . . [at the] premiere [of the film]. . . . I said [to him], 'You are a bloody bluffer.'" Nevertheless, Dortheimer acknowledges that, "thanks to him [i.e., Pfefferberg], *Schindler's List* exists. He was the initiator of the film."[46]

Because of Pfefferberg's strategic role in the realization of *Schindler's List*, survivors' acquaintance with him sometimes becomes a topic of interest during their interviews. When Maryla Susser recalls the school she attended before the war as a girl in Cracow, she mentions Pfefferberg to interviewer David Brotsky:

> Susser: Our gym teacher was that Poldek . . . , who lives now in Los Angeles, and met that Connelly [i.e., Keneally] and told him about the Holocaust, and *Schindler's List* was based on him, so, he was my teacher.
>
> Brotsky: What do you remember about him?
>
> Susser: Oh, he was wonderful, wonderful! . . . I saw him in New York, when he came to our, you know, gathering, and he looked wonderful, and also in Israel I saw him [at a survivors' gathering]. . . .
>
> Brotsky: What type of a person was he before the war?
>
> Susser: He was good looking, tall, very jolly, and he was very friendly, very nice person; we all loved him. All the girls were in love with him!
>
> Brotsky: How much older was he?
>
> Susser: Oh, he was—now he's, I don't know, eighty-five or so—Well now, the 1939. . . .[47]

Susser thus takes the initiative to return the interview from a discussion of Pfefferberg to the story of her own life.

The various ways that survivors imbricate *Schindler's List* into their accounts of wartime events they experienced suggest that they did not simply watch the film differently from other people but in effect saw a different film, into which they integrated their remembrances during the act of watching. A particularly striking example occurs in the interview with Benek Geizhals as he discusses the scene in *Schindler's List* where Schindler appears on horseback, watching the liquidation of the Cracow ghetto. Geizhals notes that in the background of the shot is a "red building," which belonged to his family, and he remarks, "I know this spot very well."[48] Geizhals can "see" a red building while watching the film, but other viewers cannot do so, of course, as it was shot in black and white. Geizhals's remark seems to validate a comment that Spielberg made when explaining his decision not to film *Schindler's List* in color: "I think color is . . . real to the people who survived the Holocaust, but . . . my own experience with the Holocaust has been through black-and-white documentaries. I've never seen the Holocaust in color. Even though I've been there, it's still black and white in my eyes."[49] For Spielberg, who was born in America after World War II, the Holocaust exists as a cinematic phenomenon of the black-and-white era. At the same time, he understands the Holocaust as a *topos* (stating, "I've been there") that he can visit but not enter fully, unlike survivors, for whom it exists "in color" both as an actual experience and in its mediation.

I I I

Survivors' discussions of *Schindler's List* that occur toward the end of their VHA interviews are more wide-ranging. Often they praise the film, some comparing it favorably to other films or telecasts, including *The Diary of Anne Frank* (1959), *The Garden of the Finzi-Continis* (1970), the *Holocaust* miniseries (1978), *Shoah* (1985), and *Escape from Sobibor* (1987). Several interviewees compliment Spielberg on *Schindler's List* as they thank him for recording their personal histories. By implicitly linking the two media works, the former making the latter possible, survivors obliquely acknowledge the mediated nature of their interviews.

The praise *Schindlerjuden* offer about the film and its director sometimes extends to describing the public acclaim these survivors garnered following the release of *Schindler's List*, as the press and public sought out Jews who had been rescued by Schindler. Chaskel Schlesinger recalls that after he was interviewed for a local television report in Chicago, "right away the *Sun-Times*, the *Tribune*, everybody started calling."[50] Leopold Rosner reports, "We had been invited eight times for the premieres, six times in Melbourne, in Canberra, Sydney, and again in Melbourne."[51] Some *Schindlerjuden* recall their contact with Schindler in the postwar years or with Spielberg in connection with the film as a source of pride. Abraham Zuckerman recounts his postwar relationship with Schindler, of whom he sculpted a bust that he gave to Spielberg. Among family pictures that are typical of what other VHA interviewees select to be filmed at the end of their interviews, Zuckerman presents snapshots he and Schindler took of each other with signs of streets bearing Schindler's name as well as pictures of filming the epilogue of *Schindler's List*.[52] In this sequence of personal photographs, Zuckerman's life history embraces both Schindler and his celebrity.

Other survivors discuss watching *Schindler's List* as a landmark event in their lives, whether it motivated them to record the interview or inspired their family members to learn about the Holocaust or from it. Esther Fiszman lauds

Photograph of Oskar Schindler by a sign for a street bearing his name, taken by survivor Abraham Zuckerman. In his VHA interview, Zuckerman discusses his postwar relationship with Schindler. Provided by the USC Shoah Foundation.

the "enormous lot of good" that *Schindler's List* "has done . . . for the young people" by citing a personal story:

> My son was dating a Canadian Vietnamese girl, lovely human being, a really beautiful person—he went to see the film with her, and [then he said,] "I decided to call it a day, that we can't." . . . I don't think that he would have called it a day if not [for] the film. . . . I don't know who decided—I think they both decided together, that they couldn't do it to me, or he couldn't do it to his heritage. I've never asked.[53]

Nor does Fiszman probe the connection between her son's watching *Schindler's List* and doing what his heritage—or his mother—apparently expected of him. In her narrative, the film's moral power to prevent intermarriage is implicitly self-evident.

In recounting their watching of *Schindler's List*, some interviewees link the film with information, affect, or remembrance concerning the Holocaust. Laura Hillman explains, when asked whether she ever found out what happened to her mother during the war, "When I saw *Schindler's List*, . . . I suddenly realized that my mother ended the way it's shown in the movie."[54] David Halpern recalls that, as he watched *Schindler's List*, "I felt I was in it, I was hiding in there, when I saw those kids hiding in the toilet, in the shot, I felt I'm in there with them. . . . I couldn't sleep that night, . . . what I went through, and here they made a picture like that, I couldn't believe it."[55] George Hartman describes crying when he saw *Schindler's List* as a "curious" response: "When . . . seeing the reality you don't cry, there's nothing to cry about, you know you're going to die tomorrow probably, you see all this horror. . . . When that's happening, it doesn't have any emotional impact. It's only when I see it now, when . . . everything is normal, and I look at this horrible film, which was really much better than what I went through, . . . it's much more emotional than actually being there."[56] For Hartman, the film's affective power is not its verisimilitude but rather its difference from the actuality, with regard not only to time and place but also to the structuring of catharsis provided by a work of drama.

The disparity between cinematic representation and the remembered past engenders reflections among some *Schindlerjuden* on the film's form, genre, or content. Lore Smith describes watching *Schindler's List* as feeling "like being on the outside and looking into something here. And when I was looking at it, I couldn't believe that this is—I was there. And still to this day, I couldn't believe it. Of course, I must say that it was worse than it was portrayed. But I understand in order for people to be able to accept the film, it needed to be done the way it was done. I still feel that documentaries are better."[57] Smith doesn't explain why she holds documentaries in higher esteem but suggests that she believes this genre resolves the disparity between actuality and how it is represented in fictional film, which strives to render its representation "acceptable" to audiences but induces an uncanny experience for her.

Harriet Solz also reflects on the implications of cinematic genre in order to reconcile the disparity between *Schindler's List* and her actual experiences as well as to come to terms with the film's public success despite this difference:

So, the movie I couldn't wait to see. But when I came out from the movie, I was really disappointed. So my daughter calls me, and she says, "Ma, you went through so much? You never told me what you went through. . . . " So I said, . . . "This is nothing what they showed in the movie." And then I've been thinking about that movie a lot. And I came to a conclusion: That it's not a Holocaust movie. This is a biography of Schindler. If he [i.e., Spielberg] would have put more morbid scenes into the picture, people wouldn't have seen it. Like this, that movie woke up the whole world, which he did a marvelous job. But really the movie is a biography of Schindler, who saved us our lives, and [for] which he deserves it.[58]

In the course of these discussions of *Schindler's List*, survivors offer impromptu thoughts on the nature of mediating Holocaust narratives generally. Even as they praise the film, several survivors note the discrepancy between their actual experience and the medium's capacity to represent the Holocaust, citing the greater enormity of the actuality as well as the element of time. Israel Arbeiter explains that *Schindler's List* was the "closest that I have ever seen to the truth" of what happened in Auschwitz, but "it gives you only about five, or ten, or fifteen minutes. . . . I went through this five years." He questions whether any writer or filmmaker could represent the genocide in its full extent, "day in and day out. . . . How can this be shown?"[59]

Sometimes survivors and their interviewers debate the issue of cinematic verisimilitude and its limits. After Karol Saks talks about his gratitude to the people in France who hid him during the war, Mark Turkeltaub asks Saks whether he has seen *Schindler's List*:

Saks: Yes.

Turkeltaub: Here it is, fifty years after the war—just in your opinion, how did that affect you after all this time, seeing on the movie screen what happened?

Saks: It's a very, very hard movie to take. It affected me to the point where I saw myself sometimes among these children. So I'm sure that thousands of people like me could see themselves, standing there in these lines. . . .

Turkeltaub: It's probably very hard to recreate in a movie, you know, what really—

Saks: Well, as much as you can recreate, I mean, you can't have the authenticity, so to speak, the reality, but as much reality as you can give, I think this movie had a tremendous amount of, of realism.

Rather than pursuing this discussion of cinematic realism (perhaps as it was not his reason for raising *Schindler's List* in the first place), Turkeltaub returns to Saks's personal history, asking, "Why do you think you survived?"[60]

In these reflections, survivors sometimes engage the trope that the Holocaust is an event that tests the limits of representation. Zoltan Gluck struggles with this notion as he recounts his deportation to Auschwitz:

> It's almost impossible to describe. I have seen the movie *Schindler's List*, this was one of the closest to the situation what . . . I went through, anyway, the closest to the reality. . . . I have seen many movies about that, but nothing came close enough to say, "Oh, it happened like this." That's impossible, to get it so close, what really happened over there. *Schindler's List* was one of the closest, what I could say that was close—still not close enough, I mean, not perfectly close, but close. It was unbearable, really, I mean, just imagine.[61]

For Gluck, the act of imagining addresses the unbridgeable gap between the Holocaust's actuality—whether for those who experienced it or for others—and its representation in *Schindler's List* (or any other mediation). Yet other survivors find in *Schindler's List* a productive impetus to imagining as a point of entry to remembrance. Goldy Zylberszac-Junger, who spent the war in hiding in Belgium, commented, when speaking of a relative who had died during the war, "You know, there was a movie from Spielberg, . . . and you saw a little . . . blond girl with a red dress? Everybody imagined it's something from them— me, I imagined it's my niece."[62] And Horst Senger, who had fled Germany during the war, reflected on the film's impact on survivors: "The remaining people who come from that era, some see things, they now see illustrated in detail, of what they read about that perhaps were unimaginable, really, but the movie made it—made it imaginable. The movie made the details."[63]

I I I

Interviewees' discussions of *Schindler's List* complicate the notion that these videos offer straightforward presentations of survivors' recalled experience of the Holocaust. Their references to the film demonstrate the extent to which these memories are not only contingent, responsive to the context in which the interviews took place, but also permeable, given how readily this feature film is incorporated as a referent. The facility with which survivors integrate *Schindler's List* into their personal histories might seem to confirm some observers' anxieties about the film's impact on Holocaust remembrance generally or on video interviews with survivors in particular. Walter Reich, a former director of the US Holocaust Memorial Museum, decried what he termed the " 'Schindlerization of Holocaust memory,' which may suppress stories that refuse life-affirming and heart-warming conclusions."[64] Similarly, Holocaust studies scholar Noah Shenker posits the "cinematic origins" of the Shoah Foundation by connecting *Schindler's List*, as "a redemptive story cut from the cloth of classical Hollywood cinematic conventions," to the Archive's protocols, arguing that "Spielberg's film serves as a source narrative for the VHA, linking the archival project with [the film's] own narrative stakes in hope and tolerance." Shenker also suggests that the form of "Classical Hollywood Cinema" informed the Shoah Foundation's objectives of maintaining "narrative continuity" and that periodizing the interviews into prewar, war, and postwar segments mirrors the "three-act structure" of this cinematic genre.[65]

The interviews with survivors cited above do not validate these concerns that *Schindler's List* in some way imposes or coerces saccharine, uplifting, or conformist storytelling. Rather, *Schindler's List* figures in these survivors' narratives as a highly variable catalyst, interacting with wartime memories, other mediations of the Holocaust, and the context of the interview itself. The film can figure in a survivor's interview as a shared narrative, a master narrative, or an alternate narrative; the film's creation can become a source of satisfaction, contention, or anxiety; watching the film can be characterized as a landmark event, an encounter with an aesthetic model, or an artistic challenge.

However, survivors' discussions of *Schindler's List*, in which their engagements with the film inform the process of remembrance and become part of their life narratives, do raise questions about the widespread investment in survivor interviews as accounts of unparalleled immediacy and authority, thereby prompting a reconsideration of how to ascertain their value. First, survivors' references to *Schindler's List* evoke the moment in which these interviews were recorded. By the mid-1990s, survivors had been exhorted to tell their stories in public for two decades by an international proliferation of interviewing projects, museums, educational programs, and the like. The VHA, one of the most recent of these undertakings, interviewed survivors who were informed by years of this demand and by exposure to multiple models of storytelling, including filmed or published personal narratives of other survivors.

Some VHA interviewees attest to relying on other mediations for an understanding of their own past. Dorit Whiteman, who had fled her native Austria before the start of the war, recalls that she first became aware of the "real full extent" of the Holocaust in a movie theater in the United States: "I remember going by myself to the newsreel, and they showed some pictures [of conditions in liberated concentration camps] . . . , and I remember . . . being totally, totally horrified."[66] Harriet Solz recalls that when Keneally's book came out, "I didn't want to read it. So my daughter bought the book and was reading. And she called me up to ask questions. I said . . . , 'I don't really remember a lot. Let me go read the book.' And still I have a lot of questions, which—I remember certain things differently, but I'm not sure, I was too young to—I looked at things differently, and everything."[67]

Given how avidly many survivors attend to representations of the Holocaust (as some of these interviewees report), it is likely that the narratives they offered for the VHA are among those most extensively informed by other mediations, whether of individuals' wartime experiences or of the Holocaust writ large. Notwithstanding the videos' form—unedited, recorded in an austere aesthetic—they are no less mediated than any other representation of the Holocaust. But the extent to which mediation defines these undertakings does not undermine these interviews' significance. Rather, attending to mediation reveals their value as palimpsests of memory, which by its nature both prompts and integrates the act of mediation.

Second, these references to *Schindler's List* are of special value because they do not only arise when interviewees construct their wartime narratives. The film is also part of some survivors' metanarratives, explaining why they tell their story—to offer eyewitness accounts of the genocide, moral exhortation, or a legacy for future generations—or reflecting spontaneously on the issue of experience versus representation, life versus art. Rather than offering clarifying insights, survivors voice an honestly inchoate awareness that their interviews are situated amid a complex, dynamic array of Holocaust mediations and their metadiscussion as well as the actuality of survivors' own experience and its recall. Indeed, the same aesthetic issues arise in the aforementioned "Schindler's List" tours, the *Seinfeld* episode, the *Ha-hamishia ha-kamerit* skit, Godard's film, and Fast's video piece, as these works, each in its own way, interrogate *Schindler's List*.

The interviewees cited above, especially the *Schindlerjuden*, repeatedly remark that the film cannot represent wartime experiences comprehensively.

Survivors distinguish among competing narratives—"my," "his," or "her" story vis-à-vis "the" story—implicitly juxtaposing various individual survivors' accounts with a master narrative. Survivors leave unspecified what might constitute that master narrative—a scholarly history? a documentary film? an abstract ideal?—or who facilitates its telling. Nor are survivors self-conscious about their own agency as narrators. They seem more aware of the complex of contributions that went into the making of *Schindler's List* (reflecting on the roles played by Spielberg, Keneally, Pfefferberg, and others) than of their own stories' video documentation (such as the impact of the interviewer, camera operator, or VHA protocols).[68]

Indeed, while survivors probe the aesthetic limitations of *Schindler's List* in relation to the actuality of the Holocaust, they do not subject their own narratives to the same scrutiny. Their attention to the discrepancies between *Schindler's List* and the actual events of the Holocaust is tellingly selective. Especially noteworthy is the fact that, though these survivors discuss the length of the film, the verisimilitude of its setting or its actors, and the accuracy of information in its plot, they fail to mention language, including the fact that the film is largely in English. Of course, they, too, have been mediating their own wartime experiences in English—which none of them spoke as a first language and which, in most cases, they learned after the war. If these survivors' discussions of *Schindler's List* address the metaissues of narrating the past, they seem to be limited to scrutinizing retellings of the Holocaust other than the ones that the survivors themselves are in the midst of creating. Rather, they assume the task of narrating their lives unself-consciously, whether it is something they have never done before or have undertaken repeatedly.

Survivor as Celebrity

Most Holocaust survivors interviewed for the VHA or other similar projects were "ordinary" people—that is, they were not famous or members of a social, political, economic, or cultural elite—before World War II, when, as members of civilian populations targeted for persecution by Nazi Germany, they were caught up in extreme, life-threatening circumstances. After the war, these survivors typically strove to establish new "ordinary" lives for themselves, after having been abruptly and cruelly deprived of the context and means of leading such a life as they had known it before the war. Holocaust survivors often found themselves at the war's end without a family, community, or country; lacking in education, language fluency, job skills, capital, or other means of support; and coping with physical or mental ailments. In light of these daunting circumstances, the ability to become "ordinary" people in radically new milieus constitutes an extraordinary accomplishment in its own right.

Among the many thousands of interviews in the VHA are a small number conducted with individuals of renown. They include people recognized for accomplishments apart from being Holocaust survivors, such as actor Robert Clary (best known for appearing in the 1960s American sitcom *Hogan's Heroes*), Rebbetzin Esther Jungreis (the founder of Hineni, an Orthodox Jewish outreach organization), US Representative Tom Lantos, and psychologist and media personality Ruth Westheimer.[69] In addition, the VHA includes interviews with a number of people well known for being Holocaust survivors. By the time they were interviewed for the Archive, they had already related their wartime experiences in widely known books or films. Among these survivors are Abraham Bomba, whose interview about the Treblinka death camp figures prominently in Claude Lanzmann's documentary *Shoah*, and Leopold Page (known before the war as Poldek Pfefferberg), the initial source for Thomas Keneally's book that is the basis for the film *Schindler's List*. The VHA also includes an interview with Binjamin Wilkomirski, author of the 1995 book *Fragments: Memories of a Wartime Childhood*. Shortly after the interview was recorded, this widely read autobiography was exposed as fraudulent, and Wilkomirski's actual identity as Bruno Dössekker (né Grosjean), who is neither a Jew nor a victim of Nazi persecution, was established.[70]

Some survivors interviewed for the VHA had become well known for their commitment to causes directly related to the Holocaust, including Benjamin Meed, founder of the American Gathering of Jewish Holocaust Survivors, and Simon Wiesenthal, long famous for his efforts to track down fugitive Nazi war criminals. Other interviewees have turned their public recognition as survivors toward causes less directly connected to Holocaust remembrance, such as Gerda Weissmann Klein, the subject of the award-winning documentary *One Survivor Remembers* (1995), based on her memoir *All but My Life*. In 2008 Klein founded Citizenship Counts, a nonprofit organization committed to promoting the value of citizenship among American youth.[71]

The VHA's interviews with renowned survivors raise two key issues. First, what is the particular value of interviews with individuals who have already related their life stories previously, in some cases frequently, in various media, and to large audiences? Second, what role does celebrity play in these survivors' narratives? In particular, how do their life stories incorporate previous tellings of their story and the attention it has garnered? Given survivors' rise to public prominence generally, these are important questions for the study of Holocaust remembrance beyond their relevance for the relatively small number of well-known survivors. In the course of being interviewed, many survivors mention their involvement in Holocaust remembrance as presenters of their personal histories—for example, when speaking at schools, houses of worship, or local community organizations. (The VHA index references these discussions with the search term "Holocaust education.")[72] Examining an interview with a celebrated survivor in which discussing the telling of one's life story figures prominently can shed light on this practice among hundreds, if not thousands, of survivors at the turn of the millennium. At the same time, a survivor who has honed her story over the years and has dedicated a considerable part of her postwar life to telling that story to many others is of interest for the study of personal narrative as well as Holocaust memory.

I I I

In 2015, at the age of eighty-nine, survivor Kitty Hart-Moxon (née Felix) appeared in the documentary film *One Day in Auschwitz*, produced by the Shoah Foundation to mark the seventieth anniversary of the camp's liberation.[73] This was far from the first time that Hart-Moxon had related her wartime experiences on camera, including her interview for the VHA almost two decades earlier. Indeed, having devoted much of her life since the end of the war to telling her story of surviving the Holocaust through books, documentary films, audio and video recordings for archives, press interviews, courtroom testimony, and public speaking, Kitty Hart-Moxon exemplifies the celebrity survivor.

Kitty, who was born in Bielsko, Poland, in 1926, first presented her story of survival to the public in her 1961 memoir, *I Am Alive*, in which she details how her immediate family tried to escape Nazi persecution. After the war began, Kitty was confined to the Lublin ghetto and then worked under a false identity as a Pole in a German factory in Bitterfeld. When her Jewish identity was

Poster for the 2015 documentary film *One Day in Auschwitz*, featuring survivor Kitty Hart-Moxon. Provided by the USC Shoah Foundation.

exposed, Kitty was interned in a series of prisons and camps, including spend-
ing almost two years in Auschwitz, before her liberation from a concentration
camp near Salzwedel, Germany. She survived these ordeals together with her
mother, Rosa Felix, with whom Kitty settled in England in 1946; all the other
members of their family in Poland were killed during the war.

Though *I Am Alive* was reprinted in the mid-1970s, Kitty's international
renown was established by the 1979 documentary *Kitty: Return to Auschwitz*,
produced for ITV Yorkshire. One of the first films to record a survivor's return
visit to the site of the death camp, the documentary was widely seen both in
the United Kingdom and elsewhere, including telecasts in the United States on
both public and commercial networks in 1981.[74] Widespread acclaim for the
film prompted the publication of a second memoir, *Return to Auschwitz*, in
1981. Kitty subsequently testified at a Nazi war crimes trial in West Germany
in the mid-1980s and appeared in other documentary films, including *Another
Journey by Train* (1993), in which she confronts British neo-Nazis at Auschwitz,
and *Death March: A Survivor's Story* (2003), in which she retraces the forced
march of prisoners from Auschwitz to Germany. Her life history was recorded
on audio by the Imperial War Museum in 1996,[75] and she was interviewed on
videotape for the VHA in 1998. For her commitment to Holocaust education in
the United Kingdom, Hart-Moxon was awarded the Order of the British Empire in 2003 and an honorary doctorate from the University of Birmingham in
2013. In 2016, the National Holocaust Centre and Museum in Nottinghamshire
announced that Hart-Moxon was among a small number of survivors whose
life history the institution would be recording with interactive holography, in
order to keep their "testimonies alive forever."[76]

Hart-Moxon's interview is among the longest in the VHA, running eight
and a half hours, during which she recounts her life in prewar Poland, the series
of ordeals she and her family endured during the war, and her efforts to start
a new life after the war in England. In addition, Hart-Moxon reflects throughout the interview on the task of recounting her experience of the Holocaust
and discusses the consequences of this memory work for her and others in
her life. The VHA interview includes narrative episodes and descriptions that
closely resemble what Kitty wrote in her first published memoir and continued
to articulate over the years through various media and to different audiences.
At the same time, these reiterations reveal shifts in Kitty's approach to the task,

reflecting differences in context, form, and medium as well as the dynamic of her postwar life, especially her evolving commitment to telling her life story.

By the time Kitty set about writing her first published memoir, she had begun a new life in England: she had settled in Birmingham, trained to become a radiologist, and married Rudolf Hart, a German Jewish refugee who had arrived in England before the war, thanks to the Kindertransport; the Harts had two young sons. *I Am Alive* chronicles Kitty's struggles to survive the war, beginning in the summer of 1939, when the Felix family abruptly fled Bielsko on the eve of Germany's invasion of Poland. The memoir ends shortly after the author and her mother were liberated in Salzwedel and, having found a temporary haven in a displaced persons camp in Germany, learned of the deaths of the rest of their family.

I Am Alive opens with a foreword by Lord Russell of Liverpool, who served as deputy judge advocate general to the British Army in Germany during the war and then advised British prosecutors at war crimes trials in Germany and Japan; his book *The Scourge of the Swastika: A Short History of Nazi War Crimes* appeared in 1954. Russell's foreword to *I Am Alive* focuses on Kitty's refusal to seek revenge on her persecutors after the war, citing a passage from the book's final chapter in which she recalls stopping short of killing German civilians (the passage is also excerpted on the back of the book's dust jacket). Russell writes that Hart's "own experiences and what she saw others suffer were horrible enough to have embittered her for life, but they did not. . . . She believes that there is almost no limit to what one can endure mentally," though "all that is left is a kind of indifference," which "probably explains the complete lack of emotion in her fascinating account of those terrible years."[77]

What likely prompted Russell's characterization of the narrative as unemotional is its evenhanded candor. Hart relates countless harrowing events, as well as poignant and even risible moments, but she is consistently, bluntly straightforward in her accounts of the many abuses she and others endured and her daring exploits to keep herself and her mother alive, as well as her desires to seek revenge—and their limits—at the war's end. Unlike other, more widely read memoirs of Auschwitz survivors published shortly after the war—notably Primo Levi's *Se questo è un uomo* (*If This Is a Man*) and Elie Wiesel's *La nuit* (*Night*)[78]—*I Am Alive* does not imbricate its account of surviving genocidal persecution with philosophical or theological discussions, nor does the text

offer much personal introspection. Rather, Hart's memoir hews close to her
wartime experiences and only occasionally extends to offer a larger contex-
tualization, such as providing background information on the economy and
demographics of prewar Bielsko or explaining the operations of various parts
of Auschwitz. The narrative's tight focus is sometimes expanded with brief passages of foreshadowing ("Little did I know then what lay ahead of me!") and
reflections on Kitty's changing self-awareness ("It was a crazy life. For a time I
could hardly believe I was myself").[79]

As these brief passages intimate, *I Am Alive* is configured somewhat like
a bildungsroman. Within Hart's account of her survival she offers an ellipti-
cal narrative of entering adulthood under the most adverse circumstances,
occasionally marked by reflections set apart from the wartime chronicle ("I
had learned a lot . . . and no longer asked childish questions"). Moreover, Hart
frames her narrative within the topic of coming of age. In the book's dedication,
she mourns the loss of educational opportunities during the war, describing
her memoir as "the story of the years which I should by rights have spent at the
schooldesk, years upon which I might have looked back as the happiest of my
life." Recounting her departure from Auschwitz in November 1944, she characterizes the nearly two years she spent in the camp as a formative experience:
"I think I had learned a lot in that time. I had grown up, and grown old in my
experience, and I knew how to fight for my life in any circumstances. In a way
it had been a good schooling."[80]

Seventeen years after *I Am Alive* was published, Hart related her wartime
experiences again, this time focusing primarily on her internment in Auschwitz, in a medium that fostered a very different kind of storytelling. She was
approached by British documentary filmmaker Peter Morley, who was considering her for one of a series of hour-long film portraits of women's resistance against Nazism during World War II. Upon meeting Hart, Morley was
convinced that hers was such an extraordinary story that it would not fit
within the envisioned series. Instead, he proposed making a longer, "one-off"
documentary about Hart, centered on what would be her first postwar visit
to Auschwitz (returning to the sites of wartime resistance was a criterion of
the original documentary series). When he first visited Hart at her home in
Birmingham, Morley was impressed by both the "unstoppable eloquence" with
which she related her wartime ordeals and the Holocaust's looming presence

in her daily life. For example, Hart showed Morley an item she kept on the mantelpiece: "a small transparent Perspex presentation stand. Mounted inside it were two separate pieces of human skin, each one bearing a camp number—one was Kitty's, the other her mother's."[81]

Concerned about the psychological impact that revisiting Auschwitz might have on Hart, Morley invited her son David, then working as a doctor in Canada, to accompany his mother on the film shoot. Morley also decided that the filmmaking must exercise "restraint" and be "purely observational" in style. He rejected suggestions that an interviewer accompany the Harts to Auschwitz, which Morley feared "would stifle Kitty's natural, eloquent style of delivery—it would blunt the impact of a mother telling her son what she and his grandmother had to endure." Upon their arrival in Poland, Morley explained to the Harts that he and his crew "would keep our distance and simply observe them with the camera, and follow [Kitty] wherever she chose to take David. I would not offer any suggestions or instructions. There would be no prompting or cueing; in fact, I would not be speaking to her at all."[82]

The Harts' visit to Auschwitz was filmed over three consecutive days in November 1978, during which, Morley recalls, "we just followed [Kitty] with the camera running, not knowing where she was taking David to next, and time and time again she surprised him, and us, with the most dreadful revelations."[83] From these hours of filming, plus some additional footage of the camp that was shot afterwards, Morley composed the documentary's core, framing it with shorter interviews in which Hart, seated before the camera in her home, discusses her prewar and postwar life. During the film's long central section, the camera follows the Harts around the seemingly deserted grounds of Auschwitz, often filming them at a distance or from behind, thereby presenting the camp and the Holocaust in a different cinematic idiom from that used to present Hart's life before and after the war.

Hart's encounter with the landscape of Auschwitz, which inspires spontaneous storytelling responsive to particular locations, structures the extended sequences that make up the documentary's core. She engages the environment aggressively, striding across the campgrounds in search of places she remembers. Hart strives to conjure her wartime experience in Auschwitz by evoking repeatedly the presence of many thousands of people, living and dead, amid the vast spaces and empty structures that she and her son now visit. Morley's selection of footage is not sequenced according to the chronology of Hart's time as a prisoner in Auschwitz but appears instead to reflect the flow of her return visit to the campgrounds. For the most part, Hart speaks directly to her son, who provides her recollections with a direct, intimate audience. Though at the beginning of this section of the documentary she states, "I've come to speak for all the people who died" in the camp, Hart's narrative is in large measure offered as personal, family lore, in this respect similar to the close focus of *I Am Alive*. As a result, *Kitty: Return to Auschwitz* is as much a documentation of the process of remembering—shaped by charged encounters with the environment and the immediate context of a mother explaining her past to her son, as well as by Hart's earlier published memoir—as it is about the harrowing experiences she relates.

Kitty: Return to Auschwitz was first aired in the United Kingdom in November 1979, attracting an unusually large audience ("close on 13 million") and strong reviews. Soon Hart was "inundated with letters," some simply addressed to "Kitty, Birmingham." Over the ensuing years, the documentary was broadcast in Canada, Germany, Japan, the United States, and other countries, garnering critical accolades and winning awards. Morley later credited his documentation of Hart's "cathartic return" to Auschwitz with her enduring commitment to Holocaust education in the public sphere:

> Ever since the film's transmission . . . , she has been in huge demand. She has
> lectured in dozens of schools on the holocaust. She has visited her hometown,
> Bielsko, where the Jewish community, which included thirty members of her
> family, perished in the holocaust. She has taken student groups on numerous
> trips to Auschwitz and has played an active role in countering those who have
> denied that any of this ever happened.[84]

The surging interest in Hart's story, as a result of Morley's film, led to the publication of her second memoir in 1981. Its title, *Return to Auschwitz*, links the book to the documentary, as does promotional copy on the dust jacket, which invokes "Yorkshire Television's award winning documentary" and proffers within the volume "the full account of [Kitty Hart's] remarkable experiences." *Return to Auschwitz* presents a more developed narrative than *I Am Alive* and frames Hart's wartime account within episodes that center on her postwar life and her motivation to recount her experiences during the Holocaust. Whereas the first memoir begins on the eve of World War II, *Return to*

Auschwitz opens at another threshold moment in the author's life: her arrival, along with her mother, in England in 1946, anxious to begin new lives. There they were met by Kitty's uncle, who had fled Vienna with his wife shortly before the start of the war and then settled in Birmingham. This memoir's first chapter recounts Kitty's travails during the early postwar years, struggling to get an education, find a profession, and establish friendships. So challenging were these experiences that Hart describes this as "one of the unhappiest times of my life," her months in Auschwitz notwithstanding.[85]

Central to Kitty's frustration at the time were efforts to suppress her wish to talk about her wartime ordeals. Hart reports that when she and her mother arrived in England, her uncle told her straightaway: "On no account are you to talk about any of the things that have happened to you. Not in my house. I don't want my girls upset. And *I* don't want to know." Kitty responded by resolving to speak and write about her experience of the Holocaust. This conviction, she explains, epitomizes her determination to "Never obey," which Hart describes as "a motto I had made up for myself long ago."[86] Hart conceptualizes Holocaust remembrance as an act of defiance, in keeping with the noncompliance she deemed fundamental to surviving the genocide. Indeed, her willful dedication to public recollection of the Holocaust might be seen as an extension of her contrarian experience of the war as a moral proving ground.

Complementing the opening of *Return to Auschwitz* is its final chapter, which recounts Hart's experience of making the documentary with Morley and includes much verbatim quoting from recollections she offered in the film. Beginning this memoir with a defining moment, in which the desire to report her wartime experiences is suppressed, Hart ends with an account of vindication as she relates her story before an international audience. At the same time, *Return to Auschwitz* indicates the extent to which Hart's narrative is indebted to others. Though she is listed as the book's sole author, she holds its copyright jointly with author John Burke. He is the first person whom Hart thanks in the Acknowledgments, crediting his "patient questioning and argument," which "drew out of me so many things I thought I had forgotten, and who worked closely with me over several months sorting these out into what we both hope is the right order."[87] Hart's second memoir is informed by input from both Morley and Burke, who each attended carefully to her storytelling and shaped its structure.

Return to Auschwitz relates Hart's life story within a more developed agenda than does *I Am Alive*, expanding beyond her first memoir's close focus on the struggle to survive. In addition to providing more details of her wartime experiences, *Return to Auschwitz* offers greater reflection on Kitty's character, such as her feistiness as a child, to which Hart attributes her ability to survive the Holocaust. Hart also offers a moral reading of her experiences to make sense of her own life and to guide future generations. *Return to Auschwitz* addresses as well issues concerning the Holocaust writ large, such as Jews' limited capacity to resist Nazi oppression. This expansion of the narrative may reflect Hart's involvement in Holocaust education and her awareness of the questions that arise in public discussions of this subject. Moreover, as the book's title indicates, *Return to Auschwitz* adds to Hart's wartime account her reflections on the task of recalling these experiences and on how this task became part of her life story.

By the time she recorded her interview for the VHA in 1998, Kitty Hart-Moxon had divorced her first husband, remarried, and retired from her career as a radiologist, while continuing her commitment to Holocaust education. Earlier in the decade, she had appeared in the documentary film *Another Journey by Train* and recorded a lengthy audio interview for the Imperial War Museum. The VHA interview takes place in the wake of decades of Kitty's telling her life story, in different media and before different audiences, and of garnering international recognition for her dedication to Holocaust education.

Throughout Hart-Moxon's account in the VHA interview of her life after World War II she interweaves recollections of personal experiences with discussion of her commitment to Holocaust remembrance. Hart-Moxon foregrounds her decision to speak about the war prominently when recalling the early postwar years. She situates her decision to document her and her mother's wartime experiences in their immediate aftermath. While still in a displaced persons camp in Broitzem, Germany, Hart-Moxon explains, she set about composing "a small sort of account" of her and her mother's survival "while it was fresh in our minds," writing her recollections in English even though her command of the language was limited. When Hart-Moxon recounts the conversation she had with her uncle upon arriving in England, in which he told her not to speak about her wartime ordeals, she characterizes his words as having "altered the course of my life" and projects forward from that defining incident to the present: "From that moment on, I realized one thing I must do: keep talking! Even if nobody wants to listen, you're just going to talk for the next fifty years. . . . That was my duty. . . . I knew I'd have to make enormous sacrifices . . . , that somehow in my life I'd have to sacrifice my career or whatever, but I have to set time apart for educating people and telling them exactly what had happened."[88]

Hart-Moxon characterizes her ongoing commitment to telling her story of survival and to Holocaust remembrance generally as having taken a toll on her personal and professional life. She suggests that her marriage to Rudolf Hart ended in divorce at least in part because of his lack of interest in her wartime experiences: "My own husband never asked me one single question of what happened to me. If he hadn't read my book or seen my video, he wouldn't know what happened." Later, Hart-Moxon mentions that, though her second husband, Philip Moxon, is not Jewish, he "understands the issue of the Holocaust very much more so than my first husband." Of her career as a radiologist, she explains that, early on, "I did realize that I will never take a full-time appointment because I had to set some time aside for my Holocaust work. So, in effect, I knew I had to sacrifice part of my career."[89]

As she recalls different opportunities for telling her story, Hart-Moxon's sense of accomplishment as a renowned Holocaust survivor is clear. In particular, she notes the impact of the 1979 documentary, especially in England, where "it was just like a catalyst" in creating public awareness about the Holocaust. Because of the film, Hart-Moxon explains, in 1986 she was asked to testify at the war crimes trial in Wuppertal of Gottfried Weise, who had been a commander at Auschwitz. Hart-Moxon notes that the prosecutors screened the documentary (which she refers to as "my videotape") during the proceedings and explains that it was "absolutely crucial" to the case against Weise, who was eventually convicted and given a life sentence.[90]

I I I

In the repeated tellings of her life story, Kitty consolidates the significance of events she understands to be key, even as she modifies her narrative. Consider four versions of an episode she relates about her initiation into Auschwitz as this story appears in both of her published memoirs, Morley's documentary film, and her VHA interview. Even as Kitty's tellings of the story vary in detail and are situated differently within each work, this episode remains of strategic importance in her personal history, and not only because it begins on the first night she and her mother spent in the camp, housed in the quarantine block where new arrivals were kept. As her repeated tellings reveal, narrating this episode conveys a foundational lesson that Kitty learned about surviving the genocide both materially and morally.

Here is the earliest published telling of this episode, in *I Am Alive*:

> My immediate neighbour was a Gypsy who had been here just two weeks. I think I shall always remember her voice. She looked closely at me and said:
>
> "I can see great strength in your eyes, child. Let me have your palm, and I will see what it says. Yes," she continued, "I can see quite clearly you *will* come out of here. How, I don't know, but you will be one of the very few to see freedom again. Remember, you must never lose your will to live. Fight for your life, or you will be finished very quickly."
>
> My first day in Auschwitz was over.
>
> I was awakened at about four o'clock next morning by the deafening shout of whistles. It was still dark and for a moment I had not the faintest idea where I was. I felt cold and shivery all over. My clothes were still wet and still clung to my skin. At last I recognized the voice of the *Blockälteste* [i.e., the woman in charge of the barracks] screaming at us to get up and go outside. I shook the Gypsy, but there was no response. I touched her. She was stone cold dead. She must have died hours before, and I had been lying against her body. . . .
>
> I had kept a crust of bread from the night before and so I looked for it inside my shift. It was gone, I had lost it during the night or perhaps it had been stolen. I ran back to my bunk, where the body of the dead Gypsy woman still lay. I looked for my bread all over and could not find it. I searched the dead woman. Tucked inside her blouse were several rations of bread. She could eat no more, so I helped myself to them.[91]

In this narrative Hart links her arrival in Auschwitz with two sequences that anticipate her ultimate survival of the camp: a prophecy that she will "see freedom again" and the discovery of what would prove to be a strategy to keep herself alive by taking possessions from a dead prisoner. Both sequences emanate from the "Gypsy," thereby linking her uncanny augury with the grim reality of material survival in the face of the camp's punitive conditions.

Hart relates this episode in *Kitty: Return to Auschwitz* about midway through the film's central sequence, which documents her visit to the camp.

(The placement in this sequence is, of course, the director's decision and does not necessarily reflect when Hart told this story during the three days of filming at Auschwitz.) She is prompted to recall her first night in Auschwitz as she and her son stand inside a barracks lined with tiers of wooden bunks:

> My mother and I, we scrambled onto here somewhere, and I was lying next to some woman, and it turned out she was a gypsy, you know, and she looked at me, and she sort of looked at my hands, and she said, "You're going to come out." And I thought, "What the heck is she talking about, I'm going to come out"—she looked at my hands and—I think it was a psychological thing, it stayed with me really, right though. I kept saying, this gypsy said I'm going to come out, so I've got to live, she said so. Anyway, I slept, I slept right through the night because I was terribly tired, there had been no food for about forty-eight hours, because we'd come from prison and we'd missed the bread ration. . . . And I slept next to this gypsy, and I'm terribly cold at night, you see, because we had only one layer of clothes and those were Russian uniforms, a sort of a khaki affair. My head had been shaved and I'd never been without hair, I was terribly cold and I didn't know why I was so cold. And then a whistle blew, and everyone started rushing out this very first morning, and I shook this woman, you see, and she was cold, you see, and she'd died in the night, and she was dead for some hours, and this was why I was so cold, because she was dead. And so I said to my mother, I said, "Now look, she's dead. I know what's got to be done. We've got to have her clothes, and we've got to have her bread ration, if she's got one, because it's no good to her." And then it came to me that this was the way to live. You must have it off the dead. And this was the principle that I adhered to all the time. That you must take off the dead, you must never take off the people that are alive. But it's yours if the people are dead. You must take advantage of this. And so, my very first thing, I stripped this gypsy, I stripped off everything she had, and so my mother and I had almost immediately a second layer of clothes and a second bread ration.[97]

Recalling the incident in situ and relating it to her son, Hart both iterates the same core plot elements as written in *I Am Alive* and elaborates them with different details and commentary. For example, this time the woman's prophecy is shorter than before, and Hart departs from a moment-by-moment account of this encounter to voice skepticism about this augury, rationalizing in retrospect its impact on her as "a psychological thing," though also noting the encouragement it offered her in the months ahead. Most striking is the compression of her discovery of the woman's death with the decision to take her clothes (not mentioned in *I Am Alive*) and bread ration, which Hart here reports discussing and sharing with her mother. Moreover, Hart extrapolates from this incident to a larger "principle" of how to survive in Auschwitz. These changes in Hart's narrative, enhancing its significance for her story as a whole while compressing its sequence of events (there is no mention in this version of her leaving and returning to the barracks), may reflect the distinctive circumstances of its telling: on camera, in the camp, with her son.

The account of this incident in Hart's second memoir both expands on the first published version and incorporates elements of its telling in the documentary film:

My immediate neighbour was a gipsy [*sic*] who whispered to me that she had got here just two weeks ahead of us. She sounded very strained and feeble, but in the gloom she brought her face close to mine and said:

"I see great strength in your eyes, child. Let me have your palm, and I'll see what it has to say." She bent closely over it. "Yes, I can see you *will* come out of here. How, I don't know, but you will be one of the few to see freedom again. Remember, you must never lose your will to live. Fight for your life, or you'll be finished very quickly."

My first day in Auschwitz was over.

At about four in the morning we were awakened by the deafening shrill of whistles. It was still dark and for a few seconds I hadn't the faintest idea where I was. My cold, damp clothes clung to my skin. Then I recognized the voice of the *Blockälteste* screaming at us to get up. I rolled off the bunk and turned to shake the gipsy. There was no response. She was stone cold and must have died hours before; and I had been lying pressed against her body. . . .

Last night I had tucked a small crust of bread into my sagging blouse. It was gone: either it had fallen out during the night or it had been stolen. I ran back to my bunk to look for it. But the dead gipsy still lay there, so I searched her and found several rations of bread hidden away. I hesitated for a moment; then helped myself to the bread and to her shirt, which was less rough than my ex-army garment and could be worn underneath without showing. This was the first time I had ever taken from the dead. It wouldn't be the last.[93]

In this version, Hart enriches the narrative with new details, such as describing the sound of the woman's voice. Thanks to a tightening of language and the use of contractions, the writing more closely resembles oral narration than does *I Am Alive*. Moreover, this version shifts the framing of the episode's future significance. The first memoir includes an anticipatory comment on the woman's prophecy ("I think I shall always remember her voice"), prefiguring the end point of surviving the war. *Return to Auschwitz* comments instead on taking the woman's bread and shirt ("This was the first time I had ever taken from the dead. It wouldn't be the last"), which introduces Kitty's strategy for staying alive in Auschwitz, in keeping with the woman's exhortation to "fight for your life." *I Am Alive* offers a brief rationale for taking the bread ("She could eat no more"). The second memoir does not explain this action here (in fact, Hart mentions that she briefly hesitated to do it at first) but does discuss it more generally a few pages later, implicating Kitty's mother in formulating this strategy for survival:

> Very early on, Mother and I agreed that no matter what happened, we would not play the Nazi game. Life in Auschwitz was a matter of organizing, of grabbing the bare necessities whenever you could find them. But we would never let ourselves be demoralized into cheating the living. If we took anything, it must be from the dead. People today may flinch from such an idea. But what use had the dead for their clothes or their pitiful rations? Mother, [who was working] in [the camp] hospital, had plenty of opportunities for taking bread and the occasional slice of cheese or salami from a corpse; the body suffered no extra misery. To rob the living, or the half-living, was to speed them on their way to death. To organize the relics of the dead was to acquire material which helped keep the living alive, and keep the half-living breathing, with just enough strength maybe to survive until the gates opened to a freer, sweeter world outside.[94]

Similarly, *Kitty: Return to Auschwitz* includes a sequence, filmed separately from the scene of Hart recounting the story of her first night in the camp, in which she discusses the morality of taking things from the dead in order to survive. While walking the grounds of Auschwitz with her son, Hart explains:

> One of the best things to do was to carry [dead] bodies. Why? It was very hard work. But (a) you worked inside the camp; you didn't do external work, you see,

and (b) the dead body had a ration, a piece of bread; the dead body had one change of clothes, and it wasn't any good to this dead body, was it? I mean, I don't have to feel guilty about this, do I?[95]

When recalling this episode in her VHA interview, Hart-Moxon once more offers different details in the course of relating the same core narrative, linking the arrival in Auschwitz, the prophecy of Kitty's survival, and the formulation of a morally circumscribed means of surviving the extreme conditions of the camp:

The first night we spent just like sardines, eight people on a bunk, and I was lying next to, it transpired, a gypsy, who had been there a few days before, and— she was a German gypsy, actually a true German gypsy—and she asked me if I speak German, "Yes, yes," and I spoke to her, and she said to me, "Give me your hand." She said, "I can foretell the future. Give me your hand." She looked at my lifeline and she said, "Well, I don't know, but you are going to come out of here. It's written here on your wrist. I know it. And never give up. Because this is what's going to happen." And I laughed at that, really, it was a joke, I think, anyway, she—and we settled down for the night. We didn't have any food, we settled down for the night, and then whistles blew the next morning, four o'clock, I had no idea where I was. . . . And I shook this woman I was sleeping next to, and I couldn't wake her. And then I kept on saying, "Come on, wake up, you've got to get up." And she was cold. And I was terribly cold, and I was terribly cold through that night, because you only had one layer of clothes, don't forget, nothing to cover yourself up with—and she was cold. And she died during the night. And I was lying next to her dead body. And she was dead. And my mother was very close by, and I said to my mother, "She's dead." And I said, "I know what we've got to do. Immediately. We've got to do something. And that is, we've got to have everything that she's got. Everything. If she's got any bread"—because we hadn't eaten—"if she's got any clothes, we must take it. Because it's not good to her; it will never do any good to her at all, she is dead." And my mother agreed. And we stripped her. Took everything off her, and immediately, I gave my mother a second layer of clothes. And she had a few bread rations, which you had to keep on your body, because if you didn't, you didn't have it by the morning. And so, eventually it came to me that day, first night, this is the way to survive in this place. If anybody dies, you have everything off them. But you must never touch anything of anybody, of a living prisoner. But when they're dead, that's fine, that's yours. You must preserve life, this is what you must do. Try and live off the dead. And I used this principle over the next twenty months of existence in Auschwitz.[96]

In this telling, Hart-Moxon compresses discrete elements of the episode into a compelling moment of initiation into the ways of Auschwitz. In particular the realization "immediately" of how to survive by "living off the dead" occurs to her "that day." Her mother is present straightaway, as both an interlocutor and a fellow beneficiary of the dead woman's belongings (which is also mentioned in the documentary film but not in either published memoir). Both the telling generally and the recounted process of determining how to survive in Auschwitz are expedited, while the articulation of this episode's moral parameters is expanded, demonstrating how the author derived enduring life lessons from extremely harrowing circumstances. At the same time, Hart-Moxon offers tangential information about camp life generally (prisoners having only one layer of clothing, the necessity of hiding bread rations in one's clothes), informing listeners about the workings of Auschwitz that she was to discover later.

Over time, the retellings of this episode clarify the instructional value of this defining moment in Kitty's initiation into Auschwitz. Attention to the dead woman shifts, as does the understanding of what she imparted of value to Kitty. She ascribes enduring worth less to the woman's prophecy, which is treated with skepticism in both oral accounts, than to her death and the opportunity it provided Kitty. Beyond the immediate acquisition of extra clothing and bread from the woman's body, her death endowed Kitty with insight into how to survive Auschwitz and to do so with a moral integrity responsive to the camp's extreme, crushing conditions.

Linguist Deborah Schiffrin's analysis of a retold survivor narrative reveals that "it is not only time and circumstance that add to the ever widening contexts of later experiences that reconstruct the meanings of the past, but also story telling itself. Thus [the survivor's] first public telling of her [wartime experience] becomes part of the scaffolding of knowledge that underlies how she will retell the past again."[97] Kitty's oft-told story of surviving the Holocaust similarly evolves with each telling, so as to address a growing, changing audience, further removed temporally from World War II, yet more likely to have some prior awareness of the Holocaust than was the case when Kitty first set about relating her story to whoever would listen. With time, her telling becomes that of a famous survivor, who is already renowned for her ability to offer a compelling, detailed narrative, and whose authority is bolstered by her ongoing commitment to Holocaust education.

By the mid-1990s, when Hart-Moxon was interviewed for the VHA, the greater part of her life had been taken up with the task of Holocaust remembrance; it had become a defining presence in her adulthood. The story of her life is therefore about both survival and its narration. Like the challenge of staying alive during the Holocaust, telling her story after the war tested Kitty's resolve and compelled her to thrive by disobeying. Just as she deems the Holocaust an experience that taught her much, even as she resents its having robbed her of a proper education in her youth, Hart-Moxon characterizes her commitment to Holocaust remembrance as both an accomplishment in which she takes pride and a constraint on her professional and personal life. In the concluding moments of this lengthy interview, Hart-Moxon characterizes her postwar life as being centered on Holocaust remembrance: "I've never stopped being involved in Holocaust activities," which includes serving on educational committees, lecturing, and participating in many school projects in both England and the United States, as well as leading group trips to sites in Poland. When asked, at the end of the interview, why she decided to tell her story to the VHA, she replies simply, "I've been telling it since 1945."[98]

I I I

In his pioneering study of videotaped interviews with Holocaust survivors, literature scholar Lawrence Langer champions the medium for facilitating "above all a freedom from the legacy of literary form and precedent" for interviewees, suggesting that the recordings provide "an unmediated text on this subject."[99] Yet both a renowned survivor's oft-told life story, exemplified by Kitty Hart-Moxon's narratives, and survivors' personal histories that include discussions of the same widely familiar Holocaust narrative, such as *Schindler's List*, manifest the extent to which these videotaped life histories are conditional, informed by differences in time, setting, medium, and audience, among other factors. Moreover, these recordings reveal how porous survivors' narratives can be, not only incorporating other narratives but also open to metadiscussions of the act of narrating. Awareness of these complications does not undermine the interviews' value. Rather, this attention enhances understanding their significance as works of remembrance, rooted in recalling the past as an ongoing activity in which narrators revise their understanding of their lives, negotiate external influences, and reflect on the activity of storytelling.

The structure of the VHA likewise complicates the nature of these narratives. By dint of its digital constitution, the Archive configures its holdings as simultaneously a library of individuals' life stories and a vast inventory of discrete narrative segments, which are defined by the Archive's indexing rubric as topics of information rather than by the interviewees who provide the information. The VHA's online platform enables users both to observe a survivor offer a lifetime of recollections as the narrative unfolds in real time and to disrupt this process by locating, aggregating, and comparing multiple survivors' accounts of specific subjects.

The VHA's holdings and the ways that users engage them thereby complicate any simple correlation between storyteller and story. Both the medium of video used to record survivor interviews and their digitized online delivery within a multivalent search mechanism provide new ways of mediating memory that are significantly different from more established forms, such as the written memoir or documentary film. Moreover, these two technological innovations facilitate complementary engagements with survivor narratives, demonstrating their integrity as well as their contingency. For users of the Archive, a sign of this double-edged engagement is ever present, even as they are engrossed in watching and listening to a particular narrative. As each survivor speaks, the apposite indexing terms appear below the video frame, segment by segment, providing viewers with an ongoing reminder that the survivor's story does not stand alone. Rather, each of these life histories exists in relation to other stories—and to other means of narration.

LANGUAGE

In Other Words

Much has been made of the importance of audio and video interviews providing opportunities to hear a Holocaust survivor speak in "his [or her] own words."[1] But what exactly are survivors' "own words," given the complex range and dynamics of language use so frequent among them? Most Jewish Holocaust survivors have spoken more than one language over the course of their lives. Many grew up in richly polyglot environments, shaped by contact among multiple ethnic communities, shifting political powers, and expanding educational and cultural possibilities in the decades before World War II. To cite but one example, Flora Benveniste, a survivor who grew up in Salonika, Greece, reports in her VHA interview that during the prewar years her family spoke "Ladino Spaniol" (also known as Judeo-Spanish and Judezmo, among other names) at home and that they heard Italian, French, and Greek spoken on the street. At the time, Benveniste attended an Italian private school, where she also studied English, the language in which she is interviewed.[2]

Displacement, hiding, and imprisonment during the war years often forced Jews to learn new languages or suppress the use of languages they knew—for example, not to speak Polish, lest a "Jewish accent" betray one's identity. In addition, Jews, along with other peoples imprisoned in Nazi concentration camps, grappled with the singular use of language in these places, which evolved their own argot. Some people fleeing Nazi persecution even tried to survive by abandoning language altogether and pretending to be mute. After the war, many

Jewish survivors immigrated to new countries, where they learned still more languages (especially English, Israeli Hebrew, or Spanish), while languages they already knew sometimes fell into disuse or were deliberately discouraged.

David Boder addressed the issue of language use in the course of recording and analyzing his audio interviews with Holocaust survivors in postwar Europe. Aware of their linguistic diversity, Boder envisioned his project as a multilingual undertaking from the start and eventually conducted interviews in nine different languages. As a rule, he asked survivors to speak in their language of choice, usually their mother tongue. Boder was motivated to do so in part by the conviction that speaking in a language of "familiarity and comfort" was key to obtaining the fullest account from his subjects. By contrast, he observed, "The flow of speech with recently acquired second languages is greatly restrained and the expression of ideas in most cases substantially hampered." Moreover, Boder considered his interviewees' choice of language to be valuable information in its own right, including those occasions when a survivor switched from one language to another during the interview.[3]

For example, Boder interviewed Bella Zgnilek, a Jewish survivor, in English, which, she explains, she learned in her native Poland before the war. Toward the end of the interview, Zgnilek responds to Boder's inquiry about songs she learned while a prisoner in Gross-Rosen concentration camp by reciting some lyrics in German. Boder then asks Zgnilek, by way of concluding the recording, whether "there [is] anything you want to tell your own people in America," and she replies briefly in English: "Well, I will just send them regards, and I am happy that not everybody of the Jews went through such a hard life as we did." Next, Boder explains, "Bella wants to add a few remarks in Polish," and she says the following (per Boder's published translation): "I would like to tell you, my friends, that all of us Jews ought to strongly hate the Germans because of the wrongs which they did to us and our families, because they broke our hearts, broke our homes, and we ought never to forget that." Boder ends the interview by commenting:

> This was a kind of a postscript that I wanted to have, because it's exceedingly important to have the feelings of these young people. We notice here that she spoke in German, in English, in Polish, and when it came to express her feelings she preferred to express it in Polish. This polyglotism, or multilinguistics if we want to call it that way, represents a psychological and ethnic problem at the same time.[4]

As Alan Rosen notes, Zgnilek's final remarks, offered in different languages to distinct Jewish audiences, "dramatically" manifest tensions "between evidence and audience, between native and acquired languages, and . . . between retribution and conciliation." Boder's final comment in this interview attests to his more general conviction that "not only what [survivors] said but how they said it . . . could best attest to the privations they had recently suffered."[5] At the same time, Boder was concerned about making the information he had gathered from his informants accessible to an American audience. When he published transcripts of these interviews, they were all rendered in English.[6]

Decades later, the Museum of Jewish Heritage addressed the same concerns about language use when it began to videotape Holocaust survivors' life histories. The museum's Video History Project, inaugurated in 1989, recorded interviews with hundreds of Holocaust survivors in English, French, Hebrew, Hungarian, Polish, Russian, Spanish, and Yiddish. The project's academic coordinator, folklorist Toby Blum-Dobkin, was familiar with Boder's pioneering interviews as well as more recent projects. She explained:

> On the one hand, . . . I believe that for accuracy of expression and elicitation of native terminology, a person should be interviewed in the language in which he or she is most comfortable, preferably in the language that person spoke at the time of the events being described. . . . On the other hand, the Museum's Video History Project is an educationally oriented project with the goal of creating an archive accessible to both scholars and the general public in the United States and elsewhere. The interviewees themselves are given a choice of which language to be interviewed in. Those living in English-speaking countries usually prefer to be interviewed in English, so that their interviews will be accessible to their younger family members and to the general public.[7]

Though the VHA boasts interviews with Holocaust survivors conducted in thirty-two languages, its model for the individual interview is monolingual, consistent with most oral history collections, such as the Museum of Jewish Heritage project. This decision reflects a pervasive "monoglot standard," which, anthropologist Michael Silverstein has observed, is hegemonic in American public culture, despite the rich multilingualism of the nation's population.[8] The Shoah Foundation asked survivors to indicate in advance the language in which they wished to be interviewed, so that appropriate interviewers could be assigned to them. This monolingual model is understood as facilitating not only interviewing but also indexing interviews and, eventually, listening to them. Moreover, this model rests on the assumption that a, if not the, primary value of the interview is informational and that the successful transmission of information from interviewee to auditor is best accomplished in a single language, which serves simply as a conduit of meaning and has no inherent meaning itself. In effect, once a survivor's choice of language for the interview has been made, the significance of the language itself becomes nominal.

Yet language use is key to the design of the VHA, though not without complications. On one hand, conducting interviews in dozens of different languages is fundamental to the global dimension of the Shoah Foundation's aspiration to record as many Holocaust survivors as possible. On the other hand, the language in which the VHA was created and in which its website, index, and database operates is English. Also, there are many more interviews with Jewish Holocaust survivors, the Archive's predominant group of interviewees, conducted entirely or partially in English (24,966 out of 49,871) than in any other language.[9] The extensive inventory of English-language interviews reflects the large number of survivors who settled in Anglophone countries after the war, as English played no direct role in the preponderance of these Jews' lives before or during the Holocaust. Moreover, this corpus of interviews exemplifies a major shift toward the use of English by Jews generally in the postwar years, as it became the predominant world language.[10]

Deciding which language to speak in their VHA interviews constrained most survivors' full range of linguistic resources. This was especially true for those survivors who had spoken Yiddish before the war. On the eve of the Holocaust, there were an estimated eleven million Yiddish speakers in the world.[11] Though many of them lived in large immigrant communities in the Americas, South Africa, and Palestine, the majority were found in Europe, especially eastern Europe, where Yiddish had been established centuries earlier as the vernacular of what was by the 1700s the largest Jewish population in history.

As prevalent as Yiddish had become by the first decades of the twentieth century, the language has never stood alone throughout its long history and was part of an especially complex set of multilingual constellations in eastern Europe during the decades before World War II. Prewar native speakers of Yiddish typically had some familiarity with at least one other language, as a consequence of where they lived, as well as their gender, class background, education, and religious and political convictions. These languages included those used in Jewish religious life (the Hebrew and Aramaic of worship and devotional study); one or more vernaculars spoken by their non-Jewish neighbors (Belorussian, German, Hungarian, Lithuanian, Polish, Romanian, Russian, or Ukrainian, among others); a state language, used for official communications, but not necessarily spoken by most locals (for example, German in eastern Galicia before World War I, Romanian in northern Bukovina during the interwar years); a language studied in a secular school (such as French or Latin) or on one's own for intellectual enrichment; or a language learned because of ideological convictions (Esperanto, modern Hebrew). Consider, therefore, the challenge posed by the imperative to conduct interviews with Holocaust survivors in a single language in light of the dilemma described by one prewar Polish Jewish adolescent when he set about writing his autobiography for a contest organized by the YIVO Institute in the 1930s:

> As I sit down to write my autobiography, I don't actually know which language to use: Yiddish, Hebrew, or even Polish. There are issues that I think about in Yiddish; these are primarily matters connected to daily life. I think about questions concerning Palestine and Zionism in Hebrew. Then there are also many issues that I think about in Polish: things that have to do with school, Polish history, world history, and the like. I've decided, however, to write in Yiddish, as I expect that my autobiography will consist of my everyday experiences.[12]

The majority of Jews murdered during the Holocaust spoke Yiddish. Their annihilation cut in half the number of Yiddish speakers in the world and destroyed major centers of Yiddish cultural activity, all within a few years. This devastating loss imparted new symbolic value to the language; the sudden absence of Yiddish speech became "a compelling metonym for the tragic loss of its speakers."[13] Questions about the language's prospects prompted a new self-consciousness about its viability in the wake of the Holocaust. At the same time, other factors contributed to the declining use of Yiddish: the suppression of Yiddish culture in the Soviet Union, the imperative to establish Hebrew as the exclusive Jewish language of the new State of Israel, and large-scale linguistic assimilation by American Jews. The long-standing tautological relationship among the Yiddish language, the Jews of East European origin, and their culture had come undone.

This dramatic shift in the instrumental and symbolic value of Yiddish after the Holocaust distinguishes it from most other languages in which VHA interviews were conducted.[14] The frequent perception of Yiddish as a "dying" language parallels concerns for the future of Holocaust remembrance, heightened by the aging of survivors. However, these two issues prompt diverging responses: a commitment to the future of Yiddish typically centers on encouraging people to continue using the language, but a commitment to remembering the Holocaust usually prioritizes doing so in languages that are now widely known, especially by younger generations, including non-Jews as well as Jews.

It may therefore surprise some users of the VHA to discover that it includes 633 interviews listed as conducted either entirely (556) or partially (78) in Yiddish, for a survivor's decision to be interviewed in this language may seem inimical to the future of Holocaust memory. The number of Yiddish speakers in the world at the turn of the millennium was estimated at six hundred thousand,[15] including a demographically disproportionate number of older speakers. The one substantial area of recent growth in the Yiddish-speaking population has been among Hasidim and other *haredim*, who, as a rule, are unlikely to make use of the VHA. These circumstances might prompt some people to wonder why a survivor would choose to tell his or her life story in Yiddish: Who will ever listen to an interview conducted in this language?

That such questions could arise is noteworthy in itself. Using Yiddish in this context seems to demand an explanation: Was it the only language that the survivor could speak fluently? If not, could there possibly be some instrumental value in making this choice? Or was there an ideological or symbolic reason for choosing Yiddish, if the survivor could also speak another language? Might there be some psychological motive at work, especially among those survivors who switch to Yiddish from another language in the course of their interviews? Such desires to rationalize the survivors' choice of Yiddish rest on assumptions about the purpose of the VHA as a vehicle of Holocaust remembrance directed toward the largest possible audience at the time of recording the interviews in the 1990s and beyond. By contrast, it might seem that interviews conducted in Yiddish are addressed to the past rather than the future and are directed inward—available largely either to an aged, dwindling Jewish speech community or, in the case of *haredim*, to a community of Yiddish speakers largely isolated from the cultural mainstream—rather than to a general audience.

Precisely because of the great ruptures in Yiddish language use wrought by World War II, some scholars, including those studying Holocaust remembrance, have sought to interview people who grew up speaking Yiddish in prewar eastern Europe in order to document their use of the language, regarding their Yiddish as itself worthy of preservation. When Blum-Dobkin advocated for interviews conducted in Holocaust survivors' native tongues, she also argued that this would provide "important documentation of language and dialect use," having Yiddish especially in mind.[16] Postwar interest in recording prewar Yiddish speakers engendered several documentation projects, including Ben Stonehill's collection of over one thousand audio recordings of Yiddish songs performed by Holocaust survivors in New York in 1948;[17] the hundreds of audiotaped interviews for the *Language and Culture Atlas of Ashkenazic Jewry* (*LCAAJ*), initiated by Uriel Weinreich at Columbia University in the 1950s; The World of Yiddish: The Voice and the Image, a collection of "video testimonies given in Yiddish in which informants talk about their lives in Jewish Eastern Europe before the Holocaust," a project begun in the 1990s by the Yiddish Department of the Hebrew University in Jerusalem;[18] and AHEYM, the Archives of Historical and Ethnographic Yiddish Memories (the acronym means "homeward" in Yiddish), launched in 2002 by two Indiana University professors, linguist Dov-Ber Kerler and historian Jeffrey Veidlinger. Over the course of a decade Kerler and Veidlinger videotaped several hundred interviews with elderly Jews living in small towns in Ukraine, Moldova, Romania, Hungary, and Slovakia, who were sought out as "Eastern Europe's last native speakers of Yiddish."[19] These interviews document Yiddish language use and traditional Jewish folkways that the interviewees had maintained in the face of revolution, genocide, and postwar oppression.

In these projects, unlike the VHA, language use is the defining interest. Therefore interviewees' recollections, including those of Holocaust survivors, are attended to because they evince the endurance of prewar Yiddish language or culture, manifested in speaking a regional dialect, singing folk songs, or describing venerable folkways. Conversely, though the VHA has about as many Yiddish-language interviews as the *LCAAJ* and more than the number in AHEYM, the Shoah Foundation made these recordings primarily to document informants' recollections of their lives before, during, and after the Holocaust. In the VHA, survivors' choice of speaking Yiddish is, in itself, considered to be of peripheral interest.

VHA interviewees who speak in Yiddish seldom discuss forthrightly the fact that they do so. In one such exceptional instance, Dov Lewanoni explains at the beginning of the recording that he is giving his interview in Yiddish because it was the language spoken by most of the six million Jews murdered during the war.[20] But in all these interviews survivors' use of Yiddish has an inherent, if tacit, significance: it enacts the value of Yiddish as a living language at a time when notions of its obsolescence, if not demise, were widespread. The use of Yiddish in hundreds of VHA interviews also testifies, if obliquely, to the survivors' understanding of the project as rooted in a specifically Jewish context, notwithstanding the universal values that the Shoah Foundation has invested in the moral imperative of Holocaust remembrance. These survivors' use of Yiddish also implicitly associates the language with Jewish endurance, rather than destruction.

Yiddish is manifest in VHA interviews in several ways: In addition to the hundreds of recordings conducted entirely in the language, there are dozens in which Yiddish is used as well as another language. Some survivors use Yiddish specifically to perform a poem, song, or other text in the course of interviews in which they otherwise speak another language. Moreover, in interviews conducted in other languages, survivors often interject occasional Yiddish words or phrases, sometimes to telling effect. To cite but one example, Lusia Puterman describes how she played tricks on Germans during the war, when she concealed her identity as a Jew by passing as a Pole. Commenting on this risky behavior, she explains: "I was getting very *khutspevate* [insolent], you know. . . . I started to be quite *frekh* [cheeky]."[21] Puterman's interjecting of Yiddish terms here is homologous—that is, she expresses the audacious nature of her wartime behavior by using Yiddish words that are, given their disruptive inclusion in her English-language narrative, themselves brazen "exposures" of her then-covert Jewishness.

Even in some VHA videos in which Yiddish is never or only seldom uttered, it can be detected as the interviewees' first language by dint of how it inflects their speech. In many interviews conducted in English, for example, survivors use idioms that, though consisting entirely of English words, are calques derived from Yiddish constructions, such as the following: "This is a time what I don't want to remember it"; "He made a living on them"; "I like you should kill me."[22] Finally, there are interviews in which Yiddish is only a topic of discussion. Under the search terms "Yiddish language" and "Yiddish culture" the VHA indexes hundreds of Jewish survivors discussing these subjects, all doing so in a language other than Yiddish.

The various modes in which Yiddish is present in VHA interviews not only indicate how the language has endured in shaping the way survivors tell their life stories but also evince different ways in which Jewish survivors relate to the language: as a former or current vernacular, as an unfamiliar or disparaged tongue, or as a postvernacular language—that is, a mode of using Yiddish in which its secondary, symbolic value is privileged over its primary value as a means of communicating information, feelings, or ideas. In postvernacular Yiddish, "the very fact that something is said (or written or sung) in Yiddish is at least as meaningful as the meaning of the words being uttered—if not more so."[23] Examining these different ways of engaging Yiddish in the course of the VHA's interviews reveals how language use and cultural ideas about language inform the meaning of what survivors tell their interviewers and their imagined future audiences. Though often oblique, this information contributes to our understanding of how survivors recall the past and how language figures in the act of remembrance, whether as a vehicle of remembering, a subject of recollection, or both.

Yiddish Interpolated

The contingency of Yiddish as a language survivors use to relate their life stories is most readily evident in interviews that the VHA indexes as bilingual. These are videos in which interviewees, and sometimes interviewers as well, code-switch—that is, they shift from using one language to another. Code switching is a frequent, wide-ranging practice among people who know more than one language. Linguist Anne Szulmejster-Celnikier notes that, "as a diasporic language belonging to a minority, Yiddish, which became an authentic Jewish language within a heteroglossic context, favors code-switching."[24] For VHA interviewees, code switching is more than a commonplace; it constitutes a long-standing definitional Jewish practice. As literary critic Shmuel Niger once observed, "one language has never been enough for the Jewish people."[25]

Of the 154 interviews with Jewish survivors listed as bilingual in the VHA, half (78) are in Yiddish plus another language, and most of these are in Yiddish and English (52).[26] Because of the large number of interviews in Yiddish and English, there are almost as many bilingual interviews in English plus another language (75). Videos in Yiddish and English thus provide the most extensive opportunity to examine code switching in VHA interviews.[27]

Code switching occurs in these recordings within the rubric of interviews intended to be monolingual and with distinct roles for interviewers and interviewees, who, in most cases, were not acquainted with each other prior to the arrangement of the interviews. However, interviews conducted in Yiddish plus another language vary considerably as to how the two languages are used by both the survivor and the interviewer. Much depends on what was arranged in advance of the interview and the extent to which interviewers were able to adapt to survivors' spontaneous code switching. Consequently, use of Yiddish in bilingual interviews entails a test, sometimes unanticipated, of the interviewers' linguistic competence. An interviewer may choose to ask a survivor to translate unfamiliar Yiddish words or phrases—for example, when the interviewer and the survivor speak different dialects of the language. When the two share a compatible command of Yiddish, interviews can become fluid and conversational. The common language, used in the context of recalling the survivor's past, forms a discursive bond between interviewer and survivor. This bond could have had added value at a time when the ability to converse in Yiddish—especially with someone previously unknown to the survivor—was becoming less and less common.

Occasionally, an interview's bilingual format is clearly a fixed, prearranged configuration. In one recording, for example, Carol Stulberg interviews Chil Rajchman in German, while he answers her in Yiddish.[28] More revealing are videos in which an unanticipated switching of language takes place during the interview. These instances highlight the dynamics of recalling and narrating one's past, thanks to video's ability to document the process of remembrance unfolding in long, unedited sequences. At the same time, the nature of the medium may influence a survivor's switching from one language to another. Language shifts sometimes appear to be linked to the fact that VHA interviews are recorded in thirty-minute units, defined by the length of each videotape, which structure the flow of the interviewing process. Thus Eva Guttman (whose interview is identified at the start of the recording as being conducted in English and Yiddish) speaks almost entirely in Yiddish on the first three of her interview's eight videotapes. Beginning with the fourth tape, however, she speaks almost entirely in English; this shift, which proceeds unexplained on the video, suggests that, while changing tapes, there may have been a discussion between Guttman and her interviewer about language use.[29]

More often the impromptu switch of languages takes place during the recording itself. Survivor Chaim Bornstein begins his interview in English, occasionally groping for words and saying to himself in Yiddish, "*Vi zogt men?*" (How do you say?). After several minutes, he switches to narrating in Yiddish: "After the war, *mayn tfilin* [my phylacteries] got in fire. I didn't have *tfilin*. After *m'hot zikh bafrayt* [we were liberated]—" and he asks, "*Ken ikh araynvarfn a por yidishe verter?*" (Can I toss in a few Yiddish words?). Interviewer Naomi Rappaport replies, "*Yo, ir kent araynvarfn*" (Yes, you can toss [them] in), and on the rest of the first thirty-minute videotape Bornstein speaks largely in Yiddish.[30] Rappaport asks some questions in English, some in Yiddish, and occasionally translates Bornstein's narrative into English. The pattern repeats with the start of the next two tapes: Bornstein and Rappaport speak in English for the first few minutes, then Bornstein switches to Yiddish, with Rappaport following suit; by the fourth tape, the interview begins and continues entirely in Yiddish.

Usually a survivor's shift from one language to another does not appear to be a conscious choice. However, there are exceptional moments when switching to Yiddish seems deliberate, enabling survivors to say something they may feel can be voiced only in that language, or to address a different kind of listener, or to articulate something in a different affective register. At the end of an interview otherwise conducted entirely in English, interviewer Rosaline Krusner asks Kalman Rubner if he has something to add. He replies, "Do you understand Jewish [i.e., Yiddish]?" and then begins to speak for several minutes in the language:

Ayn zakh ken ikh nokh nisht farshtayn: Di gantse velt hot gevist vos kimt for in Poyln, un me harget yeydn tug, me hot geharget tsendlike touznter yidn, un dos iz meglekh, me hot gurnisht gekent epes tin, me hot gevist genou alts vos me hot getin. . . . Aza medine vos in Poyln iz geveyzn, . . . erlekhe yidn, tsadikim, me zeyt

ous nisht hant azelkhene yidn. . . . Vi mit aza mise-meshine oustsehargenen azoy
fil yidn, azoy fil yidishe kinder. . . . S'iz nisht tsi farshtayn, vos iz geshen.

[One thing I still can't understand: The entire world knew what was happening
in Poland, and every day they were killing, they killed tens of thousands of Jews,
and it was possible that no one did anything, they knew exactly everything that
was being done. . . . There was such a (Jewish) nation in Poland, . . . righteous
Jews, sages, you don't see Jews like that today. . . . And with such a gruesome
death, murdering so many Jews, so many Jewish children. . . . It can't be understood, why this happened.][31]

Though Rubner has already wondered, in his English-language reflections
on the war, how the genocide of Jews could happen, his anguished condemna-
tion of a world indifferent to the destruction of Polish Jews, whom he describes
in beatific terms, is articulated more elaborately and with greater emotional
intensity when he speaks in Yiddish. As in Bella Zgnilek's interview with David
Boder, Rubner offers different messages to separate audiences, distinguished
by language use. This practice resembles a distinction that literature scholar
Naomi Seidman observes between Elie Wiesel's Holocaust memoir *La nuit*
and his earlier work from which this French text was adapted, *Un di velt hot*
geshvign (And the world was silent). Whereas in the Yiddish memoir Wiesel
voiced a "survivor's political rage," Seidman notes, it is absent in his French
reworking of the text. She argues that this constitutes a telling shift in how
Wiesel conceived of his account of the Holocaust for two different audiences:
Yiddish-speaking Jews, many of them also survivors, versus a largely Christian
Francophone readership.[32]

The paper "slates" displayed at the beginning of each VHA video, which
provide basic cataloging information, confirm that the decision to conduct
these interviews in two languages was not always made in advance. Slates for
videos that the VHA identifies as bilingual variously describe the interview as
"Yiddish–English," "English and Yiddish," or even just "English"—the last vari-
ant indicating that the survivor's use of Yiddish during the interview was impromptu. Such is the case in Masha Loen's interview of Jacob Meller. At first,
he answers Loen's questions in English, though one can hear that Yiddish is his
native language. For example, a small but telling sign is his use of *un* (and) as a
conjunction in sentences that are otherwise in English. Early in the interview,

Meller switches to Yiddish when talking about his father, describing him as "*a yid a seykher*" (a Jew [who was] a merchant). As Meller continues to recall his family in Yiddish, Loen asks him more than once to respond to her questions in English, and when he persists in speaking Yiddish, she begins to translate his remarks. After a few minutes, Loen asks Meller to "tell the story in Yiddish. Let's speak Yiddish; it's much easier, OK?" He does so straightaway, and Loen (who is also not a native speaker of English) switches to asking questions in Yiddish for the most part. She occasionally asks Meller to translate a Yiddish word with which she is apparently not familiar (e.g., *tokeray*, machine shop). Conversely, Meller sometimes uses English terms in the course of his narrative (e.g., when describing a wedding, he uses the words *catering* and *waiters* rather than their Yiddish equivalents).[33]

As a result of their shared fluency in Yiddish, as well as what is eventually revealed to be a prior acquaintance with one another, Loen's interview of Meller becomes more of a conversation.[34] Deviating from VHA guidelines for interviewers, which specify that "the interviewer's remarks (except for questions)

Paper "slates" such as this one appear at the beginning of each VHA video with basic information about the recording, including the language used. Although this slate indicates that survivor Sol Heitner is to be interviewed in English, the interview is conducted in both English and Yiddish. Provided by the USC Shoah Foundation.

should be kept to a minimum," Loen freely prompts Meller and comments on his recollections, in addition to serving as his impromptu translator.[35] At the conclusion of the interview, Loen interjects that Meller donates money to Holocaust institutions in the United States and Israel, "and I am very proud . . . *dir tsu kenen, un ikh dank dir* [to know you, and I thank you]."[36]

The nature of code switching in these interviews and the reasons for doing it vary from one interviewee to the next. The slate at the start of Lilly Goldstein's video also states that the interview will be conducted in English. Like Meller, Goldstein begins answering Alan Oirich's questions in English with occasional Yiddish words inserted, and her speech soon becomes a mix of English and Yiddish. At one point, Goldstein begins to tell a story in Yiddish about someone named Fleischman; Oirich begins to translate but then stops:

> Oirich: When you were—in English please, *af* [in] English.
>
> Goldstein: English. OK, I say English. The name is Gizzy Fleischman, *zi iz geven* [she was] a divorced woman, very nice, *elegánt, in* [elegant, and] a rich woman, but she try *arousgayn* [to go out] from the ghetto. She go to the subway, to the *vonat* [Hungarian: "train"], you know, to the *ban* [Yiddish: "train"], you know, she want maybe—and the gendarme look, as the *frou* [woman] is over here, she bring back *blitik* [bloody], the *kop* [head], and everything red—
>
> Oirich: She came back—
>
> Goldstein:—and the gendarme bring back to the ghetto, and unbelievable what they doing, only *halbe toyte* [half dead], unbelievable.[37]

As the interview proceeds, Goldstein tries to speak in English but keeps shifting to Yiddish until she speaks almost exclusively in that language. Oirich offers English summaries of what she says in Yiddish before posing his next question, always doing so in English. By the start of the third tape, Oirich identifies the interview as being conducted "in Yiddish and English." Ironically, Goldstein begins to use more English at this point, as she recalls the 1956 revolution in Hungary and then her coming to America the following year. Goldstein's shifting between languages may reflect her usual practice of code switching as a Hasidic woman living in the Brooklyn neighborhood of Williamsburg. Anthropologist Ayala Fader notes that the Hasidic women in Brooklyn whom she studied at the turn of the twenty-first century told her that their children were "unable to keep Yiddish and English distinct" from one another, and Fader also reports that the women themselves "were often unaware [when] they had switched languages."[38]

These "bilingual" interviews often entail additional languages as well. When searching for the English word *train*, Goldstein turns first to Hungarian, then to Yiddish. Chil Rajchman's German-Yiddish interview also includes, if nominally, a third language, Spanish. Rajchman, who was living in Argentina, spells his name at the beginning of the video using the Spanish names for the letters of the Roman alphabet, his interviewer addresses him as "Señor Rajchman," and he calls her *querida* (dear). Susa Marcusohn's interview, slated as "English," shifts back and forth between English and Yiddish; in addition, Marcusohn recalls and renders in Yiddish information she originally read or heard in Romanian when she was sent from her native Bukovina to a concentration camp in Transnistria in 1941. Throughout the recording, interviewer Paula Bultz both translates Marcusohn's Yiddish and uses her code switching to pose questions that advance the survivor's narrative.[39]

Bultz is able to guide the interview in this manner because of her command of Yiddish as well as the topic at hand. Not every interviewer faced with an interviewee who decides on the spot to speak in Yiddish is able to do so. Indeed, a survivor's impromptu code switching can pose an intractable challenge for the interviewer. Such was the case when Rosalie Franks interviewed Michael Wenger. Within the first few minutes of the video, slated as being conducted in English, Wenger begins speaking Yiddish. Franks is able to translate only bits of his answers and continues to ask him questions in English, to which he replies mostly in Yiddish. Franks repeatedly asks Wenger about terms she does not understand, which he translates. Though Franks's very limited command of Yiddish soon becomes apparent, Wenger continues speaking in the language.

Franks tries doggedly to glean the gist of what Wenger says from context, but her lack of language comprehension hampers her ability to follow Wenger's narrative, especially when it does not conform to her cultural expectations. When Franks asks Wenger about his family's religious life, he explains that his family was not religious but secular. Nevertheless, Franks asks Wenger to describe his family's observance of the Sabbath, and he replies, laughing, "*Shabes flegt men nit arbetn, ikh fleg nokh arbetn . . . , ikh bin geven a goy*" (On the

Sabbath [Jews] didn't work, I still used to work . . . , I was a gentile).[40] The linguistic and cultural disparity between interviewer and interviewee continues to create misunderstandings on Franks's part:

> Franks: So how did you get to America? How were you able to come here?
>
> Wenger: It isn't legal *fun Daytshland. Mir hobn geshmoglt dem grenets fun Peyln un me hot farlozn. Ir zet* [from Germany. We sneaked across the border from Poland, and they let (us). You see], we left Poland, *geganvet dem grenets. Zey flegn visn az mir, di yidn, geyen aroyset fun Peyln* [stole across the border. They knew that we Jews were leaving Poland].
>
> Franks: So you were able to get some visas.
>
> Wenger: *Nisht kayn vize, mir forn mit—di "brikhe" hot gearbet* [No visa, we traveled with—the Bricha was working]. Do you know what the Bricha is?[41]

Despite these impediments, the interview proceeds in this fashion for almost two hours. Wenger, undaunted by his interviewer's inability to understand much of what he is saying, offers his life story, considerably independent of her participation in the process. He is apparently able to understand and speak English, though not as fluently as he speaks Yiddish. In fact, toward the end of the interview Wenger talks about his life in the United States and introduces his family in English. Yet Yiddish is clearly the language in which he speaks more confidently and, perhaps, more candidly. Toward the end of the interview, Franks (who evidently never grasps Wenger's secularism) asks him, "After everything that happened, do you still have faith in God?" and he replies, with a chuckle, "Well, *ikh bin nisht geven kayn religyezer, keyn mol, un ikh bin itst nisht kayn religyezer* [I wasn't religious, never, and I'm not religious now], but I have faith in God, why not?"[42]

The value of this interview might seem compromised, given the limited ability of interviewer and interviewee to communicate. Yet precisely this shortcoming—and how each participant addresses the challenge on the spot—is of interest in its own right. Franks is determined to facilitate the telling of Wenger's life story, even though she can barely understand what he is saying. Wenger proceeds with his narrative, unhindered by his interviewer's predicament. In fact, their misalliance exemplifies the disparity between survivors and many of their auditors who are eager to hear eyewitness accounts of the Holocaust. Language is only the most obvious manifestation of this disparity, which also entails historical awareness, cultural literacy, and differences in sensibility (here, in particular, Franks's assumption, common among many VHA interviewers, that Jews in prewar eastern Europe were invariably observant of religious tradition). However formidable the distances separating survivors and their audiences, each group is nonetheless eager for the other—even if, as in this case, they often talk past each other.

In a few instances, Yiddish is heard in these interviews as not only a second language but also a third voice, even though the VHA protocols prohibit having anyone else in the room during videotaping other than the interviewee, interviewer, and camera crew. When Leon Welbel is asked at the start of his interview to say and spell his name, he replies, "*Ir hot gehat* [You had] my name here, *farvos darfstu mir fregn* [why do you have to ask me]?" and he calls to his wife, who is apparently nearby, though not on camera, for assistance. When Welbel cannot remember how to say something in English, such as the different types of grain that were ground in his family's mill in prewar Poland, he again asks his wife in Yiddish for help.[43]

This impromptu summoning of the familiarity of Yiddish, spoken by a close family member, to assist the survivor in articulating memories does not always prove successful. From the start of Paul Bacher's interview of Bela Gelbard, it is apparent that she cannot readily respond to his questions, though it is not clear whether this is because she has difficulty in hearing, in processing and articulating her thoughts, or in recalling details of the past. Although Gelbard finds it especially hard to remember names or the specifics of time and place, Bacher persists in asking her for this information, as she struggles to tell her life story. At the beginning of the third of the interview's four videotapes, an additional voice is heard off camera. It is a woman's voice, and she speaks to Gelbard in Yiddish (until this point, the interview has been conducted in English). This second woman turns out to be Gelbard's daughter, Gilda Hurwitz, who joins Bacher in pressing Gelbard for information. Hurwitz even prompts her mother to relate stories that she has apparently told her daughter in the past but that Gelbard claims, at first, not to remember. She continues to struggle to answer the questions put to her by both Bacher and her daughter, answering sometimes in Yiddish, more often in English. Though Yiddish is introduced into the interview as a memory aid, the language proves unable to facilitate Gelbard's limited ability to recount her past.[44]

In one VHA video, a third voice speaks in Yiddish posthumously. During Arlene Katz's interview, which is conducted in English, she recounts being temporarily separated from her husband during a roundup of Jews in Budapest in 1944, where they had found a temporary haven in a safe house. At this point, she plays an audio recording of her late husband, David Katz. Speaking in Yiddish to an unidentified interviewer, he describes the incident that ensued (the circumstances of his taped interview are not explained). The audiotape plays for several minutes, as Katz listens to her husband's voice. Then interviewer Raquel Grunwald suggests to Katz that she switch off the tape and explain what her husband said. Katz relates that, after being separated from her husband during the roundup, she suddenly heard him calling to her. Speaking to her in Yiddish, he told her to get out of the line, where she had been standing with the other Jews, and thereby saved her life and that of their baby. She then holds up a blanket in which, Katz explains, she had wrapped the baby. With these two relics—the recording of her husband and the blanket, kept for half a century—Katz reenacts this pivotal moment of her family's survival. The sound of her late

Survivor Arlene Katz, holding in one hand a cassette tape player, on which she played an audio recording of her late husband recounting, in Yiddish, a key incident in their survival of the Holocaust. In her other hand, Katz displays a blanket that figured in this incident. Provided by the USC Shoah Foundation.

husband's disembodied speech poignantly invokes his absence as well as the crucial role that hearing his voice, speaking in Yiddish, played in his family's rescue decades earlier.[45]

In these recordings the third voice disrupts the binary structure of the interview and complicates the interviewee's subjectivity by collaborating in the narration of the survivor's memories. The third voice in the interviews with Welbel and Gelbard speaks in Yiddish to assist in articulating a narrative in English, in the belief that what cannot be recalled in this language could be in the survivor's mother tongue. The third voice in Katz's interview, however, brings Yiddish into the narrative with a different value. Introduced by the survivor, this voice is meant not as a prompt for information but as an echo of both a crucial wartime experience and a lost loved one.

There is no regular pattern of code switching shared across these bilingual interviews or even a consistent manner of shifting from one language to another within a single interview. Rather, these recordings evince a wide range of possible movements between languages in the course of each survivor's ongoing effort to communicate. On the whole, survivors in these bilingual interviews speak Yiddish more quickly, with more complex syntax, richer vocabulary, and less groping for words than when they speak English. Their relative ease in speaking Yiddish is not necessarily a psychological response, as Boder and others have suggested, nor is it always tied to the topic of narration; what is clear is the survivors' greater linguistic competency in Yiddish. At the same time that their code switching manifests these interviewees' facility in Yiddish as their native tongue, this phenomenon can reveal the limitations of interviewers (and, by extension, many auditors) with the language.

The interviews in which survivors mix Yiddish with another language evince different ways survivors draw on their multilingual history to relate a life story despite the expectation of offering a monolingual narrative. Deviating from this norm should not be regarded as a sign of ineptitude. Barbara Kirshenblatt-Gimblett argues that the code switching one frequently hears in immigrant storytelling is "not the result of incompetence or illiteracy" but rather exhibits the narrators' "considerable skill in the manipulation of the available linguistic resources."[46] Occasionally, survivors' switching into Yiddish appears to be an intentional demonstration of this skill. More often their code switching seems unself-conscious, reflecting the merged nature of their everyday speech. At times this phenomenon exemplifies speakers' use of what linguist Sarah Bunin Benor terms a "Jewish linguistic repertoire"—that is, the ability to draw on "the linguistic features Jews have access to that distinguish their speech or writing from that of local non-Jews."[47] The language mixing heard in these interviews—entailing differences in language, kinds of code switching, and motives for doing so—evinces the mediated nature of telling one's life history in one's "own words" when that life has been lived amid a shifting constellation of languages, including the language of one's imagined future audience.

Yiddish Recalled

Many survivors discuss the roles that multiple languages played in the course of their personal histories, even when offering these accounts in a single language. The VHA index identifies hundreds of Jewish survivors who address "Yiddish language" (233 interviewees) or "Yiddish culture" (574) during interviews conducted in another language.[48] These interviews in the aggregate reveal the varied, complex dynamics of using and thinking about Yiddish over the course of the twentieth century, especially in relation to the Holocaust and its aftermath. Uniting these wide-ranging discussions of Yiddish is their articulation in other languages. Implicit in each reference to Yiddish is the survivor's remove from its use as a vernacular; at the same time, these reflections evince a common awareness that the language is significant to survivors' personal histories, whether as a means of communication or as a symbolic presence in Jewish life.

When recalling prewar life, survivors situate Yiddish within different multilingual contexts, reflecting where they lived, their gender, class background, educational opportunities, religiosity, and ideological convictions. Though these accounts are at times generic, in response to the often broad nature of interviewers' questions about prewar Jewish life, survivors usually recall Yiddish culture of the period in relation to their personal experience of literature, education, theater, music, or film. Survivors typically identify these phenomena as modern, as opposed to aspects of traditional Jewish life, and sometimes link this contrast to the disparity between older and younger generations. Alex Reifer, for instance, recalls attending performances of Yiddish theater and cabaret as a boy in Oświęcim. He was chaperoned by the family's non-Jewish maid (who did not understand Yiddish) but was never accompanied by his parents, whom Reifer describes as "very religious."[49] East European Jewish survivors offer relatively little discussion of Yiddish as part of prewar traditional religious life, perhaps because in that context they understood the language as an inevitable presence, remarkable only when its normality was disrupted. Sidney Glucksman recalls a teacher in *kheyder* (the traditional school for Jewish children's introductory religious education) who spoke an unfamiliar dialect of Yiddish, which amused Glucksman and the other pupils: "He [i.e., the teacher] called potatoes *bulbes*, and we made fun of him because we never heard anyone call a potato a *bulbe*."[50]

Often survivors recall changes in the use of Yiddish during the prewar years. Some East European Jewish survivors note that Yiddish was not their first language, though it often was for their parents, and that the language spoken at home was Polish or Russian. A few of these survivors report that their parents used Yiddish to communicate among themselves when they didn't want their children to understand, similar to the concomitant experience of many Anglophone children of Yiddish-speaking immigrants in America.[51] For other interviewees, Yiddish was primarily a language of home, but they spoke other languages elsewhere, for example, while attending schools where Polish, Romanian, Russian, or Ukrainian was the language of instruction. Some survivors also report studying other languages in school, including French, German, and Moldovan. Several survivors who grew up in the Soviet Union attended newly established state-sponsored Yiddish schools, but more report getting their education in Russian-language schools.[52]

Survivors who grew up in western Europe include those whose parents had immigrated there from eastern Europe and who report that Yiddish was a home language. In some cases, Yiddish formed the center of these survivors' Jewish identity. Max Wunderman grew up in Brussels, where he attended a Yiddish school and performed in the Yiddish theater.[53] Suzanne Gross, born in Paris to immigrant parents from Russia, recalls hearing Yiddish stories and songs from her mother and aunt: "We were cultural Jews. The home was very Jewish," she explains. "I was thoroughly conscious of being Jewish; I loved it."[54] Gross and other survivors make these assertions in the face of interviewers who assume that Jewish identity is inevitably a matter of religion. When Bronnie Tait asks Danielle Levy about her religious life, she responds by pointing out that the question assumes "a totally different framework from the one that I grew up with. We were Jewish, we spoke Yiddish. I went to . . . a [secular] Yiddish school. . . . *Khumesh* [Yiddish: "the Five Books of Moses"] was learned as a history of the Jews."[55]

By contrast, Jewish survivors born into families that had lived in western and central Europe for generations often report having little or no knowledge of Yiddish before the war and sometimes express a low regard for the language. Peter Glaser grew up in Bohemia speaking German and Czech, one language with each parent, and didn't know anyone there who spoke Yiddish.[56] Arno Cronheim explains that, like other Jews in his native Berlin, he spoke German and knew only a few Yiddish words. Cronheim adds that some German Jews used Yiddishisms in their speech "to make it a little more spicy," but he asserts that "to me, Yiddish was no language, and unfortunately it would have been easy to pick it up in the concentration camp." Instead, he explains, he conversed in German with Polish Jews there.[57]

When discussing Yiddish during their accounts of the war years, survivors typically recall very specific, personal engagements with the language while struggling to stay alive. As in the prewar years, these experiences vary considerably but generally reflect upheavals in established patterns of language use. Survivors occasionally mention Yiddish when recalling how drastically the war transformed daily life during the first years of the war, especially for Jews living under Soviet occupation. Several interviewees recall attending Yiddish-language schools run by the Soviet government. Ben Zion Schuster, who served as a school librarian in Soviet-occupied Poland, remembers a state inspector removing Yiddish books from the library that were deemed counter-revolutionary or too "Western."[58] Flight from persecution sometimes brought Yiddish speakers into contact with Jews who did not speak the language. Rose Schwartz, who worked in a children's home in the Kosice ghetto during the war, recounts the arrival of children who had escaped from Poland and were trying to make their way to Palestine via Czechoslovakia. In particular, she recalls a Yiddish song, performed by one young boy at a concert, about Moses's mother having to give up her son to strangers.[59]

Several Jewish survivors who did not grow up speaking Yiddish remember first encountering the language as prisoners in ghettos or concentration camps or in places where Jews sought refuge from persecution. Helga Alcone, a native speaker of German, learned Yiddish in Harbin, China, where her family found a haven during the war, along with Jews from the Soviet Union. She recalls that her mother, who prided herself on speaking a "beautiful" German and considered Yiddish a "botched-up" version of her native tongue, would warn Helga not to mix up the two languages.[60] Some of these interviewees, such as Esra Jurmann, a native of Dresden who was imprisoned in a concentration camp in Latvia, describe having been eager to learn Yiddish: "We children were fascinated by it, and we made it our business to learn it; we picked it up wherever we could."[61] However, others recall their lack of Yiddish as a source of strife. Gunter Faerber explains that he had no choice but to learn to speak Yiddish in Blechhammer concentration camp, instead of his native German, which other Jewish prisoners considered "a bad language."[62] When Gilbert Metz, a native of Alsace, recounts his experience of a forced march, he comments that French Jews suffered a higher mortality rate because "we didn't speak Yiddish; therefore, we could not make ourselves understood. . . . Language had a lot to do with [survival]."[63]

Indeed, Yiddish figures strategically in some survivors' accounts of staying alive during the Holocaust. Renee Grobart explains that her family was able to survive the war because her father had been an actor in the Yiddish theater; when the war started, he was on the Russian side of the border and wound up continuing to perform during the war under Soviet government sponsorship.[64] Cecilia Einhorn recalls singing for fellow prisoners in Auschwitz, mostly performing Yiddish songs. At the request of interviewer Zepporah Glass, Einhorn offers a lively rendition of "Khave-Leye, gut shabes" (Khave-Leye, a good Sabbath), a Yiddish theater song about the arduous task of preparing the elaborate Friday evening meal for celebrating the start of the Sabbath.[65] She then recalls the song's comforting impact on her fellow prisoners: "They loved it, and they get a little bit smile, and remember what it was. And that's how we lived, to remember that."[66]

In some instances, knowing Yiddish proved critical when survivors faced life-threatening situations. David Faber recounts being captured by Russian partisans in a forest after fleeing a work camp in Pustków. When he spoke to them in Polish and German they thought he was a spy. But then he spoke in Yiddish, which one of the officers in the partisan unit understood, and this, Faber explains, saved his life.[67] Conversely, Bronislava Fuks explains that when people approached her during the war and spoke to her in Yiddish, she had to pretend that she did not understand, lest it reveal her Jewish identity.[68] And Fira Yezerskaya tells Anna Feldman the following uncanny incident, which took place in 1942, when Yezerskaya and her family were in German-occupied Russia:

> Yezerskaya: One time I was home with Mama. . . . All of a sudden, Germans walked in, dressed in German uniforms. . . . One of them looked at us and said to the others, "You go, I'll catch up." They left, and he spoke in pure Yiddish: "*Yidn* [Jews], why are you sitting here? Do you know what you're doing? You should run! You should hide! Go wherever you want, otherwise you will be killed right away."
>
> Feldman: Your parents understood Yiddish?
>
> Yezerskaya:. . . . Yes. They even spoke Yiddish as well.
>
> Feldman: You also understood a little bit?
>
> Yezerskaya: I understand, but I cannot speak it. . . . This rattled us so much. We thought, "Oh my God, how can this be? He is a Jew, but why is he serving with the Germans? How is this—what is this?" . . .
>
> Feldman: Do you remember this man, what he looked like?
>
> Yezerskaya: He was young, average height . . . in a military hat and a German uniform, blue-eyed, fair. We didn't know what to think. . . . When Papa came home, we told him, and he said: "You know what? He could have been a Jew who served as a translator, if the Germans forced him to be a translator. Or maybe he's a German communist who saw that you are Jewish and decided to save you."[69]

In recounting their postwar lives, survivors occasionally mention the role that Yiddish played in their ability to find new homes. Esther Brunstein was able to receive permission from the Home Office to immigrate to England after the war as a teacher of "Yiddish elocution"; this enabled her to work in London's Yiddish theater, where there was a dearth of young performers.[70] After Georges Cojuc traces his family's peregrinations before, during, and after the war—through Russia, Romania, Poland, Germany, France, and Mexico—he concludes that "the survival factor is Yiddish. Because wherever we arrived, we looked for the Jewish people, it was the common language in Europe, the Yiddish, so you had an ID with the Yiddish, and you had assistance immediately."[71]

But for other survivors, Yiddish was a language newly encountered in their postwar lives. Ruth Bernard, who grew up speaking German, notes that she didn't speak Yiddish until she came to New York and met Jews working in the garment center.[72] Indeed, the expectation that, as Jews recently arrived from Europe, they must be Yiddish speakers proved disconcerting to some survivors who did not know the language. Gilbert Metz explains, "I could speak German, so I could understand Yiddish, but I could never speak Yiddish. And people don't believe me." In response to others' incredulity he asserted, "Alsatian Jews don't speak Yiddish; it's just a fact of life."[73] Similarly, Stella Engel, a native of Amsterdam, reports that, when she came to Boston after the war, "people couldn't understand why we didn't speak Yiddish," and she recalls that in Auschwitz language use was a source of animosity between Jews from western Europe and eastern Europe.[74] Kurt Schloss, a native of Cologne, likewise claimed that American Jews who had come from eastern Europe took umbrage at his lack of knowledge of Yiddish. He surmises that they thought, "This man hasn't learned anything" from his experiences during the war, "he probably came here and wants to hide his identity" as a Jew. However, Schloss asserts, "Nothing could be further from the truth."[75]

Those survivors who, while speaking another language, attest to the fact that they still speak Yiddish evince the extent to which maintaining the language was not taken for granted a half century after the war's end. Allen Feig, a native of Czernowitz, remarks that before the war the city's Jews were known for their "beautiful, magnificent Yiddish." Once, he recalls, he met another Jew from Czernowitz in Toronto after the war. They spent the evening conversing in Yiddish, "and I enjoyed every second of it, of that beautiful Yiddish that we were speaking."[76] Having suppressed her use of Yiddish during the war, for fear of being discovered as a Jew, Lea Kronenberg explains that "after the war I couldn't speak Yiddish, which is so unbelievable. My whole life was Yiddish." When asked if her ability to speak the language returned, Kronenberg replies, "Oh, yes, oh, yes. After I come to [the displaced persons camp in] Feldafing, I start straightaway, it came back. But I [had] suppressed it, because I thought in my dream maybe one day I'll scream out. You know I was so afraid, but oh, it came straightaway."[77]

Several survivors voice their pride in Yiddish culture in general terms. Sara Fershko remarks, "Can you imagine another people who took a language like *zhargon* [Yiddish: "jargon," a colloquial, and sometimes derogatory, term for Yiddish] . . . and they transform it into a literary, beautiful, speaking language, until today. The whole world literature was translated into Yiddish. And many, many [Yiddish] writers . . . were translated into other languages, . . . like [Isaac] Bashevis Singer. He got a Nobel Prize—for Yiddish!"[78] This devotion can include survivors seeking to inspire others to embrace the language. Masha Leon, who, at the time of her interview, was a journalist for the *Forward*, an English-language American Jewish weekly newspaper, explains that "instill[ing] a sense of pride in Yiddish. . . . [is] one of my missions."[79] When asked about her recent activity in the Melbourne Jewish community, Doba Apelowicz discusses her commitment to Yiddish culture, which often finds her at odds with other local Jews:

> Yiddish is—you have no idea how much I love that language. . . . And those people . . . in Melbourne from the Jewish community . . . —I can't stand it— . . . they never speak Yiddish. They know Yiddish from there, from birth. . . . I can't understand it, because I don't like snobbism. I like the natural thing. . . . They don't like Yiddish because the poor people spoke Yiddish. . . . This is a division of classes. . . . Yiddish, it might be because it was rejected, even in Israel, and is rejected here. I go into a coffee [i.e., café], there's a table with six Jewish ladies, they all speak Polish! They don't know Yiddish—how can it be? I know them all, where they come from, from homes like me. Well, that makes me angry; I can't help it. . . . And I'll do everything . . . to promote Yiddish here in Melbourne.[80]

On the whole, survivors' discussions of Yiddish in VHA interviews appear to grow more charged over the course of their lifetimes. Prewar recollections are largely descriptive of the language's place in the survivor's milieu, attending primarily to cultural innovations. In wartime accounts, Yiddish sometimes plays a key role in stories of life-or-death moments, or else it figures in recalling the upheaval of life as it was known before the war, whether the survivor had to abandon the language or suddenly encountered it. Discussions of Yiddish in connection with postwar life, though fewer, are most concerned with the significance of the language beyond its instrumental value. They center on symbolic associations with Yiddish, positive as well as negative, as a signifier of Jewishness, at times implying a particular locale or class. Some of those who grew up speaking the language express either sorrow over its loss or pride in its maintenance.

This survey of the dynamics of Yiddish as a presence in Holocaust survivors' lives over the course of the twentieth century is a composite account, con-

structed from segments of dozens of different survivors' narratives identified
and aggregated by the VHA's index and search mechanism. However, none of
the interviewees whose recollections contribute to this account provide such
an overview. Rather, they mention Yiddish only on occasion, usually just once,
in the course of relating their life histories. The limited, inconstant presence
of Yiddish in these narratives, offered in a different language, is itself revealing. These survivors' personal histories demonstrate the linguistic disruption in
twentieth-century European Jewish life that is, in turn, emblematic of great cultural, political, geographic, and demographic upheavals. This is true even for
those survivors who proclaim in another language their fondness for Yiddish,
for in doing so they evince its limitation or displacement as their vernacular.

Yiddish Performed

After her aforementioned disquisition on attitudes toward Yiddish in Melbourne, Doba Apelowicz reads a Yiddish poem that she wrote in 1965 for the
children's magazine *Khavershaft* (Comradeship). Her poem, titled "Baynakht"
(Nighttime), recalls the suicide of Goldele, a Jewish prisoner whom Apelowicz
knew in Auschwitz-Birkenau. Before reading the poem, she explains to the interviewer: "You will have to forgive me if you don't understand it, but I want it
to be included in my testimony a Yiddish poem."[81] Apelowicz is one of several
dozen survivors who perform a Yiddish text in the course of their interviews.
These moments endow Yiddish with yet another symbolic value and demonstrate how performances generally transform the nature of these recordings.
The VHA's index tags as "recitals" those moments when interviewees sing a
song, play a musical instrument, recite a poem, or read an essay. In some of
these sequences survivors present works of their own creation; in others, survivors perform works by another author or composer.[82]

Several survivors interviewed for the VHA are Yiddish poets who, like
Apelowicz, read samples of their work during their interviews, having prepared
to do so in advance. Some of these interviewees, like Rywka Braun and Rut
Kaplan, are published authors and read from their books; others recite unpub-
lished works from memory or from manuscripts.[83] Among these is Abraham
Bomba, who appeared in Claude Lanzmann's documentary *Shoah*. In one of
the most memorable sequences of this eight-and-a-half-hour-long film, Bomba

is filmed cutting someone's hair as he answers Lanzmann's questions about having been a barber while a prisoner in Treblinka, where he cut off the hair of women prisoners who were about to be gassed to death. Lanzmann, who is off camera, presses Bomba to answer questions about details of the killing operation that he resists recalling. At one point, he protests:

[Bomba:] I can't. It's too horrible. Please.

[Lanzmann:] We have to do it. You know it.

[Bomba:] I won't be able to do it.

[Lanzmann:] You have to do it. I know it's very hard. I know and I apologize.

[Bomba:] Don't make me go on please.

[Lanzmann:] Please. We must go on.[84]

At the end of Bomba's VHA interview, which is conducted in English, he reads two poems, which he states must be read in Yiddish; with each, he offers rough translations in English. Bomba explains that he wrote the first poem, titled "Nekome" (Vengeance), while a prisoner in the Częstochowa ghetto in 1941–42. The poem voices his vexation that the Allies had yet to come to the defense of Europe's Jews, whom Bomba exhorts to rise up against Germany and avenge the murder of their fellows. The poem ends: "*Far der velt zugn zay az zay firn milkhume, / nor kimen vet di tsayt fin nemen nekume*" (To the world they say that they are waging war, / But the time will come to take revenge). Bomba's second poem describes the roundup of the ghetto's Jews on the day after Yom Kippur in 1942, during which thousands were deported to Treblinka, while hundreds of others were shot on the spot.[85]

In contrast to his appearance in *Shoah*, Bomba's interview for the VHA enables him to offer a fuller account of his wartime experiences, including his participation in Jewish resistance at Treblinka, to a less persistent and controlling interviewer. Bomba's readings of his poems exemplify this contrast, as they demonstrate how performing provides survivors with opportunities to assume command of the interviews with regard to form as well as content. In these moments, survivors shift the video, if temporarily, to their preferred medium of expression—poetry, song, or essay. As literature scholar Leah Wolfson observes of survivors' many musical performances during VHA interviews, these sequences, in effect, constitute "a new kind of testimony."[86] Rather than responding to interviewers' questions, survivors proactively demonstrate their creativity.

Taking control of the interview at such moments can also entail a shift to the survivor's preferred language. Thus Apelowicz, Bomba, and others deliberately switch to Yiddish, their choice for literary creativity. "In English I don't write," Bomba explains; similarly, Emil Goldbarten explains, "I write only Jewish [i.e., Yiddish] poetry," and Sophia Elbaum announces, after discussing her liberation from Bergen-Belsen concentration camp, "And now I have to read in Jewish something."[87] These moments exclude those interviewers who know no Yiddish from the possibility of engaging with the substance of the survivors' performance. Indeed, during these sequences, the videos cease to present interviews per se, which are by their nature dialogic, and instead temporarily become vehicles for monologues.

These performances can be very brief—a few lines of a song or poem that survivors recite impromptu—or quite lengthy, especially when survivors intentionally present complete works. As a rule, interviewers do not interrupt survivors during these sequences, even when they run long. Nor do videographers intervene when survivors hold up the books or papers from which they recite and obscure their faces from the camera. David Gutman gives two extended performances in the course of his interview. First, he reads a lengthy article from a Toronto Yiddish newspaper about burying Torah scrolls, in an effort to protect them from an imminent attack, in his hometown of Iwaniska in 1942. Later in the video he sings "In a litvish derfl vayt" (In a remote Lithuanian village), a wartime ballad about a Jewish woman who leaves her child with a non-Jewish family for safekeeping. With this song, ironically, Gutman offers a Yiddish performance about silencing the language, as the woman instructs her child to keep quiet: *"Keyn yidish vort, keyn yidish lid, / vayl du bist nit mer keyn yid"* (No Yiddish word, no Yiddish song, / Because you are no longer a Jew).[88]

An extreme example of a survivor using the occasion of being interviewed to record an extended performance appears in the video of Wolf Scheinberg. Toward the end of his interview he reads aloud a Yiddish text that he wrote in 1947, which offers an overview of prewar Jewish culture, especially in his native Warsaw. Including explanatory asides that Scheinberg offers as he reads, this performance lasts over thirty minutes, beginning on one videotape and continuing on the next.[89] Though these segments deviate from the VHA's primary objective of recording survivors' recollections of their experiences, performances reveal how survivors conceive of their role as repositories of memory that extend beyond their own eyewitness accounts. With these performances survivors demonstrate their ability to draw on a personal store of sources that they have compiled on prewar Jewish life or the war years, whether memorized or on paper, and to present them with the authority attributed to someone who has lived through the Holocaust.

Most of these recitals take place toward the end of interviews, situated apart from the narrative arc of life review, as discrete entities, both chronologically and formally. In these instances, the recited works are treated more like the photographs and artifacts documented in a separate sequence after the interview proper. Survivors usually initiate these performances and have preselected the texts or songs they wish to include in their videos. They frequently frame these performances by explaining the substance of the work or the context in which it was created. At the end of Rywka Braun's interview, she reads "Elnt eynzam" (All alone), a poem from her book *Lider fun payn* (Poems of pain), which was published in Paris in 1957. When she finishes the poem, Richard Bassett asks

Survivor Rywka Braun (née Akerman) displaying *Lider fun payn* (Poems of pain), her 1957 book of Yiddish poems, from which she reads during her VHA interview. Provided by the USC Shoah Foundation.

Braun when the poem was written. She replies that she wrote it during the war, when she was hiding in a bunker and prayed to God for help. Bassett asks her how she got materials to write, and Braun explains that a man who provided her with bread while in hiding also brought her a pen and paper.[90]

Sometimes survivors contextualize their performances in a language other than Yiddish, thereby marking the language, if implicitly, as postvernacular. Before singing "A din-toyre mit Got" (God on trial), a folk song attributed to Rabbi Levi-Yitskhok Berditshever, Michael Deutsch explains in English the song's text, in which this important Hasidic leader during the late eighteenth and early nineteenth centuries confronts God over the harsh treatment of the Jewish people. Deutsch then offers his reason for performing this song as exemplifying his own relationship with God, which is both critical and devoted.[91]

In other videos, performances take place within the survivor's life narrative, linked in some way with a topic the survivor addresses at that moment. After Harold Weiss describes his bar mitzvah in prewar Vilna, Lucy Samorodin asks him if he remembers the speech he gave on the occasion. Weiss recites a few lines in Yiddish and then translates them into English.[92] Over the course of her interview, Bronislavah Rabinovits recites from memory three Yiddish poems that she wrote. She launches into them in response to Mina Graur's questions about Rabinovits's life experiences, including her involvement in Jewish political youth movements before the war and her experience hiding from the Germans during the war. When Rabinovits offers postwar reflections at the conclusion of the interview, she recites the last of her poems, which takes the form of a letter addressed to God, demanding an explanation of the Holocaust. In this poem's last lines, Rabinovits explains her choice of language as tautological, expressed in the use of the word *yidish* to refer to both "Jewish" people and "Yiddish" language. The language is bound up with her Jewishness and her relationship with God, whom she addresses with an emotionally charged urgency and also, ultimately, with reverence:

> *Ikh shrayb af yidish, vayl ikh bin a yidish kind,*
> *Shrayb ikh tsu mayn yidishn Got take nor af yidish.*
> *Vilst gevis farsteyn vos ikh vil un vos ikh meyn.*
> *Antshuldik mir, tate, liber foter in himl,*
> *Vos ikh farnem dir di tsayt mit mayn sipur.*

[I write in Yiddish, because I am a Jew,

So I write to my Jewish God only in Yiddish.

Surely You understand what I mean.

Forgive me, dear Father in heaven,

For taking up Your time with my tale.][93]

The associations that prompt survivors to sing spontaneously in the course of being interviewed are not all of a kind, just as the songs they recall suggest the varied repertoire of Yiddish song before and during the war. Describing his prewar life, Joseph Blitz remembers his first efforts to talk to girls when he was in his teens and sings a few lines of a folksong: "*Ikh hob a maydl, iz zi shayn. / Ikh vil zi kishn, zogt zi 'Nayn.' / Nor dos tensl vil zi gayn*" (I have a girl, she is pretty. / I want to kiss her, she says "No." / She only wants to go dancing).[94] When asked about religious life in the small village in which he grew up, Abraham Blumenthal chants a bit of the Passover haggadah, translating from Hebrew into Yiddish.[95] As Minna Grand describes the food given to prisoners in the Kauen concentration camp, she mentions a song that prisoners sang about how bad the soup was. At the urging of interviewer Masha Loen, Grand sings a verse and remarks, "*Dos gedenk ikh biz haynt*" (I remember it to this day),[96] distinguishing her ability to recall the song after a half century as noteworthy in itself.

Memories that prompt a survivor to sing can vary within a single interview. While describing her family's efforts to flee German persecution during World War II, Eva Guttman recalls a song from World War I, which her mother used to sing, about the violence Jews suffered at the hands of Russian forces. Guttman explains that before World War II Jews had been more fearful of the Russians than the Germans; as a result, Jews couldn't believe how merciless the German army was during the Holocaust. This discussion also prompts Guttman to sing part of a Yiddish song about the Kishinev pogrom of 1903 and the 1905 revolution in Russia.[97] Later in her interview Guttman recalls that during the war her family tried, without success, to burn some books for fuel. This memory inspires her to sing the beginning of a Yiddish folksong, "*Shikt a har a poyerl in vald arayn*" (A nobleman sends a peasant into the forest), in which nothing will do what it is supposed to do, including wood refusing to catch fire, much like the books that Guttman recalls. The song has no historical connection to this event; rather, she explains, it came to mind because she had recently sung it at a Passover seder.[98]

Several times survivors perform Yiddish songs when prompted by interviewers, rather than at their own initiative. Often these invitations result in incomplete or altered performances, leaving the interviewers' requests unfulfilled. At the end of Adam Brandys's interview, Phyllis Dreazen asks him to sing something and suggests the Partisan Song—that is, Hirsh Glik's Vilna ghetto poem "Zog nit keyn mol" (Never say), which was set to music and adopted by Jewish partisans as an anthem during the war. In the postwar years this song became well known as a fixture of Holocaust commemorations.[99] When Brandys replies that he doesn't know the words, the interviewer asks him if he can sing something else, and he performs two songs in modern Hebrew. Later, when he appears with his wife in the video's final segment, they sing the 1930s American Yiddish theater song "Bay mir bistu sheyn" (To me you are beautiful).[100] Brandys thus fulfills the request to perform something, though not the Holocaust anthem that his interviewer had in mind. Rather, his choices draw on a postwar repertoire of familiar Jewish songs. While recounting her experience in Mielegjany concentration camp, Rachela Braude mentions that she used to sing there, and Ana Suchodolski-Tarnaruder asks her to sing a song. Braude recites some of the lyrics of a children's song but does not remember them well; then she starts singing a love song, which she also has trouble recalling. She comments, "I knew all the songs; I sang and they wept," directing attention to the songs' affective impact, a more prominent memory for her than the songs themselves.[101] Emotion likewise predominates when Sol Glaser recalls his family's prewar celebration of the Sabbath. When Fay Nicoll asks him if he remembers what they sang on Friday night, Glaser begins a traditional *nign* (Yiddish: "melody"), but his voice breaks; he stops singing and starts to weep.[102]

One of the most elaborate examples of a Yiddish performance in a VHA video is remarkable on several counts, including the ways that it breaks with the Shoah Foundation's interviewing protocols. The performance takes place not in a survivor's home but in a gallery of the Jewish Holocaust Museum and Research Centre, established in 1984 in Melbourne, Australia. Two survivors, Adek Stein and Chaim Sztajer, participate in the performance; the interviewer, Mary Ziegler, who is Stein's daughter, also appears on camera with them.[103]

Both Sztajer and Stein were among the only survivors of Treblinka to settle in Australia. The performance, which runs about thirty minutes, centers on a large model of the Treblinka death camp, which Sztajer had built at some time in the 1950s or 1960s and donated to the museum at the time that it opened.[104]

At the beginning of this sequence, Ziegler asks Sztajer to talk about the model. Standing to one side, and using a long wooden pointer to indicate particular locations on the model, he explains how prisoners entered the camp. Ziegler asks her father, who is seated beside the model, if he remembers this experience. Stein describes what he encountered when he came to Treblinka, which occurred at a different time from Sztajer's arrival. The camera pushes in on Stein as he points to the model's entry gate, at Ziegler's suggestion. *"Der veg firt tsim toyt"* (This way leads to death), he states, summing up his account of entering the camp, and he proceeds to recall seeing other people whom he knew when they arrived there, some selected for forced labor, others sent directly to the gas chamber.[105]

Survivors Chaim Sztajer (left) and Adek Stein, with interviewer Mary Ziegler, in the Jewish Holocaust Museum and Research Centre in Melbourne, Australia. The two men, among the few survivors of Treblinka, recount their experiences there before a model of the camp, which Sztajer made and donated to the museum. Provided by the USC Shoah Foundation.

Ziegler asks Sztajer for more of his recollections of Treblinka, and he uses the model to point out what took place at different locations. Then Ziegler directs the interview back to Stein, who talks fervidly about the extermination of Jews in the camp's gas chambers. As he recounts his escape from Treblinka, exclaiming, "*Un ikh bin geboyrn gevorn afs nay*" (And I was born anew), the tape—and this performance—ends.[106]

The survivors' performance in this sequence is compelling, not merely because of the recording's unusual format or even the horrifying stories that the two men relate, but because the performance manifests their resolve, both during the war and afterwards. Each man has a forthright sense of what he wishes to relate about Treblinka and how to do so. The singular configuration of this sequence—the two survivors present at the same time, the model as the interview's centerpiece—enhances their impassioned commitment to recounting the events that took place at the death camp, as two of the very few people to survive imprisonment there. Sztajer's model exemplifies a creative response to surviving the genocide and addressing the onus of its remembrance, as offering their recollections in Yiddish signifies both men's tenacity. Contemplating the model, Stein wonders, "*Efsher bin ikh ayner fin di gliklekhste, velkhe ikh bin aroys un ikh ken ibergeybn dus vus mentshn hobn gemakht tsi mentshn*" (Perhaps I am one of the most fortunate, as I got out and I can convey what people did to people).[107]

The moments in VHA interviews indexed as recitals reveal how survivors regarded the interview more generally as an occasion for the performance of oneself. Rather than regarding these sequences—or the interviews as a whole—as suspect "playing to the camera," and thereby conceptualizing performance as a kind of dissembling, we can better understand them as epitomizing moments in which survivors use the videos to enact their lifetime of memories. These recording sessions not only provide interviewees with opportunities to voice recollections that usually remain within their minds but also offer survivors moments of elevated attention and recognition. Barbara Myerhoff, in her fieldwork on elderly American Jews, which included recording their personal histories on audiotape and film, observed that her subjects came "more completely alive" in response to the attention of "a camera, a tape recorder, or . . . any indication that a record was being made of their existence."[108] Performing similarly enables an especially intense form of self-presentation for survivors interviewed for the VHA.

Moreover, as some of these examples demonstrate, recitals in VHA interviews can recall wartime performances that constituted acts of asserting one's humanity in the face of efforts to degrade and destroy it. As survivor Charlotte Delbo wrote in *La mémoire et les jours* (translated as *Days and Memory*), "When I would recite a poem [in Auschwitz] . . . , it was to keep myself alive, to preserve my memory, to remain me."[109] In the VHA, life-affirming performances, recalled from decades earlier and reenacted on camera, demonstrate these narrative acts of resistance and validate survivors' endurance.

Performing in Yiddish animates not only the survivors but also the language and all that it had come to represent a half century after the Holocaust. Their recitals constitute performative speech, as defined by the philosopher J. L. Austin: "The issuing of the utterance is the performing of an action—it is not . . . just saying something." In the performative mode of speech, language is operative; "saying" can "make it so."[110] Interviewee recitals in Yiddish are speech acts in which *yidishkayt* (literally, "Jewishness"; the term is often used to refer to the culture of Yiddish-speaking Jewry) is called into existence. Through the charged use of this language, so strongly identified with a culture and a people, a survivor affirms the endurance of his or her Jewish self and of a collective Jewishness in the face of genocide. Given that the Holocaust is the central subject of these interviews—indeed, the reason for their being recorded—this performative assertion of Yiddish can be read as an act of defiance. Through these recitals, survivors implicitly insist that their lives be realized, and be heard, not only in the context of destruction and loss but also in terms of Jewish cultural persistence and creativity in their first language.

❚ ❚ ❚

Though the primary interest in survivor videos is the information they provide about the Holocaust and the lives of people who endured the genocide, turning attention to how language is used to convey this information enhances the value of these interviews as resources of history and of remembrance. Because most survivors dealt with multiple languages over the course of their lives, the topic of language is vital to understanding their prewar circumstances, their wartime experiences, and how they made new lives for themselves after the war's end—including deciding what should be the language in which they would be interviewed for the VHA.

The insights that can be gained from attending to the secondary, metavalue of language in survivor videos is readily apparent in the distinctive case of Yiddish, for in these recordings the postvernacular mode of engaging the language comes to the fore. The choice made by hundreds of survivors interviewed for the VHA to speak in Yiddish on these videos—whether entirely or partially, decided in advance or occurring on the spot—or even to talk about Yiddish in another language calls attention to the language's symbolic significance, informed by the dynamics of Jewish multilingualism before and during World War II and by the very different nature of Jews' language use in the second half of the twentieth century. By the time that these interviews were conducted, conversing in Yiddish had increasingly become a practice not to be taken for granted. The use of Yiddish as a vernacular had been in decline in most Jewish communities for decades. Survivors might have continued speaking the language with Jews of the same age who had also grown up with Yiddish, but they typically spoke another language with younger Jews, including their own children and grandchildren, and, of course, with non-Jewish acquaintances. Passive knowledge of Yiddish was also receding, and even members of younger generations who know Yiddish often have a different command of the language than the survivor generation, as these younger speakers have grown up in other speech communities or may have learned Yiddish in classrooms, rather than at home. Yiddish is therefore emblematic of the upheavals of Jewish life during the past century. The presence of the language in these interviews exemplifies the perseverance of the survivors' cohort as well as its waning.

Though Yiddish is this chapter's apparent focus, it is more precisely the place of this language in survivors' experiences and their recollections. It is therefore telling that, when survivors talk about Yiddish, these discussions inevitably relate to some extralinguistic issue, such as social negotiations, cultural literacy, or political change. Implicit in the discussions about Yiddish that native speakers offer in another language is their relegation of Yiddish either to the past or to a marginal place in the present. When survivors interpolate Yiddish words while speaking another language or shift between Yiddish and another language, information emerges not only from the different languages involved but also from those interstices, however brief they might be, when the switch between one language and another occurs. Whether they are clearly deliberate shifts or appear to be automatic, these instances of code switching evince the speakers' ability to draw on multiple linguistic resources toward a variety of ends, including emphasis, histrionics, irony, polemics, or playfulness. These "bilingual moments" do not confound a survivor's expressive capability but extend it. As literature scholar Doris Sommer notes, "These moments can free up communication that seems blocked" and can be "engagingly contrapuntal."[111] Given the multiglossic nature of the Jewish communities in which most of these survivors have lived, the movement between languages in these interviews may be thought of as enactments of the speakers' Jewishness.

Whereas code switching in these interviews is mostly a spontaneous vernacular practice, recitals in Yiddish—especially in interviews otherwise conducted in another language—are often more self-consciously postvernacular. Not only is a particular text being performed, but so is the language itself. Implicit in these moments is the ambivalent value accorded to a postvernacular language—on one hand, no longer used regularly as part of daily life; on the other hand, more highly prized, in part precisely because of its rarity. The language becomes an end in itself, its performance an enactment of an increasingly tenuous tenacity.

The Yiddish spoken by Jews who grew up in Europe before World War II hovers on the verge of disappearing. It has been superseded by other varieties of the language: the Yiddish spoken by some of their descendants, who use the language in new circumstances, and the Yiddish learned in classrooms by an international assortment of students, including quite a few non-Jews. But the Yiddish heard in these videos betokens a loss beyond language, extending to the demise of communities, environments, and cultural practices. As the VHA documents survivors in the later years of their lives, it records the Yiddish spoken by many of them at a moment when their passing is imminent. In doing so, the Shoah Foundation has preserved speech, the most evanescent of human activities, as a resource for the future.

4

SPECTACLE
Seeing as Believing

The visual element of Holocaust survivors' videotaped interviews most readily distinguishes them from life stories documented by other means, as the name Visual History Archive demonstrates. Yet most scholarly discussions of these recordings center on language, focusing on what survivors say or, less often, how they speak. Champions of these videos often invoke in general terms the additional information video provides, especially the affective power of watching survivors talk, "showing us an individual's appearance, expressions and gestures, . . . presenting the human face of history."[1] The Fortunoff Video Archive for Holocaust Testimonies notes that, when its founders decided to begin videotaping Holocaust survivors in the late 1970s, "It was felt that the 'living portraiture' of television would add a compassionate and sensitive dimension to the historical record."[2]

Affect is, of course, also manifest in audio recordings; in fact, much of its discussion in survivor videos concerns the audible—sighs, sobs, hesitations in speech. And, of course, emotions can be expressed powerfully, though differently, in the written word. If watching survivors talk is, in fact, a more (or, at least, a distinctly) engaging experience, compared to reading their words or listening to them, how exactly does this spectacle inform the viewer? The challenging nature of this question is illuminated by artist Esther Shalev-Gerz's 2005 video installation *Entre l'écoute et la parole: Derniers témoins: Auschwitz, 1925–2005 (Between Listening and Telling: The Last Witnesses: Auschwitz, 1925–2005).*

This installation, first displayed in the Hôtel de Ville in Paris, included a multi-screen presentation composed entirely of segments, culled from interviews the artist filmed with local Holocaust survivors, consisting of those moments between the questions asked by interviewers and the survivors' responses. Shalev-Gerz explains that this "montage of faces captured not their spoken words, but rather the silent moments that occur between words, opening up a different space-time outside the logic of language, that of sensuous and corporeal memory."³ Watching this wordless spectacle is as enigmatic as it is engrossing.

Nevertheless, seeing survivors tell their life stories on video is often characterized as facilitating a more direct connection to these remembrances, even though the spectacle of elderly survivors serves as a constant, if tacit, reminder that wartime events are being recalled from a vantage decades later. Indeed, watching a survivor on video might constrain the viewer's ability to imagine the past events being recounted, given the contrasting spectacle of a considerably older interviewee, in ways that reading a printed text might not.⁴

Photographer Jeffrey Wolin addresses the complicated interrelation of survivors' wartime recollections with their appearance decades later in *Written in Memory*, a series of portraits of Holocaust survivors he created in the 1990s.⁵ Before taking these photographs, Wolin recorded interviews with the survivors about their experiences during the war. He then inscribed portions of the transcribed interviews onto the portraits. In some of his compositions, the text frames the survivors, seeming to fill the air around them and obscure the photographs' setting; in other images, the text embeds survivors in a sea of language that threatens to overwhelm them. In these works, the survivor's portrait and narrative are simultaneously divergent—they entail distinct actions on the part of the viewer, reading versus gazing—and interdependent, each relying on the other for its significance. Whereas the texts recount ordeals of the past, the photographs manifest decades of postwar endurance. Wolin's portraits acknowledge the passage of time and the disparity between outward appearance and memories held within, between speech and silence. What is integrated in videotaped interviews with survivors is refracted in these photographs.

The dearth of academic attention to the spectacle of survivor videos may reflect the disciplines of most scholars examining these interviews, who study history, literature, or psychology and are therefore primarily interested in the information survivors provide or in their narrative practices. But another rea-

Jeffrey A. Wolin, "Rena Grynblat, born 1926, Warsaw, Poland," from the photographer's series *Written in Memory: Portraits of the Holocaust.* © Jeffrey A. Wolin, courtesy of Catherine Edelman Gallery, Chicago.

son for the limited discussion of the videos' visual element may well be that they are by design visually austere. Typically, these videos (in their full, original form, not excerpted and combined with other material, as they are in documentary films or museum installations) consist of close shots of survivors' heads and upper torsos, with little or no camera movement and no editing. Though videotaping practices vary according to the protocols of each project, survivors are most often filmed while seated before a plain backdrop or in an interior, such as a living room or office. In most of these projects, including the VHA, interviewers are located off camera, though they can be heard asking questions.

The VHA's guidelines to videographers strive for a standardized, straightforward visual aesthetic by specifying a consistent composition across "all interviews. Basically, we are expecting a very soft 3/4 key look. . . . To achieve a more 'portrait' look, use a longer lens at a wide open F-stop, softening the background."[6] These protocols express particular concern that the camerawork engage the survivor's gaze, in keeping with the conventions of interview videography: "Be sure there is adequate light in the survivor's eyes. . . . If a survivor wears glasses . . . , ask the interviewer if he/she could gently ask the survivor if he/she would feel comfortable . . . removing his/her glasses. . . . While speaking, the survivor should look at the interviewer [who sits next to the camera], not at the camera."[7] By contrast, David Boder reported that he sat behind Holocaust survivors when asking them questions in his pioneering audio interviews of 1946, "as is customary in psychological interviews, . . . so that [the interviewee] would not be influenced by the expression on the face of the interviewer."[8]

The VHA's guidelines connect these protocols for videography to concerns about the videos' documentary integrity:

> At the beginning of the interview, start with a shot that is wider than you might prefer. We want to show a glimpse of the surroundings, especially if it's in the survivor's home. Once the interview has begun you should very slowly zoom in to a comfortable close shot. Be sure to avoid extreme close-ups. Once the close shot has been established, do not zoom in or out. Such camera moves would add editorial comment to the testimony, thereby compromising its historical validity.[9]

The guidelines further explain that "the videographer should never intrude on the relationship between interviewer and survivor" and instruct:

> While the interview is in progress do not cut the camera. There may be periods of long pauses or emotional breakdowns. Under no circumstances (other than an emergency or if the survivor needs to leave their chair) should the camera be cut. These are historical testimonies, raw archival footage, the content of which is considered valuable material to scholars, researchers, academicians, etc.[10]

The "zero-degree" aesthetic prescribed in the VHA's guidelines—uniform in approach across interviews, minimizing the camera's role as mediator—is intended to mark these recordings as documents of evidentiary value. The formal standard ostensibly insures the interviews against photographic subjectivity, lest videographers' choices distort or interfere with survivors' recollections, conceived as "testimonies." Voicing similar concerns about videography's visual element, literature scholar Geoffrey Hartman asserts that the Fortunoff Archive's austere aesthetic signified the project as "facilitat[ing] and preserv[ing] archival documents in audiovisual form" and was, moreover, a strategic remedy for broadcast television's distorted presentation of the Holocaust: "Our technique, or lack of it, was homeopathic: it used television to cure television, to turn the medium against itself, limiting even while exploiting its visualizing power."[11]

In fact, the hundreds of camera operators involved in filming VHA interviews around the world realized these guidelines differently. Some interviewees are shot in close-ups that show little beyond the survivors' heads and necks; other videos present the survivors in a medium shot that also includes their arms and torsos as well as the environment in which the interview was filmed. And, despite instructions not to cut or move the camera, there are moments in some videos when the camera pans or zooms to track a survivor's movements or when interviews are broken into segments other than those dictated by the thirty-minute length of individual videotapes.

The VHA's goal of visual uniformity parallels the formal consistency sought in the interviews themselves, which begin and end with prescribed questions and request interviewers to ask survivors to specify dates, names, spellings, and the like. On one hand, the Shoah Foundation's guidelines address the desire to present survivors' narratives as original in content and unadulterated in form; on the other hand, the Foundation's protocols reflect its agenda of creating a massive data set of interviews, for which modular standardization facilitates their incorporation into the Archive as a whole.

Equating a film's formal austerity with its substantive authenticity is not without precedent. This notion hearkens back to concerns addressed when atrocity footage filmed by the Western Allies in recently liberated Nazi concentration camps was screened at the international war crimes trial convened in Nuremberg in 1946, a landmark use of film as evidence in the courtroom. The compilation film *Nazi Concentration Camps*, created for presentation at this trial, opens with shots of a series of typewritten affidavits, signed and witnessed by US military personnel. As these documents appear on screen, a narrator reads them aloud. The documents aver that the footage constitutes a "true representation of the individuals and scenes photographed" and presents an authentic replication of the original film record, which has "not been retouched, distorted, or otherwise altered in any respect."[12] Paradoxically, incorporating these affidavits, which are mediated visually and audially, into *Nazi Concentration Camps* demonstrates, if tacitly, the film's constructed nature.

The notion that an austere, regulated aesthetic transcends the mediated nature of motion pictures is, of course, misleading. As media scholar Wolf-gang Ernst notes, "The obsession with an unmediated representation of the past is itself a media effect."[13] The VHA's protocol for videographers constitutes an aesthetic choice. It straddles, rather than circumvents, the tension between the Shoah Foundation's mandated standardized form for the visual element of the videos and the many thousands of individual recordings that the project produced, created by different personnel in an international array of settings. This tension is readily evident in the VHA's decision to videotape survivors, when possible, at home, so that they appear framed by a wide variety of quotid-ian environments. The Fortunoff Archive filmed interviewees against a neutral background, which isolates the survivors and their personal histories as indi-viduated case studies, consistent with Fortunoff's practice of identifying survi-vors not by their full names but by first names and the initial letter of their last names.[14] Literature scholar Anne Rothe posits that this aesthetic choice is also meant to "reinforce the bleakness of the interviewees' atrocity narratives and the unbridgeable differences between the witness and the audience."[15]

The VHA's choice of setting for its interviews, by contrast, configures the Archive as a memory palace that contains tens of thousands of living rooms. Recording interviews in the familiar intimacy of their homes may have proved reassuring to survivors, as they embarked on the daunting task of recount-ing their past. This setting may also affect viewers, who encounter survivors of extreme experience within a domestic setting, as if paying them a virtual social call. Moreover, the VHA's extensive inventory of interiors evinces the diversity of interviewees' postwar lives with respect to nationality, class, reli-giosity, and taste. Each interior framing the survivor's face informs the inter-view, if obliquely. Some of the videos' backgrounds appear to have been staged strategically, surrounding the subject with family photographs, religious ob-jects, books, musical instruments, flowers, or works of art. (In most cases, it is not readily evident who made these choices: the interviewee, family mem-bers or other acquaintances, the interviewer, the videographer, etc. However, at the very start of the first videotape of Leizer Portnoy's interview, his wife, Bertha, whose back is to the camera, can be seen arranging photographs in small frames on a shelf, in front of which the interviewee then sits when the interview proper begins.)[16] These staged backgrounds configure the spectacle of survivor videos as something more akin to painted or photographed portraits than to documentary records of, say, witnesses testifying in courtrooms or subjects filmed for psychological studies. As with formal portraiture, the composition of the shot situates interviewees in environments that they dominate, surrounded by attributes that exemplify their character.

Injuries

Within the visual austerity of the VHA videos, moments that deviate from the prescribed spectacle of "talking heads" stand out. Though exceptional, these moments are key to understanding the signifying power of the recordings' visual element. Among the most striking instances occur when survivors display injuries they received during the war (369 interviews, according to the VHA index) or numbers that were tattooed onto their forearms when they became prisoners in Auschwitz (4,407 interviews). These shifts in how survivors are filmed, though often brief, disrupt the videos' established aesthetic and, as a result, enhance how they signify, both during these particular sequences and in general.

The range of injuries that survivors display in VHA interviews evinces the pervasive physical violence inflicted on targeted populations during the Holocaust: assaulted by soldiers, camp guards, and others with beatings, stabbings, gunfire, or dog bites; subjected to torture or medical experiments; suffering accidents while working as slave laborers, fleeing capture, or in hiding; scalded with hot water or exposed to extreme cold, and so on. The sites of injury are variously found on a survivor's head, face, arms, hands, legs, shoulders, buttocks, or back.

Survivors usually display injuries at their own initiative, though occasionally an interviewer's question prompts them to do so. Thus Richard Basset asks Mayer Tremblinski if he was ever beaten during the war:

Tremblinski (*tapping his right shoulder with his left hand*): In Poland, my
    shoulder was broken, here, with a rifle.
Basset: Who did this?
Tremblinski: A Gestapo [officer].
Basset: Why?
Tremblinski: No reason. Because I'm a Jew.
Basset: When was this?

Tremblinski: In 1939, when they [i.e., German forces] arrived.

Basset: Were you in the street? Were you doing anything?

Tremblinski: No, I wasn't doing anything. I was looking for a bit of bread to eat. And here (*gesturing to his shoulder again*), with a rifle, he broke my shoulder.

Basset: Can you show me?

Tremblinski: Yeah. (*He undoes the top buttons of his shirt, then pulls it and his undershirt back to expose his shoulder. Beneath the skin, the place where the bone was broken is readily visible.*) See?

Basset: Was it broken? (*The camera pushes in on the exposed shoulder.*)

Tremblinski: Sure! You can see it.

Basset: It never healed?

Tremblinski: No, no. The whole shoulder was broken.

Basset: Has it hurt over the years?

Tremblinski: Ooh, ooh! (*He grimaces as the camera pulls back out to a shot of Tremblinski's face and upper torso.*) I haven't been able to work. . . . There was nothing to be done. . . . OK? (*He pulls his shirt back over his shoulder.*)[17]

During his VHA interview, survivor Mayer Tremblinski displays his shoulder, which was broken when a German officer attacked him during World War II. Provided by the USC Shoah Foundation.

Sometimes survivors show their wounds quickly and spontaneously, especially if these are readily visible on the face or hands.[18] But displaying other injuries requires survivors to move from their chairs or to undress. In these instances some videographers set up a separate shot, filming the display of the injury and its discussion as a discrete narrative unit. After the conclusion of her interview proper, Frieda Jakubowicz appears again on camera, having removed her jacket and now wearing a sleeveless dress. Off camera, interviewer Debbi Portnoy explains that Jakubowicz, who survived a mass shooting in Trawniki concentration camp in 1943, "has asked to show her wound [received] during the mass killings." (Jakubowicz recounted the incident earlier in the course of her interview, gesturing to where she was shot in the shoulder.) As she pulls back the shoulder strap of her dress and points to the scar on her upper left arm, Jakubowicz notes that "it's already had plastic surgery on it." Then the camera pushes in for a close-up of the scar, and she points to her left wrist, explaining how, as she was lying face down during the shooting, the bullet entered her body there and then exited her upper arm. The camera pulls back as she adds, "It looks awful now, but it was worse before I had plastic surgery."[19] Jakubowicz's narrative exposes the full extent of the injury, undoing its postwar history of cosmetic repair. Similarly, when survivors bear no visible scar they may indicate where the injury took place. As Frank Burstin recounts the injuries he suffered when a guard in the Wittenberge concentration camp struck him in the face with a shovel, the survivor points to where his eye was swollen shut, his nose was broken, and his teeth were damaged; he explains, "All my front teeth were capped."[20]

Sometimes interviewers restrain survivors, who are eager to display their wounds in the course of recounting the war years, and ask the interviewees to wait until a separate shot can be set up to film the injury. Such is the case in Barbara Sewell's interview of Michael Deutsch, who describes suffering from frostbite while on a forced march from Mauthausen to Gunskirchen in the winter of 1944, resulting in scarring on his leg. "This is my gift from the concentration camp," he comments, as he leans over and rolls up his pant leg, out of the camera's range. "Even today, if it gets ulcerated, I get terrible pains."[21] Later in the interview, after the start of another videotape, Sewell asks Deutsch to return to his story of contracting frostbite while on the forced march. The camera pans down from his face to his right leg. As he continues to speak,

Deutsch rolls up the cuff of his pants to display a dark scar that covers most of
his shin, as well as a bandage near the top of his sock, where, he explains, the
wound has become ulcerated. Sewell inquires whether it still causes him pain
or inhibits his movement and whether he continues to get treatment. Deutsch
says repeatedly, "As I get older, it's getting worse and worse." When Sewell asks
whether the wound affected him during the march, Deutsch replies, "I'm sure
it did, but I had so much pain everywhere else, I'll be honest with you, in my
heart and my mind and my body, that I just couldn't care less if my legs fall off.
. . . I could have asked for compensation from the Germans and I never did, I
don't know."[22]

 This deviation from VHA guidelines prohibiting camera movement reveals
the camera's potential to disrupt the videos' "zero-degree" aesthetic. At the same
time, the videographer's decision to pan down from Deutsch's face to his leg follows the interviewee's words and movements. Though this decision reflects the
camera operator's agency, it nonetheless reflects the intent of the survivor being
interviewed. Such moments as this call attention, if tacitly, to the mediated
nature of these videos generally. Moreover, these moments complicate widely
held assumptions about video's direct conjoining of sight and sound. Geoffrey
Hartman champions video recordings of survivors because "the voice as such,
without a visual source, remains ghostly. That is, when you take away the visual,
when you just hear the voice, the effect is that of disembodied sound."[23] But in
these sequences, as the camera pans away from the survivor's face to film the
wound, video separates the sound of speech from the spectacle of speaking. Or,
in the case of Tamara Andriushina, who sticks out her tongue to show where a
German soldier tried to cut her after she refused to reveal where members of
her family were hiding, the survivor must stop talking to display her scar.[24] At
such moments the medium refracts the interviewee into two entities: informant
(the "talking head") and evidence (the scarred body). The survivor's voice is not
disembodied; rather, it is embodied differently.

 During these sequences, survivors' accounts, like the spectacle, center on
the injury, even as they move back and forth between the Holocaust years
and the 1990s, linking wartime events with this moment of recounting the
past. The exchanges between survivors and interviewers in these sequences
sometimes resemble familiar conversations about an injury—discussing how
it happened, what sort of treatment was sought, the lingering consequences—

even as interviewees address singular features of Holocaust persecution: the routine character of sadistic and deadly anti-Semitic violence, the possibility of postwar reparations. The wounds serve as evidence of both wartime assault and postwar endurance, exemplifying how survivors live with—and, more-over, embody—memories of the Holocaust. Yet the acts of embodiment that survivors offer in the course of being interviewed differ from how they live with their injuries and the memories they evoke. Before the camera, survivors uncover scars usually concealed from view or point them out and offer ac-counts of how they occurred and describe their aftermath. Survivors mediate their injuries through display and narrative, and these performances are fur-ther mediated by the video.

Reflecting, perhaps, an awareness of these displays' distinctive implications, a survivor's discussion of injuries can extend to addressing the challenge of pre-senting them as well as the obligation to do so. When Leon Schmetterling re-counts to Deborah Slobin the assaults he suffered during the war, the survivor implicitly links showing his wounds with the imperative to relate his wartime experiences:

> Schmetterling: Take a look—this, it happened when he beat me up. (*He ges-tures to his left knee.*) Here was growing wild meat. Here, here. (*The cam-era pans down to the knee, where Schmetterling, who is wearing shorts, gestures to indicate where he was struck.*) . . .
> Slobin: Who hit you?
> Schmetterling: That Ukrainian, in the camp. (*The camera pans back up to his face.*) . . . To tell you the truth, I don't want to talk about it. . . . This is a time what I don't want to remember it. When you tell somebody that stories they don't believe you. Nobody believes you. . . . "This has never happened," they say. That's why we should show how what happened. All the young people should see it. . . . Because when I die, . . . nobody will know if something has happened like that.[25]

As survivors point to the sites of injuries while recounting these assaults, their bodies become arenas of memory, conjoining landscape and theater. Though scars are the bodies' most pronounced landmarks, memories of injury are rendered through storytelling in words and gestures. Survivors may ges-ticulate to reenact the attack, simultaneously playing the roles of assailant and victim, while positioning themselves as narrators of a past event as well as the subjects of narration.

Much of Simon Friedman's interview is filmed in a medium-close shot, showing most of his torso, thereby accommodating his highly gestural story-telling. Friedman's display of injuries comes amid an animated account of being shot during a mass execution at the Treblinka I forced labor camp, as he shifts between past and present tense, between English and Yiddish, and between narrating and voicing various characters (including his own inner monologue during the shooting), as well as imitating the sound of gunfire. Friedman explains that he and a group of men were led toward a mass grave, which they had dug earlier, and were told to drop their pants:

And I said to myself, "Shimen, what are you going to do? You're going to put your head in, they should shot you there? Run! So you wouldn't feel when you get killed." . . . As I'm thinking to myself, I grab my pants, and I start to run. I start to run, and I feel the first bullet here. (*He points to his left wrist.*) See? The marks are still here. (*The camera pushes in on his forearm, then pulls out again.*) And I fell down. I couldn't hold up my pants. I fell down, and I'm laying. Two minutes, three minutes later, an SS man, a *ukrainer* [Ukrainian], came over to me, he looked at me. "Are you alive, you son-of-a-this-this-this?" . . . . And he took that rifle and he put it right over here. (*He gestures with both hands to the nape of his neck, turns away from camera, which pushes in on the back of his head.*) You have marks here, you see. He took that rifle and he aimed it, and then, bingo! He shot. And it looks like the bullet went down here (*he gestures to below and behind his right ear*) and didn't hit that nerve. And I lay down and the blood start to run. (*The camera pulls back out.*) And I'm laying. And a minute, two minutes later, I hear, "*Shema Yisroel! Reboyne-shel-oylem! Vi geyt es?*" *In me firt di grupe alts tsi tsi der grib. Ba-ba-ba-ba-ba-ba-ba-ba-ba-ba! Shtil.* ["Hear, O Israel! Master of the Universe! What's happening?" And the group is led closer to the grave. Pow-pow-pow-pow-pow-pow-pow-pow-pow-pow! Silence.] And they shot them and I'm laying there. And I feel drop after drop after drop of blood come out, and I'm afraid to move from that place, because somebody's going to notice that; he's going to shoot me.[26]

Throughout this sequence, Friedman articulates the shifting modes of narration through gesture. He uses his hands to indicate when he is the narrator, as opposed to when he is one of his narrative's subjects (the shooter, the other victims, himself), and he gestures to show when he is reenacting the past moment, in contrast to when he is examining it from the present. By using both his voice and hands to indicate the places on his body where he was shot, Friedman links storytelling with material corroboration. In those moments, he is simultaneously the narrator, the narrative's protagonist, and the body of evidence. Moreover, he serves as the implicit director of the videographer, who moves the camera in sync with Friedman's gesturing.

Not all survivors gesture, nor does every video capture those moments when this does occur; spontaneous hand movements often fall outside the frame of the stationary shot. In general, the on-screen image in VHA interviews centers on the spectacle of speech as a vehicle of remembrance, thereby situating the survivor as a presence of mind more than of body. This convention of videotaped oral histories reflects a widely shared understanding of remembering one's past as a mental process that responds to an embodied experience but at a physical as well as temporal remove. Survivors' displays of wounds in the course of recalling wartime experiences trouble this notion of memory by seeming to collapse the distance between recollection and the recalled experience and by directing viewers' attention beyond listening to the mental activity of remembering to beholding the embodied trace of the remembered experience. Gesturing while relating memories of these injuries further complicates this notion of memory by rendering the cerebral act of remembering visible. "When we see a gesture," notes psychologists David McNeill, Liesbet Quaeghebeur, and Susan Duncan, "we see part of the speaker's current cognitive being, her very mental existence, at the moment it occurs."[27]

The display of injuries in VHA interviews constitutes a particularly complex example of what anthropologist Paul Connerton terms "bodily practices" of social memory, in which "the past is . . . sedimented in the body."[28] Survivors often speak about their injury both as a separate entity and as something they live with, its history part of the chronicle of their aging bodies. The injury is both persistent and dynamic, either getting "worse and worse" or ameliorated through treatment, such as plastic surgery or years of healing. For these survivors, the embodied memory, in the form of the wound, is always there. Yet during their interviews, they elect whether and, if so, when to discuss it—and, if the injury is not on a regularly exposed part of the body, when and how to reveal it. The display of injuries concretizes and enhances the testimonial aspect of these videos, as the survivors become evidence incarnate. At the same time, the bodily evidence depends on narration to explain the context of the injury, especially its absent agency (inflicted by the Gestapo officer, the Ukrainian guard, etc.). On one hand, narrating the story of the injury while displaying it constitutes taking control of the attack on one's body and, by implication, prevailing over one's persecutors. On the other hand, these injuries evince the ordeal of survival and tacitly acknowledge the partial success of the survivors' assailants.

A survivor's scar inscribes the assault and its consequences onto his or her body; the video documentation of the scar's display and its narration, in turn, inscribes the survivor's memory for viewers of these videos. In doing so, displays of survivors' injuries remind viewers of the salience of corporeal suffering during the Holocaust. This attention contrasts with the focus on mental assaults that are so often the subject of these interviews, centered on the survivor as a "talking head," who is asked, "What did you think?" "How did you feel?" "When did you understand?" "What do you remember?" and so on. In this context, displaying injuries foregrounds the central feature of genocide, distinguishing it from other forms of mass persecution, as an attempt to destroy not just the minds or practices of a people but also their bodies.

The video of Maria Berger's interview includes the spectacle of someone beholding a survivor's injury, incorporating the impact that this act of viewing has on another person within the presentation of the survivor's life story. During her interview, Berger recalls surviving a mass execution of Jews in the Stepan ghetto in 1942, gesturing to where she was shot in the back: "This was the grave. (*She spreads her arms out.*) And here they put us. They start to shoot. I feel it. (*She touches her left shoulder.*) And I fell; everybody fell. (*She gestures a downward motion.*)"[29] At the end of the video, Berger stands beside her daughter, Svetlana Monas, and turns away from the camera. Berger pulls back the neckline of her dress to show the scar on her back, between her shoulder blades. The camera pushes in on her back as Monas, who holds her mother's shoulder with one hand and touches the scar with the other, comments: "Wow, this is the first time that I actually see this bullet scar. I never looked at my mother closely, she never told me about the bullet itself; I knew that there was shooting, I knew that her whole family got hurt, I knew that she

At the conclusion of survivor Maria Berger's VHA interview, her daughter, Svetlana Monas (right), examines the scar where Berger was shot in the back during World War II. Provided by the USC Shoah Foundation.

ran out of the hole, (*the camera pulls back to show the two women's faces, as Berger turns to face the camera*) . . . but I never ever saw the bullet, so to me it's another revelation."[30]

Survivors' displays of injuries recall precedents in the history of documenting Nazi atrocities. Film footage of recently liberated concentration camps, recorded by the Allied armies in 1945, shows survivors displaying injuries and, in some cases, demonstrating how they were administered. Still photographs of injuries have been used to galvanize public awareness of atrocities well before World War II—for example, pictures of victims of anti-Semitic attacks at the turn of the twentieth century in the Russian Empire or, in the early years of photography, the image of an African American slave baring the scars of repeated whippings on his back. Photographed injuries are, in turn, part of the long history of their depiction in Western visual culture, from wounds as attributes of the crucified Jesus to the maimed bodies of soldiers in post–World War I German expressionist art. In renderings of Christian "martyrdom as spectacle," artists frequently identify persecuted saints by their display of wounds—for example, Saint Roch's open sore on his leg or Saint Agatha's severed breasts. According to religion scholar Elizabeth Castelli, this long-standing practice of Christian visual culture rests, in part, on the conviction that "the very image of violence can have a salutary and edifying impact on the viewer."[31] Other saints are depicted in the act of being martyred—Saint Sebastian's body pierced by multiple arrows, the slow burning of Saint Lawrence—situating them between life and death. Survivors of genocide who display and recount injuries in these videos similarly appear as both persecuted and enduring, located among both the dead of the past, who were murdered by similar assaults, and the living of the recording's present.

The galvanizing impact of viewing a Holocaust survivor's wounds figures in Frieda Jakubowicz's aforementioned account of surviving a mass shooting, which left her with a life-threatening injury to her arm. Jakubowicz recalls how

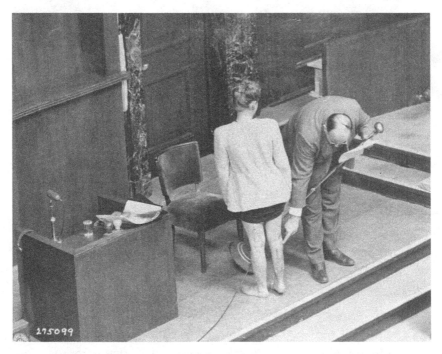

Trials of Nazi war criminals displayed survivors' injuries as evidence, using both photo-documentation and live witnesses. Testifying at the Doctors' Trial in Nuremberg on December 17, 1946, Polish survivor Jadwiga Dzido shows her scarred leg, as an expert witness explains the nature of the medical experiment performed on Dzido in Ravensbrück concentration camp. United States Holocaust Memorial Museum, courtesy of National Archives and Records Administration, College Park.

people imparted remarkable values to her survival of this assault as a sign of uncanny tenacity, variously understood as evidence of a religious miracle or as prognostication of fame and fortune:

> I was shot. And I was already dead. They left me for dead. . . . The rest of the people, everybody's dead. . . . I'm laying there . . . naked, like a wounded lamb. The [Christian] people there, what I knew them, . . . they found me, I don't know how many hours it was, how long I was dead. . . . Meantime, my blood went so far, it stopped itself, because there wasn't any more in it. I was white as a sheet. And so the *goyim* [Yiddish: "gentiles"], they had to come in to bury the dead, just to cover them with dirt. There I am, alive, there, out of the grave. So . . . they were saying, "What should we do with her? We will leave her alive, we're gonna have tomorrow to bury her." Some are saying—and I'm listening [to] every-thing—some saying, "We should kill her, throw her in together [with the other bodies]." The others say, "No, . . . we're not gonna do what they started." Anyway, they were saying, I'm not gonna survive anyway 'til morning. . . . But, happily, I survived. So I was there, and there comes in a bachelor, . . . and he says, "You know, you will come to America, and when you will tell your story, you will get rich just from telling your story what you lived through." And I'm looking at him; I'm on a deathbed, he is well, . . . so I didn't answer him. What will I say? . . . I don't know from where this comes to his mind, but just like he said, like he's a *neviye-zoger* [Yiddish: "prophet"]. . . . So I'm already there, laying, the second day, people used to come to me, as I'm a saint. I came back from the dead. I was their saint. They believed me like in Jesus. There was talk about me in all the vil-lages, what I'm the saint.[32]

Later, after escaping from another concentration camp, Jakubowicz explains that she found refuge with Christians from her village: "I was still the saint. They believed in me. They couldn't chase me out, because they believed I was the saint."[33] Though Jakubowicz's narrative and the display of her scar relate to the same incident, these presentations offer complementary responses to her injury and recovery. She narrates her experience as a tale of death and resur-rection that, albeit obliquely and skeptically, entertains the possibility of her survival as something miraculous or, at least, celebratory. Yet when Jakubowicz offers viewers her scar, which still "looks awful," it serves as a graphic reminder of the brutal effort of fellow human beings to destroy her and other Jews.

Tattoos

Displays of concentration camp prisoner tattoos in the VHA's interviews constitute a special case within these videos' attention to the body as a site of persecution and its remembrance. Unlike other bodily traces of the genocide that survivors display, tattoos are distinguished by their stature as icons of the Holocaust. At the war's end these tattoos' emblematic value was already evident in film footage and still photographs of recently liberated concentration camp survivors showing their tattoos to the camera, as well as shots of tattooed forearms isolated from the rest of the survivors' bodies.[34] Since then, showing a number tattooed on someone's arm identifies the person straightaway as a Holocaust survivor in many works of photography, painting, film, and other media, including works that make no other reference to the Holocaust. For example, late in the 1971 feature film *Harold and Maude*, viewers learn that the madcap octogenarian Maude (played by Ruth Gordon) is a Holocaust survivor, thanks only to a fleeting glimpse of a number tattooed on her arm.

Professional photographers who have made portraits of Holocaust survivors often pose them so that their tattooed arms are featured prominently.[35] One such photograph, made by Frédéric Brenner in 1991 of four survivors from Salonika, is displayed in the US Holocaust Memorial Museum, framed by dozens of other photos (not taken by Brenner) of prisoners' tattooed forearms. This massing effect, a central idiom of display in Holocaust museums more generally (lists of names of victims; piles of shoes, suitcases, etc.), exemplifies the genocide's enormity. While this display may be meant to invoke moral outrage at the scope of the Holocaust, its aesthetic strategy replicates the practice of reducing the subjects of Nazi persecution to a nameless inventory. The isolated tattooed arm as synecdoche for the survivor paradoxically iterates the dehumanization of persecuted peoples that the museum and other Holocaust memorial projects decry.

To some extent, the VHA approaches documenting prisoner tattoos similarly. They are usually recorded in extreme close-up shots of survivors' forearms during the final sequence of these videos, when family photographs and other items are filmed. This strategy isolates the tattoo from the survivor's body as it separates the tattoo's display from the interview proper, which may include recollections of receiving the tattoo or postwar reactions to it. In these final sequences, the tattooed forearm is, in effect, conceptualized as an object, located

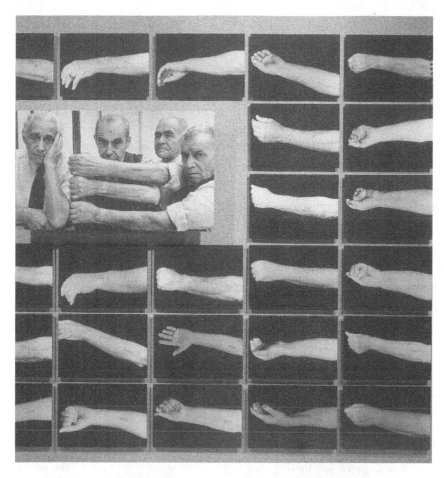

Portion of photo display depicting Jewish Auschwitz survivors from Salonika showing their tattooed arms on the third floor of the permanent exhibition at the US Holocaust Memorial Museum. The center photograph was taken in Salonika by Frédéric Brenner in 1991. Pictured from left to right in Brenner's photograph are Sam Saporta, Mois Amir, Mr. Robisa, and Barouh Sevy. Photographer: Arnold Kramer. Copyright © United States Holocaust Memorial Museum.

within the survivor's inventory of relics of his or her life. In the interview with Aharon Feldberg, the close-up of his tattooed forearm follows several photographs of his grandchildren and precedes examples of his artwork: paintings and bas-reliefs of still-lifes, Israeli landscapes, and shtetl genre scenes. This sequencing, perhaps the result of what was most expedient for the videographer, surrounds Feldberg's tattoo with material evidence of his postwar thriving.[36]

When their tattooed forearms are filmed in these final sequences, survivors are asked to recite the number. Often, survivors say nothing more during the shot. Some survivors add information about where and when they were tattooed or explain the significance of the number or symbols on their arms.[37] These standardized close-ups of tattoos are filmed even in videos where survivors display their numbers earlier, while discussing them in the course of the interview proper. When Adela Becher recalls being tattooed as a prisoner at Auschwitz, she recites the number and rolls up her left sleeve to reveal the tattoo, and the camera pulls back to include her arm in the frame. After she moves on to discuss conditions in the camp, the camera pushes back in on her face. Becher's number is filmed at the end of the video in a close-up of her forearm, and she repeats the number as well as where and when she was tattooed.[38]

Survivors' discussions of their tattoos sometimes extend to the postwar era, often focusing on deliberations about whether to have them removed. Carl Willner reflects on the tattoo he received at Auschwitz as the camera photographs a close-up of his forearm: "People tell me, 'Why don't you take it off?' Well, it could be taken off by operation, but why should I? I didn't do nothing wrong. So I got nothing to be ashamed of. . . . Well, I'm not anything proud of it, but that's what it is."[39] When Joseph Carver recalls the moment he was tattooed during the war, he recites the number and then explains that he had it removed after the war, because he was working for "a very large English company, and I had to travel in Europe." Carver also mentions that he had the tattoo photographed and that "the mark [i.e., scar] is here." He rolls up the sleeve on his left arm and points to the spot, as the camera pushes in on his forearm. "You see, they didn't do a good job; it was here," and he recites the number as he traces the spot with his index finger.[40] Though the tattoo is absent from his arm, Carver has resituated it there through photo-documentation, narrative, and gesture.

Kate Arnon offers a different explanation for having her tattoo removed. "After the war I did not feel that I wanted the number, because it was something inflicted upon me that I did not want. . . . I am not ashamed over having been in the camps, but I'm also not proud of it, it's not something I wanted. And so I had it removed, and I'm glad about that." When interviewer Fred Charatan asks Arnon if she remembers the number, "just for the record," she replies that she does not and adds: "I do not like to be labeled. . . . I even do not like the word 'survivor' too much, because it also puts a certain label. I like to be my own person, with my own values, and I do not think we should be all put in one category; everybody was different."

Though Arnon had her tattoo removed, a scar remains on her forearm. It cannot be seen during the interview proper, when she discusses having the tattoo removed, though she looks down at her arm, which is below the frame of the shot. However, the scar is filmed in an extreme close-up of Arnon's forearm at the end of the interview, along with her photographs and other personal objects. Over this shot, Arnon is heard saying, "This is where my number was removed," as she points to the location with her finger.[41] The tattoo's absence becomes the subject of both discussion and visual attention. The tattoo can be expunged, but its existence cannot be forgotten (even if the number has been). The visual trace of erasing this icon of Holocaust survivorhood from her body remains as a defining gesture for Arnon, emblematic of her resistance to being labeled a survivor.

Kitty Hart-Moxon also had her tattoo removed, but toward a very different end. When recounting her arrival at Auschwitz, she describes the tattooing process and recites both her mother's and her own prisoner numbers (they were imprisoned together, and their numbers are consecutive). Hart-Moxon then rolls up her sleeve to reveal a scar on her left forearm. The camera pushes in on the scar and then pulls back out as she explains that she had the tattoo removed in the 1950s and adds, "But I have got it; it is intact."[42] Later, when recounting her postwar life, Hart-Moxon describes the role the tattoo played in talking about her wartime experiences with people she met in England:

> It wasn't very difficult, because I had a number on my arm, and people would remark or something, and it came from there. . . . My mother, when she was in company, she used to cover her number up, because she didn't like people asking her questions. . . . But I didn't do that; I preferred to have my number visible. There was a time when I actually had to have it removed, because— . . . it didn't become an embarrassment, I wouldn't say that . . . —but there were some irritating instances, which I was no longer prepared to put up with. . . . I was working in a children's hospital at that time, and there were one or two people, and one was a doctor who, whenever he saw me, would make some peculiar remark, such as "Is this your boyfriend's telephone number?"[43]

Hart-Moxon then explains that she decided not simply to remove the tattoo but to have it "mounted in a specimen, so that it lives forever; even when I'm not here, my number will live on in some museum."[44] The specimen is photographed at the end of the interview, along with Hart-Moxon's personal photographs and documents, and she describes it, off camera, in detail:

> This is a specimen of two pieces of skin, each one showing a tattoo. The upper tattoo, which is very distinctive, 39933 with a triangle underneath, is a piece of skin that belonged to my mother. After my mother's death I asked permission to have this removed. I wanted it kept, and eventually I want it to go into a museum. The lower number, the lower piece of skin, is not terribly clear; it is 39934, which is my own piece of skin, my own tattoo. The reason this is not so clear is that it had been removed in the '50s and had just been left in formaldehyde for many years, before it was actually mounted, together with my mother's. And so it wasn't all that well preserved. But I think it does actually show the tattoo quite clearly.[45]

Hart-Moxon's removal and display of her tattoo parallel the writing of her wartime memoirs (discussed in chapter 2). With both acts, she separates the traces of experiencing the Holocaust from herself and makes them publicly available. Even as Hart-Moxon remains very closely invested in her identity as a Holocaust survivor, these acts reify this status as something that can stand apart from her and, eventually, outlive her.[46]

The display of a scar where a prisoner's tattoo was removed also occurs during one of David Boder's interviews with Holocaust survivors conducted in 1946. What cannot be shown in the audio recording of his exchange with Nelly Bondy is described, including a parenthetical explanation that Boder later added to the transcript:

> Bondy: The first thing to be done was to be tattooed. You see, they preferred . . .
>   they tattooed the number on our left forearm.
> Boder: You have a tattoo number?
> Bondy: No. I got it cut . . . I got it cut out when I came back. (*she shows a rather
>   bad scar*)
> Boder: How did you take it out?
> Bondy: It was quite an operation. It had to be cut out. It was very deep.

Boder: It was . . . it was cut out and then you had some skin re-grafted?

Bondy: Yes, yes. That's it.

Boder: Aha . . . also you have then on your left arm . . .

Bondy: Yes . . .

Boder: . . . left arm you have a scar.

Bondy: Yes.

Boder: From the removal of the tattoo.

Bondy: Yes.[47]

Here, too, narrative reverses the surgery that removed the tattoo, virtually in-scribing its presence on the survivor's body for the interview's auditors.

The VHA's presentation of prisoner tattoos, by contrast, is centered on dis-play rather than narrative and therefore often entails minimal explanation. As a result, in many of these sequences, the iconic shot of the tattooed arm is as-sumed to be self-evident. Nevertheless, the VHA records a range of survivors' responses to their tattoos: as objects of others' curiosity, as sources of discom-fort, as artifacts for posterity. Even those survivors who had their tattoos re-moved report having done so for different reasons: to escape being identified as a Holocaust survivor or to document and preserve the number, separate from the survivor's body. In survivors' responses to their tattoos, embodiment is tied to questions of volition. Survivors did not elect to be tattooed, but after the war they had the choice of whether or not to continue to bear (and bare) the tattoo. The VHA's request of survivors to display their tattoos gauges each survivor's relationship with this number as emblematic of being visible as a Holocaust survivor.

The VHA's special attention to prisoner tattoos reflects a broader attention to them as embodiments of the Holocaust and its remembrance. A recent spate of creative works involves not only the presence of Holocaust survivor tattoos but also their embodied inscription and display. Filmmaker Dana Doron pro-duced Numbered, a 2012 documentary composed of interviews with fifty Ho-locaust survivors displaying and discussing their tattoos. In Artur Żmijewski's 2004 video titled 80064, the artist persuaded Józef Tarnawa, who had been a prisoner in Auschwitz, to "renovate" his tattoo, despite Tarnawa's misgivings that having the number re-inked would render it "inauthentic."[48] For Yishay Garbasz's The Number Project, an artwork initiated in 2011, the artist branded her forearm with her mother's concentration camp tattoo. Wishing to "recon-textualize these numbers, rather than appropriating them," Garbasz chose branding in order to "produce a visually distinct image from a tattoo" and thereby "provide . . . a different experience of receiving and wearing the num-bers, until they disappear."[49] The impulse to imprint a prisoner number on one's skin, if temporarily, as an act of Holocaust remembrance is ritualized in *Night-words: A Liturgy on the Holocaust*, compiled by literature scholar David Roskies in 2000. At one point in this innovative Jewish rite of Holocaust commemora-tion, the directions instruct participants to "roll up their left sleeves," so that one of the participants can inscribe a series of consecutive concentration camp numbers on their arms with "a black felt pen."[50]

The voluntary act of inscribing a Holocaust prisoner tattoo onto one's body extends beyond works of art or ritual to descendants of survivors electing to duplicate a forebear's tattoo on their own arms as a gesture of remembrance, a practice that situates this icon of the Holocaust within the current popularity of tattooing generally, especially among young adults. A 2012 *New York Times* feature on the phenomenon quotes one practitioner, Eli Sagir, a young Israeli: "I decided to do it to remind my generation: I want to tell them my grand-father's story and the Holocaust story."[51] This practice transforms the tattoo from a mark of dehumanization into an emblem of survivors' tenacity and of Jewish solidarity and continuity.

The Holocaust prisoner tattoo has attained an equivocal status—an unwel-come external imposition as well as a persistent fixture of the body, a sign of both stigmatization and fortitude. This ambivalence is fundamental to how the VHA documents tattoos, as it is to their more recent engagement by artists, survivors' descendants, and others. In all these undertakings tattoos consti-tute visual evidence of persecution that displaying, documenting, or copying them reinscribes, even as these efforts intend, at least in part, to condemn the dehumanizing treatment that these numbers evince. Embracing these num-bers as emblems of remembrance, unity, and endurance radically repurposes their original significance. At the same time, this transformation conforms to the Western iconography of martyrdom, epitomized by the crucifix, in which an image of abject suffering becomes a venerated emblem of defining moral conviction.

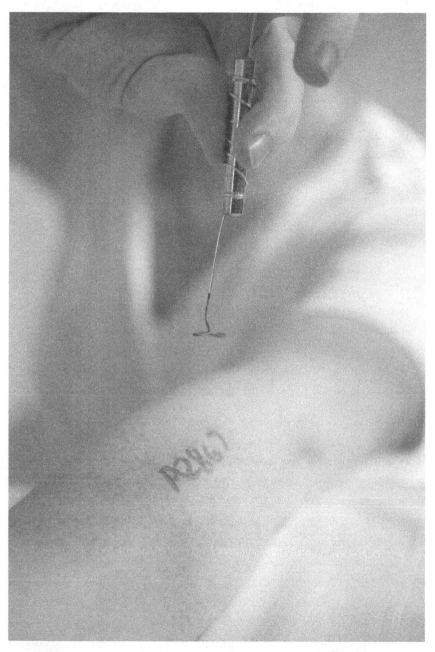

Yishay Garbasz branding her forearm with the prisoner number that was tattooed on the artist's mother when she was a prisoner in Auschwitz. From *The Number Project*, © Yishay Garbasz, courtesy of Ronald Feldman Fine Art and the artist.

Objects

Notwithstanding the salience of survivor narratives in Holocaust memory practices at the turn of the millennium, a great variety of artifacts also figure prominently in recalling the genocide. The frequent turn to inanimate objects when reckoning with the enormity of human losses during the Holocaust provides "an oblique but no less powerful encounter with the horror of genocide." While the display of artifacts in Holocaust museums may be the most obvious example of this phenomenon, it occurs elsewhere, including in literary works and in the visual and performing arts. The considerable role of objects in Holocaust remembrance reflects how ordinary items

> acquired new values of unprecedented urgency and consequence during the Holocaust. The powerful imbrication of human lives with the stuff of daily life—articles of clothing, household goods, tools—came apart as the social contract in Nazi-controlled lands was breached. Nazi Germany persecuted its victims by confiscating their property, by replacing their basic material needs with inferior goods (e.g., wooden clogs instead of shoes for concentration camp inmates, their uniforms made of coarse cloth woven from nettles), by scavenging their bodies for hidden treasures (gold, jewelry), and ultimately by reducing human beings to raw material for commodities (hair for cloth, fat for soap).[52]

Reflecting this attention to material objects, the Shoah Foundation invited Holocaust survivors to prepare photographs, documents, and other items related to their personal histories to be recorded on videotape. Though these items appear in the complete video, they were filmed separately from the interview proper and in a different manner. Per the VHA's protocols, each item is typically placed on a copy stand against a dark background and filmed, one item at a time. The survivor, sometimes prompted by the interviewer, identifies each item in voice-over. The VHA guidelines for the videographer stress that "PHOTOS SHOULD NOT BE HELD BY THE SURVIVOR OR INTERVIEWER. *Be sure to shoot beyond all four edges of the photograph and then move in if necessary for details.* Since the photographs will also be part of the archive, they must be established as being complete, unedited, untrimmed documents."[53] These protocols also apply to how survivors' other objects, both two- and three-dimensional, are filmed.

These guidelines diverge from the VHA's protocols for filming survivors in significant ways. During the interview proper, the camera is not to be moved or cut, except in extraordinary circumstances; the continuous, fixed presence of the survivor, even through periods of silence or emotional distress, is deemed paramount. When filming objects, by contrast, the camera is cut between the setups of each item to be photographed and can zoom in on details. During these sequences, the survivor's visual presence—for example, helping to set up and remove each object—is to be omitted. Though this approach to photographing objects breaks from the interviews' constant visual attention to the survivors, they are present obliquely, as they continue to speak, off camera, while their objects are filmed.

The VHA's protocols for photographing objects may well have been prompted by concerns for efficiency and formal consistency, in addition to maintaining these items' documentary integrity, but this methodology is not inevitable. The Museum of Jewish Heritage in New York City, for example, videotaped interviews of Holocaust survivors handling some objects, so as to use the videos in exhibition spaces displaying these items. This approach presents them as personal possessions rather than as archived artifacts and may even inform how survivors discuss these objects.

In the VHA, a survivor's objects are ambiguously situated within the video; they are both part of the interview and apart from it. (On the Archive's website, these sequences of objects can be viewed either within the entire video or as a series of stills in a separate "slide show," without voice-over.) Similarly, the guidelines for filming these items are equivocal. Though the VHA seeks a uniform, dispassionate presentation of survivors' possessions as archival documents, it employs a cinematic subjectivity and agency that is avoided during the interview proper. Recorded in a time-based medium, the presentation of these objects is shaped by camera movement (panning over objects, pushing in on details), survivors' comments, and even the amount of time each item appears on screen.

Occasionally either survivors or videographers break with the VHA's protocols. At the end of Leszek Allerhand's interview, he narrates the display of family photographs and painted portraits hanging on the walls of his home, some in elaborate vintage frames, as the camera moves from one item to the next.[54] Lucy Smith can be seen pointing to people in family photos and other items, all of which are laid out on a table, as the camera pans from one object to another.[55] In the middle of Leizer Portnoy's interview he displays and describes a number of photographs, papers, and books, which were placed on a table by his side. He then hands some of these items to interviewer Stephanie Fastlicht, who holds them up to the camera.[56] In such moments, the objects' significance is informed by the environment in which they are displayed or the survivor's interaction with them, in addition to the recollections they prompt.

The VHA's protocols for filming objects facilitate a different kind of storytelling, which contrasts with and sometimes complements the survivors' on-camera interviews. Not only are survivors obliquely part of these sequences as providers of off-camera commentary; they also appear in many of the personal photographs, their names appear on personal papers, and they are implicitly present throughout as the keepers of all these items. The order in which objects are filmed also rests, at least in part, with the survivor. Typically, these items (especially photographs) are arranged in chronological order. The interviewer or videographer may contribute to this sequencing, but it is ultimately determined by the survivor, who alone knows each item's provenance. Compared to their role in the interview proper, interviewers generally seem to ask fewer questions during the filming of objects, other than prompting survivors to provide identification information (such as names, dates, and places for photographs, or translations of documents written in languages other than the one in which the interview is conducted).[57] Survivors often provide only this information, but they may also choose to discuss some items more extensively, at times linking an object to the narrative they provided earlier, during the interview proper. Some of these sequences of objects are substantial enough to constitute another life narrative, articulated through images, artifacts, and the commentary they elicit from the survivor, rather than answers to an interviewer's questions.

Even as the videos' visual composition shifts away from the survivors during these sequences, it extends their spectacular presence beyond their faces and a glimpse of their homes to their possessions. At the same time, the camera's attention to these objects depends upon the survivor's speech. The length of the shot of each item is usually determined by how long the survivor speaks about it, and camera movement, pushing in on details, follows specific information that the survivor offers. Objects and narrative are interdependent: the former are offered as material evidence that substantiates the latter, while the narrative situates the objects within contexts that impart value to these items.

Some items are relics specific to the Holocaust, such as yellow cloth "Jewish" badges in the shape of a six-pointed star, concentration camp uniforms, or samples of ghetto currency. Survivors occasionally present items that testify to personal distinctions apart from the Holocaust. To cite but one example, Abraham Slucki, who became a professional baker in the United States after the war, includes a picture of a cake that he made for President Kennedy's inauguration.[58] But most objects in these final sequences appear to be "ordinary"—that is, they are neither readily distinguished as artifacts of the Holocaust nor inherently singular in some other way. Photographs—both prewar studio portraits and postwar snapshots—of the survivors, their families, and acquaintances predominate in these sequences, and there is also an abundance of personal papers and correspondence. In addition, survivors display articles of clothing, tools, jewelry, artwork, religious objects, musical instruments, and the like. Through the stories they prompt, these commonplace objects can become extraordinary relics of epochal events.

As object-driven narratives, these sequences in the VHA interviews resemble other cultural practices centered on material or visual culture. Because most items are connected to the survivor's personal history, these sequences resemble family photo albums or scrapbooks—and, in fact, some images are photographed in these assemblages. As ordered arrangements of selected, discrete items, these sequences also become impromptu exhibitions. The survivor, in the role of curator, provides information that identifies and contextualizes objects and can arrange items to impart added meaning through their juxtaposition. In addition, the survivor functions during the videotaping as a docent, guiding viewers from object to object, directing their attention to particular details and offering explanations of the items' significance. These sequences might also be thought of as virtual time capsules, into which survivors place their possessions for posterity, so that they will testify, after the survivors' death, to a bygone era.

These sequences of objects constitute a final act of summation of the survivor's life story, coming after the end of the interview proper (when survivors are often asked to offer a "message to future generations"), which is sometimes

followed by a group interview with the survivor's family members.[59] The prescribed order of recording the entire video may be expeditious in terms of
camerawork, but it also tracks the progress of the interviewee's life—a narrative that proceeds from origins (family background, birth, childhood) to the
present—followed by a series of legacies: concluding thoughts offered for posterity, resembling an impromptu ethical will; an appearance on camera together
with progeny; an assembly of material relics. Beyond these objects' value as
evidence of the Holocaust, they testify, if largely tacitly, to the survivor's postwar endurance. Kept and maintained for decades after the war, then selected
for inclusion in the video, these objects also evince survivors' sense of history,
whether personal or on a grand scale, and its materialization.

I I I

Among the many different kinds of objects that Jewish Holocaust survivors
chose to include in their videos are a small number of items that the VHA
index identifies as "Christian religious objects," appearing in twenty-two interviews.[60] Survivors usually acquired these crucifixes, rosaries, saints' med-
als, and similar items as part of efforts to pass as Christians during the war.
Displayed in the context of an interview with a Jewish survivor, these are inherently provocative objects. Their presence among the survivor's collection
of personal artifacts prompts an accounting of their place in a "Jewish" life
history. Consequently, these items sometimes engender complex narratives of
survivors' relationships with individual Christians or with Christianity in general, both during the war and, in some cases, afterwards, continuing up to the
time of the interview.

Where survivors locate Christian religious objects when organizing material to be photographed informs their significance within the implicit narratives of these sequences. Survivors sometimes place Christian religious objects
immediately before or after other objects related to their efforts to pass as
Christians, such as wartime photographs of themselves wearing crosses or participating in Christian rituals.[61] In Maurice Elbaum's video the scapular he wore
during the early 1940s precedes a photograph of himself taken at the time. He
explains that he then wore a hairnet at night to straighten his curly hair, inti-
mating that doing so was also part of concealing his Jewishness. Next comes a
photocopy of his wartime *Arbeitskarte* (German government-issued work per-

mit), which identifies Elbaum as Ignacz Dzikowski, a Pole.[62] This set of three items, together with their narrative, documents Elbaum's efforts to pass as a Christian, the external emblems of his disguise—a religious amulet, an ethnic Polish name—in tension with his Jewish physiognomy. Other survivors' videos position religious articles adjacent to photographs of the Christians who hid the survivors or helped them disguise their Jewishness, thereby acknowledging the agency of their protectors.[63]

By juxtaposing Christian religious objects with emblems of wartime Jewish stigmatization, some survivors create opportunities to comment on the complex connections between their personal histories and the identities they assumed during the war. Maurice Baron's video displays the crucifix that, the survivor explains, his mother wore "every day between 1942 'til 1944, when we were liberated," followed by a yellow star, marked with the letter "J." Of this item, Baron remarks: "I had to wear it, and that *mogen-Dovid* [Yiddish: "Star of David"] reminds me sometimes if I forget who I really am, and I'm very pleased, I'm very thrilled that I still have it, so it can remind me of what happened."[64] At the end of her interview, Daisy Shapiro-Rieke asks interviewer Eileen Molfetas, "Can I hold that rosary in my hand? Can I? And the star? . . . I'd like to end this tape by holding these two things, I really want to hold them." From her position off camera, Molfetas hands Shapiro-Rieke a yellow, six-pointed cloth star, which is under glass in a small wooden frame, and a rosary. The latter item belonged to Shapiro-Rieke's mother, who had created a false identity for herself and her children as Christians; the star was worn by Shapiro-Rieke's father, who was unable to assume a false identity during the war. Holding one object in each hand, Shapiro-Rieke raises them, framing her face. "I am both, I am here because of both. And this is—this is my story. . . . And I want this to be on the tape. And I want to hold this."[65] Though the video subsequently includes a separate shot of the rosary and the star displayed by themselves, per the VHA guidelines, Shapiro-Rieke takes command of the filming process at the end of the interview proper, so that she can be photographed clasping these objects. After having spent more than an hour and a half narrating her life history, Shapiro-Rieke offers viewers of her video an alternate form of autobiography, one that is not only, or even primarily, verbal but rather is material and gestural: the spectacle of her face framed by these defining objects within her close embrace.

At the conclusion of her VHA interview, survivor Daisy Shapiro-Rieke displays a rosary used by her mother during World War II, when she passed as a Christian, and a yellow star that Shapiro-Rieke's father wore during the war, marking him as a Jew. Provided by the USC Shoah Foundation.

Christian religious articles acquire special value when they appear first or last in the sequence of objects, separate from the chronology of the interviewee's life story, as emblems of the Christians who protected these survivors during the war. The first object photographed in Edith Simblist-Polak's video is a small, framed, metal bas-relief of the Madonna and Child. She explains: "This is the icon that Mrs. Zembruska [with whom the interviewee and her family hid during the war] gave me when we said goodbye, and this was the one she had on her little altar in her room, where she prayed that we should survive the war." As the camera pushes in on the icon, Simblist-Polak adds, "I had to promise her that I will always have it with me and it will always have a special place in wherever I will be, and it was."[66] At the very end of Sonia Liberman's video, following a photograph of her four grandchildren, the camera records a close-up of the palm of her hand holding a small crucifix on a chain. She explains that the Christian family that protected her gave her this on the day she was baptized, "and that's what saved my life."[67]

Liberman's last words exemplify the sentiments of other survivors who attest to the power that Christian religious objects held for them during the war. In addition to acknowledging their instrumental value for disguising one's Jewishness, some survivors speak of these objects' talismanic power. Irene Barkan explains that a Polish woman, Kasia Puszczynska, gave her a rosary "to help me, to bring me luck, and in case I was found, that they would think I was not Jewish by carrying this." Of the crucifix that his mother wore during the war, Maurice Baron recalls that, "after the war, she kept it and thought this was, let's say, a good luck charm to her, but she was very, very emotionally involved with that cross." These survivors' attachments to Christian religious articles are, nonetheless, distinct from what they would mean to a Christian owner, a point some survivors address directly. Eugene Winnik describes his childhood of going to church, wearing a cross, and saying Christian prayers on his knees while in hiding during the war as a matter of wanting to be "like everybody else"—that is, all the Poles—in the village where he and his mother hid after escaping the Warsaw ghetto. But when interviewer Jacob Pinger asks Winnik if having religious faith helped him, he replies, "Faith? You mean mentally? Oh, no. This won't help me survive. This helped me survive, to avoid being killed. That's all. I don't believe in this now. But in these years, yes, I was a believer."[68]

Displaying their religious objects prompts survivors to address the materiality of these items in conjunction with their symbolic value. As she finishes discussing her icon, Simblist-Polak adds, "When I came to Australia, I sent all my things by sea-mail, but this one was in my little suitcase, I never ever trusted it anywhere. It's always in a special place." Irma Grundland says of the small catechism she displays, "When I touch it I feel my mother's hand. She taught me all the Catholic prayers from this book. . . . I carried that booklet with me all through the war, and I never part with that book even now." Teresa Gericke, a Jew who had converted to Christianity before the war, describes a simple cross she found among personal items taken from other prisoners at Auschwitz. For a long time she carried it in her purse but worried the cross might be stolen, "so I put it on my neck, and that is where it is and that is where it belongs."[69]

Leo Turkell reveals an especially profound attachment to a rosary, which he discusses at three different points during his interview. Turkell first mentions the rosary when recounting how he and hundreds of other soldiers in the Polish army were captured by German forces at the beginning of the war. Another soldier, Witold Szedlecki, a Polish friend of Turkell's, gave him the rosary a few minutes before the Germans separated out the Jewish soldiers and shot them. As Turkell is about to relate this episode, he indicates that he wants to get the rosary, but interviewer Temmie Margolis tells him to wait. Turkell then explains that Szedlecki "took off from his neck his rosary and he gave it to me, and he says, 'Please, put on quick the rosary.' And I put on quick the rosary on my neck. (*He gestures with his hands as if putting the rosary over his head.*) . . . And I bent down my head, because this was a call for all the Jews to step out." After recounting how the other Jewish soldiers were executed, Turkell continues:

> Then the generals walked through the whole line, looking at faces, is there any Jew who didn't step out. I bent down (*he lowers his head*) and I fixed my shoe, that they shouldn't see my face. And here (*he indicates with his fingers alongside his neck*) was hanging the rosary. [As] soon [as] they saw the rosary, they even didn't touch me, they didn't look at me, and that's the way this rosary saved my life. And I have it 'til today. And I told my wife, "When the time comes, this rosary you will have to put in my grave." She says she will be ashamed of it. I say, "Why should you be ashamed of it? This rosary saved my life. I wouldn't be here to be your husband and have children and grandchildren." . . . And I still have it here, which I would like to show it. . . . I would like to have it on the camera.[70]

Turkell's request is soon fulfilled; at the beginning of the next videotape, Margolis asks him to return to the story about the rosary and to display it. Turkell already has the rosary in his hands; he holds it up before his face and speaks: "Please—this was my lifesaver. This what I keep 'til today, until I die, I want this to go with me." The camera pulls back in order to show more of the rosary, which hangs down to Turkell's mid-torso. He retells, more concisely, the story of how Szedlecki gave him the rosary just before the Jewish soldiers were selected for execution. All the while, Turkell holds up the rosary with both hands, as if he were about to put it on. Turkell concludes the narrative by adding, "And with this rosary I went through the whole war."[71] Then Margolis tells him to put down the rosary so that they can continue with the interview.

The rosary is seen again at the end of the video—this time laid on a dark background—following a sequence of Turkell's family photographs, wartime documents, and rubber stamps he made during the war to create false identification papers. As the rosary appears on screen, he says, off camera: "This

During his VHA interview, survivor Leo Turkell displays a rosary as he recounts receiving it from a Polish friend during World War II, enabling Turkell to pass as a Christian. Provided by the USC Shoah Foundation.

is what I can hardly talk about it. The best of my life, what saved my life. I wore this cross, who was given to me by my friend Witold Szedlecki, about five minutes before they took out the Jews to be killed, and they were killed several hundred. And this cross I wore since 1939 and I keep that 'til today; I will keep it 'til my grave." As Turkell speaks, the camera pushes in on the crucifix and then pulls back out to the full rosary. A male voice (possibly the videographer, Warren Yeager) can be heard saying, "It's so great that you have that." Turkell comments: "And this cross saved my life. The cross with the Lord Jesus Christ."[72]

Turkell conveys his profound sense of indebtedness to the rosary—and the man who gave it to him—through a compelling, thrice-told narrative as well as his insistence on displaying the rosary. He voices this desire the first time he relates the story, after being forbidden to interrupt the interview to get the rosary. During this first telling, Turkell invokes the rosary's presence through gestures that mime its placement around his neck at the crucial, lifesaving moment. Following a break between videotapes, now with the rosary in his hands, Turkell tells the story of his rescue a second time. He does not reenact donning the rosary this time but holds it up, so as to have it on camera and to have it seen with him, parallel to his wish to be buried with the rosary. Finally, when the rosary is displayed by itself, Turkell recalls, more briefly than before but as passionately, the incident when he received it from Szedlecki, whom he names each time the story is told. The spectacle in these three tellings of the same story changes from the rosary's absence to Turkell's absence. This shift, though it is serendipitous, becomes significant for viewing the narrative as a whole. At the center of this dynamic is the rosary's role as disguise, concealing Turkell's Jewishness and replacing his face, which, he implies, might give him away as a Jew. The telling of the story—without and then with the appearance of the rosary; with and then without Turkell's presence on screen—evokes the rosary's double role of saving and obscuring a Jew.

Though Turkell repeats some information in all three tellings, each one also offers different details. In his final account, as the camera offers a close-up of the crucifix, he first mentions "the Lord Jesus Christ"—a provocative locution for East European Jews, who traditionally avoided uttering Jesus's name, let alone acknowledging his divinity. Yet Turkell's oblique validation of the Crucifixion—and his forthright affirmation of the rosary as the instrument of his rescue by a Polish Christian—contrasts sharply with what ensues and concludes the video. The shot of the rosary is followed by a final image: a color photograph of Turkell standing before a sign marking the entrance to Stopnica, his hometown, taken when he visited Poland in the 1980s. He remarks bitterly: "There was no [Jewish] cemetery, no synagogue, everything was thrown down by the Polacks. That's what I couldn't believe, as I lived between people, and a lot of them were just animals, murderers."[73] The double-edged story of Turkell's rescue parallels the ambivalence with which he ends the video, recalling Poles variously as rescuers and persecutors.

Ruth Sokolecki presents an even more elaborate relationship with a crucifix when interviewed by Zahava Spitzer, beginning with an account of seeking refuge after escaping from a labor camp in Tłuste in 1943. Sokolecki explains that she prevailed upon a Polish woman, Antonina Sędzikowa, to provide the sixteen-year-old Sokolecki with a refuge.[74] Sokolecki mentions straightaway the crucifix worn by Sędzikowa as emblematic of her moral integrity: "I looked at her. She was wearing a big cross on her neck. (*Sokolecki demonstrates where the cross was by grasping the beaded necklace she wears.*) So as a child I look at her and I say, 'She must be a very religious lady. She believes in something, doesn't matter what. God—there's one God, and she believes.'"

After providing Sokolecki with temporary shelter in her barn, Sędzikowa proposed another hiding place: "She said, 'You see, there's a grave, you know, people keep potatoes over the wintertime. . . . If I make space there in that hole, . . . can you crawl in there?' And I said, 'I can do it.' . . . And I was there 'til the end of the war. She saved my life."[75] Sokolecki then adds:

> When I was there a few days, she came in to me, she said, she took out her necklace (*Sokolecki gestures again with her own necklace*) with the cross, big cross, with Jesus on top, and she said, "Put Him on. He will help you, not me. He's a saver. He saves people. . . ." You know, I come from a very strict, I told you, religious [upbringing]—but when you're in trouble, you grab a straw, you say, "This straw will help me." And I was wearing that cross, and looking at Him, and kissing Him, and loving Him, and I used to promise Him, I used to say, "Jesus, if You can hear me, I will be so good. If You will have poor people, You send them to me. I will help them; I will give them food. Please!" And He was my saver. He saved me. He saved my mind. . . .
>
> Spitzer: You prayed to him, too?
>
> Sokolecki: I used to pray Jewish to Him, what should I pray? I used to say *Shema Yisroel* [i.e., the Hebrew prayer beginning "Hear, O Israel"], then I used to say, "You are Jewish, You had a Jewish mother, maybe You understand me!" You know, I didn't know other language to say to Him. But I promised Him, I used to say, "I make a bargain with You. Give me life. I will do something for You." And this saved my mind. More than my life. Both! But the mind was the first. Yes, I believe in Him now. I'm Jewish, like I said.[76]

Sokolecki later relates how she lost the crucifix at the end of war, while running away from someone who recognized her as a Jew and tried to harm her. She explains that when she told Sędzikowa about losing the crucifix, the woman replied, "You are free, you don't need Him no more. He saved you, you are free."[77] Toward the end of the interview, Spitzer asks Sokolecki whether she still thinks about the cross, and she replies:

> Sure, sure. Listen, I have Him with me. I didn't told you, with the cross, that my daughter found it. . . . Susan was seven years, eight years old, she

went to public school. . . . She came home . . . and she yells, "Mommy! . . .
I have to show you something! . . . I was standing to talk to my friend, and
this big cross was laying next to my foot. It's like hitting my foot, I should
pick it up." As I look at the cross, and I listen to my child, and I just said,
"You picked it up, a Jewish little girl?" . . . "Mommy, I picked it up for you.
For good luck." And I never told her about it. I used to dream at night, I
have Him. I used to get up, He's not there. And if she gave me this, I said,
"Would you like to have it?" "No, Mommy, you keep it." . . . Did I cry!
I looked at Him, I kissed Him, I put Him to my heart, and I said, "You
came back to me! I love You!" I felt like I have everything, nothing will
happen to me, because I have Him. . . .

Spitzer: And you still have that cross?

Sokolecki: Oh yes, I would not give Him for a million dollars. But if I go, He's
with me. I keep Him in my pocketbook; if I go far, I'm afraid someone
will grab my pocketbook, I keep Him in my pocket in a coat or some-
place—you can have the charge accounts, you can take everything, but
not Him.[78]

The crucifix finally appears on screen, photographed on a dark background,
as the video's penultimate image. It follows photographs of Sędzikowa (whom
Sokolecki describes as "a beautiful, gorgeous, second mother of mine. I love her
dearly. She gave me my life. She saved me. She was an angel from God") and of
Sędzikowa's son ("just like a brother to me") with his own son. Sokolecki identifies the crucifix as "the cross that my beautiful lady, my second mother, gave
me when I was by her in that grave. And she said to me, 'He will save you, not
me.' And I wore that all the time there, I loved Him, I kissed Him. He is to me
everything. I just love Him. I feel like He is with me always."[79]

Sokolecki's remarkable narrative abounds with plot twists, symbolic mo-
tifs, and religious paradoxes, as it voices a strong, straightforward psychological and moral certainty. Like Jesus, Sokolecki rose from the "grave" (she likely
uses this English word as the gloss for its Yiddish cognate, *grub*, which can
also mean "pit" or "hole," to describe the underground hollow used to store
potatoes, where she was hidden). Jesus answered her prayers by not only saving
her life but also "coming back" to her. Sokolecki, in turn, kept the promise she
had made to Jesus to help people through her ongoing support of Sędzikowa

and her family. (At the time of the interview, Sokolecki was concerned that Sędzikowa's grandson was in prison for some reason and, as Sokolecki hadn't heard from him in a while, had contacted the Red Cross to find out about his circumstances.)[80] Mirroring the gift of a crucifix from her "second mother" is the one Sokolecki receives from her own daughter.

The crucifix is central to Sokolecki's life story as the sign of Sędzikowa's goodness, the focus of Sokolecki's will to survive during the war, and the validation of her inner resolve. She evokes the materiality of the crucifix during her interview by repeatedly grasping the necklace she wears, a gesture that invites the viewer to imagine the crucifix around first Sędzikowa's neck and then on Sokolecki. The delayed appearance of the crucifix until near the very end of the video heightens its signifying power. Upon hearing Sokolecki's story of its return to her, years after the war, a skeptical viewer of this interview may consider it most unlikely that the object she now treasures is the same crucifix given to her by Sędzikowa, even though Sokolecki identifies it as such when it finally appears on camera. At this moment, such skepticism confronts the survivor's conviction. For her, the crucifix displayed in the video is, in essence if not in substance, the gift she received during the war and that she credits with having saved her life.

Sokolecki's account of the crucifix is an especially rich example of what has been termed "folk religion"—that is, spiritual belief and observance conceived and enacted, not according to the official tenets promulgated by an institutional religious elite, but by dint of an "ordinary" person's particular, deeply felt convictions and self-fashioned practices.[81] Sokolecki's attachment to the crucifix as a redemptive talisman during the war and her embrace of its postwar "return" exemplify the magical thinking typical of folk religion. Such beliefs were already familiar to Sokolecki as a young woman, who grew up in a milieu rich in what historian Joshua Trachtenberg termed "folk Judaism"—the convictions, lore, and customs that "made up the everyday religion of the Jewish people."[82] In fact, the power Sokolecki invests in the crucifix is prefigured in an incident she recalls from her prewar childhood, mentioned early in the interview. As a little girl, she received a coin from a Hasidic leader, the Czortkower Rebbe, who instructed her to "wear it with you always" as a "*shmire* [Yiddish: "talisman"].[83] Sokolecki's attachment to the crucifix as a life-saving object with supernal power resembles as well accounts of other Jewish Holocaust survivors, who attest to the redemptive properties of Jewish ritual objects.[84]

Also typical of folk religion is Sokolecki's syncretism, which fuses her Catholic rescuer's belief in Jesus's power to save the girl with Sokolecki's upbringing as a pious Jew. She characterizes "praying Jewish" to Jesus as one child of a Jewish mother appealing to another; by reciting *Shema Yisroel* to Jesus she affirms, before a fellow Jew, that "the Lord is One." Remaining a committed Jew after the war, Sokolecki explains during the interview that she keeps kosher, gave her children a Jewish education, and buys Israel bonds. She also reports having attempted to make the case for a reconciliation of Jewish and Catholic concerns, shortly before the time of her interview, to none less than the pope. In a letter voicing her concern that the Vatican did not recognize the State of Israel, Sokolecki told the pope of her wartime experiences, including the story of the crucifix: "I wrote him, 'Please—Jesus was Jewish. He comes from a Jewish mother. We all are His people, too. If you love really Jesus, help, that there should be peace all over the world and Israel, too.' . . . Maybe four weeks came a beautiful letter from him, written down, 'God should be with you forever.' That's it."[85]

Together with her self-styled religiosity, Sokolecki's narrative offers insightful psychological reflection, informed not only by the distance of several decades but also by religious tenets and her subjectivity. She explains that during the war the crucifix

> gave me my life, mentally, because I was alone, there were mice and rats [in her hiding place]—and me. But I had that cross on me (*touches her necklace and holds it in her hands*), and I felt *in* me, I'm not alone. He is with me, He will save me, He loves me, He will be good to me. And this kept my mind going that I will live, I will be free. And it's something like—you take any little thing, you say, this is my good luck charm. And you believe so strong, that this *is* your good luck charm.[86]

Later in the interview, she comments, "Fear never leaves you. The mind is a very strong power. If the mind takes over your body, you're finished."[87]

Jesus helped to save Sokolecki, but not as Sędzikowa may have understood this salvation—let alone how her priest would have done so—as a supernal act in response to faithful devotion. Sokolecki characterizes Jesus as a "straw" to grasp, the crucifix as a "good luck charm," in order to save her mind and body—

as opposed to her soul—and to help her overcome psychologically paralyzing fear. Similarly, she describes how she has repaid Jesus for saving her through acts of charity as a humanistic virtue: "I love to give *tsedoke* [Yiddish: "charity"]. I like to help people, I like to give things, I'm just looking for things whom to give. Because I cannot forget what I promised Him. And this has nothing to do with me as Jewish. This is two different worlds. This is me. And I love Him."[88]

Through her story about the crucifix, Sokolecki, like some other Jewish survivors talking about Christian religious objects they had during the war, articulates an ethical or religious worldview that conforms neither to Jewish nor to Christian normative tenets. Rather, it is born of her own extraordinary experiences, in which the struggle to stay alive in the face of genocide trumps religious precepts. The fact of having survived affirms, if tacitly, her self-styled beliefs, and having done so in the face of seeming incongruities between Judaism and Christianity reinforces her convictions, rather than undermining them. These convictions are materialized in her crucifix, the instrument of her survival, thanks to Sędzikowa's kindness and Sokolecki's internal resolve. Decades later, this object serves as the emblem of her continued remembrance of this risky endeavor.

Sokolecki's interrelation of Christian iconography and Jewish historical experience resembles similar juxtapositions in works of modern Jewish culture: the cruciform poem "Uri Tsvi farn tselem INRI" (Yiddish: "Uri Zvi before the cross INRI") by Uri Zvi Greenberg, Marc Chagall's paintings of the crucified Jesus wearing a prayer shawl or phylacteries, or the Crucifixion as motif in Chaim Potok's novel *My Name Is Asher Lev*.[89] But unlike the provocative motives behind these examples, Sokolecki's intention is not to foreground the disparities between Christian tenets and Jewish suffering.[90] Rather, her narrative integrates Christian and Jewish principles into an ethos that is, in its essence, a universal, humanistic call "to help people." Her crucifix and the story of its powerful role in her life elevate this common belief in the importance of doing good by associating it with enduring belief in the supernal and with surviving a genocide. The fact that the material object she now treasures may well not be the same crucifix as the one she was given during the war testifies to the power of Sokolecki's belief to transcend obstacles, be they the constraints of religious doctrines or the upheavals of history.

I I I

The moments in VHA interviews when the camera shifts away from recording "talking heads" to filming displays of scarred or tattooed bodies and personal relics unsettle the videos' primary idiom of remembrance, which privileges the spectacle as well as the substance of speech. Exceptional displays of injuries and objects offer a different kind of evidence, which stands apart from survivors' narratives even as it relies on them to articulate its significance. The visual images don't simply corroborate narratives but signify in their own right, by dint of the striking physicality of the images' subjects, that the events recounted actually took place. The interrelation of word and image in these videos exemplifies Roland Barthes's distinction between *studium* and *punctum* in his reading of photographic images, where the former—a generalized, intellectually and culturally informed, and equable interest in the image overall—is disrupted by the latter, "an element which rises from the scene, shoots out of it like an arrow, and pierces."[91]

These images in the VHA resonate with long-standing visual idioms of evidence, associated with religiously inspired moral exhortation, that concretizes faith: the martyr's wounds, the protective amulet. In addition, the accounts of wartime ordeals that survivors offer in conjunction with these images evoke the giving of eyewitness testimony in a courtroom. The moments in these videos where survivors display and narrate their injuries or religious artifacts thereby unite the "two historical roots of witnessing": the avowal of religious faith and the giving of evidence in a court of law.[92]

Finally, the signifying power of these exceptional moments accrues to the general value of watching Holocaust survivors tell their stories. Filmed decades after the war, survivors' on-camera presence, like their wounds and treasured possessions, offers visible evidence of their endurance and roots their stories in the observable act of bearing witness. Just as the spectacle of elderly survivors validates and informs the significance of their narratives, their words transform the act of beholding survivors' visual presence. Like a scarred limb or a rosary, these people, too, may well look ordinary, until users of the Archive listen—and watch—as survivors tell their extraordinary stories.

CONCLUSION

The Shoah Foundation's Visual History Archive is rich in contradictions, and the VHA user is enriched by contending with them. The project is international in scope and expansive in its approach to Holocaust remembrance through oral histories, extending the Archive's reach to include the memory of other genocides. At the same time, it is a distinctly American endeavor and is informed by long-standing Jewish commitments to the value of ethnography. The VHA is equally concerned with documenting the historical specificity of the Holocaust and with engaging its paradigmatic value as a universal moral exemplar. The Archive addresses these commitments through its inventory of interviews, in which the individuality of personal narratives is positioned within collective remembrance of the Holocaust on a monumental scale. These interviews rely on both the oldest form of communication—face-to-face storytelling—and the latest communications technologies. The use of video is distinguished by the medium's visual element, even as attention to these recordings centers largely on the spoken word. Video enables recording the running flow of storytelling, which unfolds at each interviewee's pace, as well as atomizing this flow through the recordings' digitization and indexing. As a digital project, the Archive both centralizes on its website the stories of survivors located around the world and distributes them to new sites internationally. Similarly, the Shoah Foundation prizes the integrity of each survivor's life story, even as the VHA offers ways to select and aggregate segments of these narratives in new matrices of information. The Foundation requires that videos adhere to formal standards, and yet its protocols entail provisions that are highly variable, including the use of interviewers from all manner of backgrounds and the filming of videos in individual survivors' homes. And some of the most revealing moments in these interviews take place when survivors, interviewers, or videographers break with the project's guidelines. These exceptional moments are of interest not only in themselves but as points of entry into understanding the complex of contradictions inherent in the Archive as a whole, thereby revealing its value as a redoubt of memory and its significance as a threshold work of digital humanities.

From the start, documenting Holocaust survivors' personal histories has entailed a shifting conglomeration of personal undertakings, collaborative efforts, and institutional projects. These documentations have been realized in a variety of media and genres and are available to diverse audiences that range in scope from the intimate to the international. Intellectuals have long debated the possibilities of Holocaust representation, and some survivors have created thought-provoking personal narratives of formal daring, such as Primo Levi's *Il sistema periodico* (*The Periodic Table*) or Georges Perec's *W ou le souvenir d'enfance* (*W, or the Memory of Childhood*).[1] But most of these efforts by far are the work of amateur memoirists, who rely on familiar modes of storytelling. These works constitute a kind of folk practice, and their grassroots origins and conventions persist despite the institutionalization and professionalization of documenting Holocaust survivors' life stories. The VHA provides ample evidence of the tenacity of folk narrative, even in the face of a half century of survivors' exposure to Holocaust narratives in the mass media or of institutional and technological structures that strive to standardize these personal histories.

Nevertheless, the life histories collected by the Shoah Foundation and other videotaping projects are distinct within the larger corpus of survivor narratives, including other videos. Even as dozens of institutions began to collect recordings of Holocaust survivors in the final decades of the twentieth century, survivors' stories were also recorded on audio- or videotape by members of their own families. These private, amateur documentations offer a different kind of narrative from those housed in the VHA and other collections. The storytelling in recordings undertaken by a survivor's loved ones is more intimate, shaped by the particulars of family relationships. Though distinguished by the act of recording, these narratives are part of ongoing interactions between survivors and their families, even if the survivors reveal information on these recordings that they never previously disclosed or use the occasion to relate their stories differently—for example, offering a continuous narrative, rather than telling isolated anecdotes over time.

Family members may be more likely to interrupt, editorialize, or argue during these recordings—that is, to do the very sorts of things that interviewers are instructed to avoid. Family recordings of survivors' life stories are therefore liable to be more of a conversation than an interview, conventionally understood as having discrete roles for interviewer and interviewee. To that end, perhaps, the VHA and other videotaping projects remove family members from the act of documenting the survivor's story. Typically, they are not allowed to be in the room during the videotaping—indeed, the VHA provides family members the opportunity to speak in a separate segment of the video that is distinct in form from the survivor interview proper.

In the VHA and other similar collections, survivors tell their stories to interviewers who are usually otherwise unknown to the interviewees. Even when these interviewers are volunteers new to the task, as is often the case in the VHA, they are instructed to approach interviewing as dispassionate professionals—for example, not to make sympathetic comments or otherwise engage the interviewee except in the pursuit of information. This procedure makes for a very different kind of narrative from those offered in family recordings, in which survivors directly address a specific, intimate audience. Instead, the interviewer stands in for future auditors, who not only will likely be strangers to the interviewee but also will be at a temporal and physical remove. Therefore, though the institutional video usually documents a singular encounter with the survivor, it is not regarded as an end in itself. Both survivors and those involved in creating these videos imagine them as having some future use—contributing to scholarly research, pedagogy, or other works of Holocaust remembrance, such as a documentary film or a museum exhibition—and envision their potential outcome, whether it be historical insight, moral edification, or affirmation of peoplehood.

Because they are filmed in interviewees' homes, the Shoah Foundation's interviews may look similar to videos made by survivors' family members. However, the VHA juxtaposes the intimacy of these domestic settings with a world map, which appears alongside the display of each video on the Archive's website and pinpoints locations as they are mentioned during the interviews. The spatial character of memory in the VHA is therefore simultaneously private and global. Place is also implicitly linked to time, as the world map, which uses contemporary place-names and boundaries, contrasts with the shifting political geography of Europe over the course of the twentieth century (which is indicated in the website's annotations to the map). Moreover, the Archive constructs a virtual space of its own, configured as an architecture of memory. Searching the VHA's holdings resembles roaming a building with thousands of rooms, each housing a different conversation that, as if by magic, takes place in a different locale. Unlike television, characterized by geographer Paul Adams as constituting a "place without a location," the VHA interrelates multiple geographies: Europe of the first half of the twentieth century, the postwar diaspora of Holocaust survivors, and the international network of the Archive's users.[2]

The typical user of the Archive watches its videos on a laptop or other personal device, thereby mirroring the intimate scale of the interviewees' homes. Nevertheless, survivors will always be remote from users, who are, in effect, eavesdropping on face-to-face conversations that took place years ago. Users can sample, replay, compare, and combine these conversations but can never enter them as participants. The Shoah Foundation now grapples with the challenge of overcoming the passage of time and the social dispersion of the Internet to foster a sense of communing with Holocaust survivors. Engaging with others without actually meeting them is, of course, a fundament of virtual communities, including those of long standing that have been created through correspondence and periodicals. But because recording these videos was motivated, to a considerable degree, by mounting anxieties over losing the unrivaled opportunity to learn about the genocide from direct encounters with its survivors, the absence of this connection is regarded as perilous to the future of Holocaust remembrance.

Therefore, rather than conceding to the inevitable passing of survivors, the Shoah Foundation has turned to the technology of interactive holography to create the semblance of a survivor that is more comprehensive (a full-body moving image, rendered in a three-dimensional apparition) and with which audiences can engage in a simulation of face-to-face conversation. This endeavor appears to prioritize the experience of conversing with survivors, as holography grants them an uncanny, ersatz immortality, over archival research, the primary activity of using the VHA. Yet Holocaust studies scholar Rachel Baum proposes that the interactive holograph be regarded not as a departure from the Shoah Foundation's prior efforts but as an "extension of earlier digital artifacts," constituting "the visual representation of a database" of information in the form of survivors' answers to interviewers' questions.[3] The turn to holography calls attention to yet another tension within the VHA: on one hand, the Shoah Foundation champions the morally galvanizing power of watching and listening to Holocaust survivors relate their intimate and often emotionally charged recollections; on the other hand, it proffers the intellectual value of these interviews as sources of information about the Holocaust, life before and after the genocide, and the processes of memory. Indeed, the path to enlightening encounters with survivors' recollections begins at the gateway of the Archive's index and database, with the task of research. Interactive holographs would seem to conflate the intellectual search for information and the affective engagement with survivors' stories, but these different modes of encounter with survivors' recorded life histories remain distinct, in the form of "live" questions from the audience and prerecorded answers from the hologram, respectively.

Regardless of the extent to which holography could ever supersede the VHA's videos, it is inevitable that, at some point in the future, they will seem dated. Their technology and aesthetic will appear less than state of the art, just as the people in the videos are already evidently of an earlier era, marked by their clothes, home furnishings, and ways of speaking as much as by the stories they have to tell. During the project's first two decades, its technologies for preserving and disseminating the Archive's holdings have been updated more than once, most notably by digitizing the original analog videos, and these modifications will doubtless continue as digital media evolve. The VHA's commitment to preserving its survivor interviews "in perpetuity" is in tension with the ongoing need of digital media to be rechecked and recopied, as well as the potential that digitization provides for interviews to be atomized and reconfigured as users gather excerpts and organize them into ever new compositions. What the VHA sustains is therefore a dynamic maintenance—repeatedly upgrading the technology, working to establish an ever-widening array of users, finding new points of entry to engaging the recordings, and creating new outcomes for their use. These ongoing innovations situate the Foundation's dedication to "preserving memory" within the subjective, contingent, and relational nature of remembering.

As it straddles the transition from the "video age" to the "digital age," the VHA manifests shifts in intellectual sensibility as well as technology. Historian Wulf Kansteiner argues that Holocaust memory projects created in "linear media" such as print, film, and television are, in effect, aging out, alongside survivors. Younger generations, he contends, will want to encounter this subject through new kinds of media, especially those that provide immersive experiences, exemplified by interactive holography.[4] It is true that, over time, videos of Holocaust survivors will increasingly seem antiquated, by dint of their medium, but this will not necessarily result in their being of less interest to younger generations. Rather than constituting a loss in effectiveness, the aging of video may well endow the medium with the aura of a historical artifact, much as has happened with black-and-white film footage of the World War II era. This added value may also facilitate greater awareness among viewers that the videos are mediations of memory, rooted in the past by their form as well as their content, like eighteenth-century documents written with a flowing hand on parchment or nineteenth-century portraits in sepia-toned *cartes de visite*. The VHA also historicizes its videos of Holocaust survivors by enabling their comparison with footage of survivors of the Armenian genocide, recorded on 16 mm film as early as 1975, as well as videos of survivors of the Rwandan genocide, in which younger interviewees describe a more recent atrocity.

More than a repository for its many hours of videotaped recollection, the VHA is itself an artifact of remembrance, which is realized in its archival structure. The Archive's search terms and matrices determine users' access to its extensive holdings and direct, as well as constrain, what users can find within the collection. The inherently selective nature of the index also articulates the VHA's significance as a resource of Holocaust memory by identifying what the Archive's creators have deemed memorable. At the same time that the VHA imposes a structure of meaning onto the life histories in its collection, each individual survivor engages in archival acts as well, by choosing and organizing photographs and objects to be filmed or deciding on texts to be recited on camera. Moreover, the very act of offering a personal narrative entails the work of selecting and organizing that is the essence of archiving: considering what episodes to recount and how to fashion meaning out of the "material and symbolic composites . . . that make up the life-story."[5]

Media scholar Wolfgang Ernst argues that the Internet has engendered a new kind of archive, which is "no longer the static accumulation of dossiers" but instead a "dynamic connection of documents and links. Although their indexes are primarily search oriented, unlike traditional archive repertoires," these new archives "are not passive but themselves constitute a logistical document containing links to the pertinent data records—a finding aid in the documents themselves, a self-referent archive." The VHA is currently a hybrid of what Ernst distinguishes as the "traditional" and the "dynamic" archive and has the potential to become even more of the latter, "the essence of which is permanent updating."[6] To that end, historian Todd Presner proposes "a more participatory architecture" for the VHA's index, which would enable users "to create tags that could . . . undo—or, at least, supplement—the [Archive's] definitive indexing categories and keywords." Doing so "would constantly re-interpret and re-inscribe the survivors' stories in ways that not only place the listener into an active relationship of responsibility but unleash a potentiality of meaning in every act of . . . 'browsing'" the Archive's holdings.[7] By enabling a crowd-sourced complement to the VHA's index, the Shoah Foundation could more fully embrace the open-source ethos of the Internet. Indeed, the ideals of Internet sociability that prize egalitarian, nonhierarchical sharing are well suited to the Foundation's commitment to use its videos to promote tolerance.[8]

Presner's proposal could be facilitated by the Shoah Foundation's recent initiative, begun in 2016, to transcribe all of the VHA's interviews, which will further expand research possibilities in the Archive. The Foundation explains that these "transcripts will not replace the current use of indexed keywords. Instead, they will work together to provide scholars and researchers the best option that suits their needs. The transcripts will appear on the screen as interviewees are talking so there will not be any loss of nuance of expression or paralinguistic cues."[9] This on-screen juxtaposition of video, indexing terms, and transcription will situate these interviews within a complex apparatus that can both highlight the distinction of relating one's life narrative through this audiovisual medium and enhance the possibilities for probing the Archive, including ample opportunities to read it against the grain. Doing so proves to be less subversive than it might at first seem, for it resonates with the ways that many of the Holocaust survivors whose life histories are housed in the VHA subverted its protocols of interviewing—challenging assumptions in interviewers' questions, changing languages on the spur of the moment, insisting on holding objects or displaying injuries on camera. This may not only reflect the fact that many of those who survived the Holocaust did so by defying wartime powers that were at best indifferent to the well-being of these people and at worst intent on their destruction. For when interviewees deviate from what is expected of them, they are being true to the task of remembering as a subjective, conditional practice. The contingency of memory continues to develop as these interviews are accessed by successions of viewers, each encounter enabling new possibilities of recalling and making sense of the past.

Probing the VHA demonstrates the ongoing, complex, "mutually shaping" interrelation of memory practices and media practices.[10] Survivors motivated by an imperative, whether personal or institutional, to remember the Holocaust have sought ways to secure and share their recollections through various media. Each medium informs the work of remembering, and, in turn, the resulting mediations engender concerns for their own preservation and transmission. The memory works themselves also prompt the creation of new media practices, including technological inventions, epistemological innovations, and new ethical and pedagogical protocols. This interdependency, foundational to the cultural practices of memory, is in the midst of threshold changes, driven by watershed developments in communications media that the VHA exemplifies. The imminent passing of survivors and other eyewitnesses of the Holocaust intensifies the attention to this interrelation, as the possibility of their creating new firsthand accounts comes to an end. Nevertheless, the Visual History Archive and similar undertakings will continue to evolve, prompting new inquiries for scholars, educators, artists, and others who work at the intersection of media and memory, exploring how people will learn not only from the past but also from the accumulating efforts to remember it.

APPENDIX
Interviews Referenced

The author gratefully acknowledges the USC Shoah Foundation for allowing the use in this book of transcripts of excerpts from the following VHA interviews. For more information on the Foundation and the VHA: http://sfi.usc.edu.

Interviewee	IC No. *	Place and Year of Birth**	Interview Date	Interview Place	Interviewer	Language(s) ***
Abrashkevitch, Sofia	12345	Teresva, Czechoslovakia, 1930	March 19, 1996	Rehovot, Israel	Maria Lackman	Y
Alcone, Helga	18663	Breslau, Germany, 1925	July 26, 1996	Mission Viejo, California	Renée Firestone	E
Aleksandrovskii, Miron	37388	Bershad', USSR, 1934	October 26, 1997	Odessa, Ukraine	David Rozenfeld	R
Allerhand, Leszek	27779	Lwów, Poland, 1932	February 1, 1997	Zakopane, Poland	Irena Kowalik	P
Andriushina, Tamara	47415	Tokmak, USSR, 1935	June 3, 1998	Rovno, Ukraine	Genadii Tenenbaum	R
Apelowicz, Doba	29753	Białystok, Russia, 1917	March 28, 1997	Melbourne, Australia	Jason Walker	E, (Y)
Arbeiter, Israel	18588	Płock, Poland, 1925	August 9, 1996	Newton, Massachusetts	Paula Saltman	E
Armer, John	3638	Cracow, Poland, 1925	June 29, 1995	Sydney, Australia	Dani Katz	E
Arnon, Kate	4835	Berlin, Germany, 1925	July 28, 1995	Palm Beach, Florida	Fred Charatan	E
Bakal, Lev	34759	Briceni, Romania, 1937	August 12, 1997	Kishinev, Moldova	Maia Feldman	R

* IC No. = VHA Interview Code number.

** Municipal place-names are spelled per VHA listings. Country names are listed, per the VHA, according to each municipality's location at the time of the interviewee's birth.

*** E = English, G = German, H = Hebrew, P = Polish, R = Russian, S = Spanish, Y = Yiddish. Languages listed in parentheses are heard in the interviews but not listed in the VHA database.

Interviewee	IC No. *	Place and Year of Birth**	Interview Date	Interview Place	Interviewer	Language(s) ***
Barkan, Irene	2039	Lwów, Poland, 1931	April 13, 1995	Great Neck, New York	Marvin Miller	E
Baron, Maurice	32481	Warsaw, Poland, 1931	August 10, 1997	Melbourne, Australia	Leon Garfinkel	E
Becher, Adela	37975	Radom, Poland, 1923	November 5, 1997	Philadelphia, Pennsylvania	Sally Alsher	E
Becher, Martha	11877	Josbach, Germany, 1923	February 7, 1996	West Palm Beach, Florida	Marvin Greenberg	E
Bejski, Moshe	23848	Dzialoszyce, Poland, 1931	November 7, 1998	Tel Aviv, Israel	Nathan Lavie	H
Benveniste, Flora	47902	Salonika, Greece, 1923	November 12, 1998	Charlotte, North Carolina	Eileen Molfetas	E
Berger, Maria	32398	Równe, Poland, 1926	July 24, 1997	Brooklyn, New York	Lorrie Fein	E
Bernard, Ruth	13786	Stuttgart, Germany, 1926	March 28, 1996	Toronto, Canada	Paula Draper	E
Billys, Sophie	10850	Łódź, Russia, 1912	January 4, 1996	Beachwood, Ohio	Margaret Kocevar	Y
Biniaz, Celina	11133	Cracow, Poland 1931	January 25, 1996	Camarillo, California	Carol Stulberg	E
Blitz, Joseph	15985	Bukaczowce, Russia, 1910	June 11, 1996	Plantation, Florida	Norma Menasche	Y
Blumenthal, Abraham	16640	Bielsk Podlaski, Russia, 1905	June 20, 1996	Buenos Aires, Argentina	Ana Suchodolski-Tarnaruder	Y
Bomba, Abraham	18061	Beuthen, Germany, 1913	August 14, 1996	Monticello, New York	Louise Bobrow	E, (Y)
Bornstein, Chaim	18510	Druja, Russia, 1911	August 14, 1996	Monticello, New York	Naomi Rappaport	E, Y
Brandys, Adam	14457	Sosnowiec, Russia, 1911	April 24, 1996	Skokie, Illinois	Phyllis Dreazen	Y
Braude, Rachela	33567	Oszmiana, Poland, 1926	September 29, 1997	Buenos Aires, Argentina	Ana Suchodolski-Tarnaruder	Y
Braun, Rywka	3624	Bychawa, Russia, 1918	June 29, 1995	Toronto, Canada	Richard Bassett	Y
Brunstein, Esther	20838	Łódź, Poland, 1928	October 17, 1996	Ilford, England	Bernice Krantz	E
Burstin, Frank	37151	Lutomiersk, Poland, 1925	December 8, 1997	Bronx, New York	Martha Frazer	E
Carver, Joseph	9262	Leipzig, Germany, 1928	February 8, 1996	London, England	Susan Fransman	E

Interviewee	IC No. *	Place and Year of Birth**	Interview Date	Interview Place	Interviewer	Language(s) ***
Clary, Robert	95	Paris, France, 1926	September 12, 1994	Beverly Hills, California	Merle Goldberg	E
Cohn, Suzanne	52043	Kobryn, Poland, 1938	November 1, 2011	Philadelphia, Pennsylvania	Nancy Fisher	E
Cojuc, Georges	15904	Paris, France, 1928	May 31, 1996	Mexico City, Mexico	Anita Hecht	E
Cronheim, Arno	21483	Berlin, Germany, 1922	October 20, 1996	Columbus, Ohio	Joanne Centa	E
de Haan, Cecilia	32721	Alkmaar, Netherlands, 1923	August 27, 1997	Melbourne, Australia	Anna Epstein	E
Deutsch, Michael	1358	Vrbové, Czechoslovakia, 1923	March 15, 1995	Sydney, Australia	Barbara Sewell	E, (Y)
Dortheimer, Victor	22469	Cracow, Poland, 1918	December 3, 1996	London, England	Simone Redbart	E
Einhorn, Cecilia	49619	Bochnia, Poland, 1920	April 29, 1999	San Francisco, California	Zepporah Glass	E, (Y)
Elbaum, Morris	9317	Warsaw, Poland, 1924	November 28, 1995	Pembroke Pines, Florida	Helen Desman	H
Elbaum, Sophia	7914	Łódź. Russia, 1916	October 24, 1995	Chicago, Illinois	Anita Weiss	E, (Y)
Engel, Stella	7402	Amsterdam, Netherlands, 1921	October 6, 1995	Albertson, New York	Charlotte Rettinger	E
Faber, David	10416	Nowy Sącz, Poland, 1926	December 20, 1995	San Diego, California	Harlene Rottenberg	E
Faerber, Gunter	41847	Lipiny, Poland, 1928	May 7, 1998	Birmingham, England	Corinne Oppenheimer	E
Feig, Allen	16852	Vulcan, Romania, 1922	June 30, 1996	Toronto, Canada	Judy Breuer	E
Feldberg, Aharon	7165	Będzin, Poland, 1920	December 13, 1995	Jerusalem, Israel	Lauren Schachar	H
Ferber, Roman	43707	Cracow, Poland, 1933	July 12, 1998	Airmont, New York	Susan Peirez	E
Fershko, Sara	10825	Luck, Russia, 1917	January 9, 1996	Miami Beach, Florida	Lenore Bienenfeld Weinstein	E
Fishman, Anna	89	Briceva, Romania, 1938	September 1, 1994	Los Angeles, California	Ana Feldman	R
Fiszman, Esther	1350	Sosnowiec, Poland, 1930	March 14, 1995	Sydney, Australia	Jackie Regos	E
Frenkel, Anna	38848	Iampol', USSR, 1925	November 18, 1997	Trostianets, Ukraine	Leonid Sapozhnikov	R

Interviewee	IC No. *	Place and Year of Birth**	Interview Date	Interview Place	Interviewer	Language(s) ***
Friedman, Simon	11175	Warsaw, Russia, 1909	January 24, 1996	Coconut Creek, Florida	Bonnie Gurewitsch	E
Fuks, Bronislava	30401	Zin'kov, USSR, 1924	June 24, 1997	Rishon LeZion, Israel	Rozalia Dobina	R
Geizhals, Benek	11349	Cracow, Poland, 1921	January 25, 1996	New Hyde Park, New York	Susan Peirez	E
Gelbard, Bela	5450	Pińczów, Russia, 1908	October 22, 1995	Johannesburg, South Africa	Paul Bacher	E, Y
Gericke, Teresa	32466	Szeged, Austria-Hungary, 1913	August 5, 1997	London, England	Lesley Nathan	E
Glaser, Peter	21449	Zatec, Czechoslovakia, 1923	October 21, 1996	Lexington, Massachusetts	Paula Saltman	E
Glaser, Sol	32704	Glod, Austria-Hungary, 1896	August 10, 1997	North Miami Beach, Florida	Fay Nicoll	Y
Gluck, Zoltan	12812	Felsővadász, Hungary, 1929	April 25, 1996	New York, New York	Sheila Ainbinder	E
Glucksman, Sidney	26276	Chrzanów, Poland, 1927	February 2, 1997	New Haven, Connecticut	Jaclyn R. Jeffrey	E
Goldbarten, Emil	7722	Komarów, Russia, 1906	October 19, 1995	North Miami Beach, Florida	Rita R. Jacobsohn	E, (Y)
Goldstein, Lilly	45022	Kékcse, Hungary, 1922	August 16, 1998	Brooklyn, New York	Alan Oirich	E, Y
Grand, Minna	7853	Kaunas, Lithuania, 1925	October 22, 1995	Los Angeles, California	Masha Loen	Y
Grobart, Renee	3921	Warsaw, Poland, 1934	July 13, 1995	Buffalo Grove, Illinois	Malka Kleiman	E
Gross, Suzanne	22180	Paris, France, 1931	November 19, 1996	Philadelphia, Pennsylvania	Merrill Grumer	E
Grundland, Irma	5502	Warsaw, Poland, 1933	August 15, 1995	Northbrook, Illinois	Elayne Morgan	E
Gutman, David	20037	Iwaniska, Poland, 1920	September 25, 1996	Hallandale, Florida	Nadine Litterman	E, (Y)
Guttman, Eva	14192	Opatów, Poland, 1915	April 15, 1996	Belle Harbor, New York	Rivka Wakslak	E, Y
Halpern, David	34094	Uzhorod, Czechoslovakia, 1928	September 30, 1997	Amityville, New York	Louise Bobrow	E
Hartman, George	10110	Prague, Czechoslovakia, 1925	December 15, 1995	Seattle, Washington	Janice Englehart	E
Hart-Moxon, Kitty	45132	Bielsko, Poland, 1926	June 9, 1998	Birmingham, England	Corinne Oppenheimer	E

Interviewee	IC No. *	Place and Year of Birth**	Interview Date	Interview Place	Interviewer	Language(s) ***
Heitner, Sol	1500	Bethuen, Germany, 1915	March 17, 1995	Bronxville, New York	Naomi Rappaport	E, Y
Hertsberg, Sia	14139	Riga, Latvia, 1927	April 12, 1996	Northbrook, Illinois	Joy Goldman	E
Hillman, Laura	1208	Aurich, Germany, 1923	March 17, 1995	Los Alamitos, California	Carol Stulberg	E
Jakubowicz, Frieda	31253	Burakówka, Poland, 1923	July 24, 1997	Bayside, New York	Debbi Portnoy	E
Jungreis, Esther	518	Szeged, Hungary, 1936	January 9, 1995	North Woodmere, New York	Raquel Grunwald	E
Jurmann, Esra	36824	Dresden, Germany, 1929	November 16, 1997	London, England	Joanna Buchan	E
Kaplan, Rut	9104	Vilna, Poland, 1924	February 6, 1996	Cholon, Israel	Yeshayahu Pery	H, Y
Katz, Arlene	1531	Hajdúnánás, Austria-Hungary, 1916	March 19, 1995	Brooklyn, New York	Raquel Grunwald	E, (Y)
Kaye, Sara	23573	Węgrów, Poland, 1929/1931	November 28, 1996	London, England	Lesley Nathan	E
Klein, Gerda Weissmann	9725	Bielsko, Poland, 1924	December 7, 1995	Scottsdale, Arizona	Louise Bobrow	E
Koenigsberg, John	29548	Amsterdam, Netherlands, 1937	June 1, 1997	Columbus, Ohio	Pam McKenna	E
Koifman, Iakov	16648	Vasileuti, Romania, 1926	June 20, 1996	Kiryat Yam, Israel	Boris Zilper	R
Krichevskaia, Rosaliia	35800	Feodosiia, USSR, 1932	September 4, 1997	Beersheva, Israel	Boris Yablochnik	R
Kronenberg, Lea	32760	Łódź, Poland, 1924	August 19, 1997	Melbourne, Australia	Suzanne Hampel	E
Kurtsfeld, Sofia	35119	Minsk, USSR, 1925	August 11, 1997	Kiryat Motzkin, Israel	Boris Zilper	R
Lantos, Tom	25591	Budapest, Hungary, 1928	December 10, 1996	Washington, D.C.	Renée Firestone	E
Leon, Masha	9071	Warsaw, Poland, 1931	February 6, 1996	New York, New York	Brenda Smith	E
Levy, Danielle	38941	Brussels, Belgium, 1937	December 15, 1997	Melbourne, Australia	Bronnie Tait	E
Lewanoni, Dov	19085	Kerecky, Czechoslovakia, 1921	August 19, 1996	Jerusalem, Israel	Jehoshua Modlinger	Y
Leyson, Leon	8916	Narewka, Poland, 1929	November 16, 1995	Fullerton, Califronia	Stella Eliezrie	E

Interviewee	IC No. *	Place and Year of Birth**	Interview Date	Interview Place	Interviewer	Language(s) ***
Liberman, Sonia	2530	Kleck, Poland, 1933	May 15, 1995	Van Nuys, California	Adelle Chabelski	E
Loen, Masha	42186	Kaunas, Lithuania, 1930	May 16, 1998	Studio City, California	Dana Schwartz	E
Marcusohn, Susa	23098	Mihova, Romania, 1928	December 11, 1996	Montreal, Canada	Paula Bultz	E, Y
Meed, Benjamin	50584	Warsaw, Poland, 1922	August 5, 1999	New York, New York	Michael Berenbaum	E, Y
Meller, Jacob	8879	Kaunas, Russia, 1913	November 17, 1995	Los Angeles, California	Masha Loen	E, Y
Metz, Gilbert	45926	Bischwiller, France, 1929	September 3, 1998	Jackson, Mississippi	Adrian Hirsch	E
Nas, Blanka	6051	Turí Remety, Czechoslovakia, 1925	August 28, 1995	Pembroke Pines, Florida	Susan Neshick	E
Oikerman, Moisei	49664	Odessa, USSR, 1933	September 2, 1998	Odessa, Ukraine	David Rozenfeld	R
Page, Leopold	293	Cracow, Austria-Hungary, 1913	December 6, 1994	Beverly Hills, California	Branko Lustig	E
Portnoy, Leizer	11225	Janów, Poland, 1919	March 26, 1996	Mexico City, Mexico	Stephanie Fastlicht	S, Y
Puterman, Lusia	12897	Łódź, Poland, 1923	March 27, 1996	Sydney, Australia	Mary Ziegler	E
Rabinovits, Bronislavah	19762	Gródek Jagiellonski, Poland, 1920	September 9, 1996	Petach Tikva, Israel	Mina Graur	(H), Y
Rajchman, Chil	5	Łódź, Russia, 1914	October 24, 1994	California	Carol Stulberg	G, Y
Reifer, Alex	16792	Oswięcim, Poland, 1921	June 22, 1996	Sherman Oaks, California	Merrill Goldberg	E
Rosenzweig, Helena Jonas	23626	Cracow, Poland, 1925	November 26, 1996	Colts Neck, New Jersey	Susan Peirez	E
Rosman, Esther	14218	Warsaw, Poland, 1929	May 1, 1996	Tel Aviv, Israel	Chaya Colodner	H
Rosner, Leopold	17372	Cracow, Poland, 1918	July 14, 1996	Melbourne, Australia	Yael Hirsch	E
Rosner, Marianne	24958	Vienna, Austria-Hungary, 1910	January 21, 1997	Hallandale, Florida	Nancy Solomon	E
Rubner, Kalman	7899	Wadowice, Austria-Hungary, 1914	October 23, 1995	Toronto, Canada	Rosaline Krusner	E, Y

Interviewee	IC No. *	Place and Year of Birth**	Interview Date	Interview Place	Interviewer	Language(s) ***
Saks, Karol	11374	Sevlus, Czechoslovakia, 1934	January 21, 1996	Cleveland, Ohio	Mark Turkeltaub	E
Scheinberg, Wolf	14495	Warsaw, Russia, 1912	April 28, 1996	Brooklyn, New York	Shirley Berenstein	Y
Schlesinger, Chaskel	1680	Weilopole, Austria-Hungary, 1910	March 23, 1995	Chicago, Illinois	Donna Puccini	E
Schloss, Kurt	2057	Cologne, Germany, 1911	April 17, 1995	Bronx, New York	Martha Frazer	E
Schmetterling, Leon	2659	Buczacz, Poland, 1920	May 21, 1995	Miami Beach, Florida	Deborah Slobin	E
Schuster, Ben Zion	35883	Jezierzany, Poland, 1920	November 16, 1997	Baltimore, Maryland	Maran Gluckstein	E
Schwartz, Rose	10119	Krivé, Czechoslovakia, 1926	December 15, 1995	Margate, Florida	Rita R. Jacobsohn	E
Senger, Horst	9557	Berlin, Germany, 1924	December 4, 1995	Simi Valley, California	Temmie Margolis	E
Shapiro-Rieke, Daisy	48028	Vienna, Austria, 1937	November 12, 1998	Charlotte, North Carolina	Eileen Molfetas	E
Silberstein, Ritta	24365	Bistrita, Romania, 1924	December 20, 1996	Philadelphia, Pennsylvania	Helen Schneeberg	E
Simblist-Polak, Edith	5215	Bielsko, Poland, 1919	October 11, 1995	Sydney, Australia	Mary Ziegler	E
Slucki, Abraham	723	Warsaw, Russia, 1913	January 26, 1995	Los Angeles, California	Carol Schulberg	Y
Smith, Lore	40685	Halle, Germany, 1926	April 27, 1998	Hawthorne, California	Zepporah Glass	E
Smith, Lucy	10744	Cracow, Poland, 1933	January 9, 1996	St. Paul, Minnesota	Carol Wirtschafter	E
Sokolecki, Ruth	8420	Tłuste, Poland, 1926	November 7, 1995	Brooklyn, New York	Zahava Spitzer	E
Solz, Harriet	1491	Cracow, Poland, 1929	March 14, 1995	New York, New York	Sherry Amatenstein	E
Stein, Adek	3169	Białystok, Russia, 1914	June 13, 1995	Sydney, Australia	Rosemary Block	E, (Y)
Susser, Maryla	26484	Cracow, Poland, 1922	February 27, 1997	Clifton, New Jersey	David Brotsky	E
Sztajer, Chaim	5184	Częstochowa, Russia, 1909	October 29, 1995	Melbourne, Australia	Mary Ziegler	Y
Tremblinski, Mayer	40446	Wyszków, Poland, 1920	April 16, 1998	Toronto, Canada	Richard Bassett	Y

Interviewee	IC No. *	Place and Year of Birth**	Interview Date	Interview Place	Interviewer	Language(s) ***
Turkell, Leo	41507	Stopnica, Russia, 1917	May 18, 1998	Los Angeles, California	Temmie Margolis	E
Weiss, Harold	22039	Stettin, Germany, 1920	October 30, 1996	Baltimore, Maryland	Lucy Samorodin	E, (Y)
Welbel, Leon	1770	Lunna, Russia, 1916	March 30, 1995	Skokie, Illinois	Phyllis Dreazen	E, Y
Wenger, Michael	16162	Białystok, Russia, 1912	June 20, 1996	Brockton, Massachusetts	Rosalie Franks	E, Y
Westheimer, Ruth	43928	Wiesenfeld Germany, 1928	June 8, 1998	New York, New York	David Altshuler	E
Whiteman, Dorit	34738	Vienna, Austria, 1924	November 6, 1997	Hollis Hills, New York	Larry Rosenberg	E
Wiesenthal, Simon	35104	Buczacz, Austria-Hungary, 1908	November 18, 1997	Vienna, Austria	Albert Lichtblau	G
Wilkomirski, Binjamin	29545	Latvia?, 1938/1939?	March 20, 1997	Amlikon, Switzerland	Karin Merzbacher	G
Willner, Carl	1899	Dąbrowa, Poland, 1924	April 6, 1995	Palm Beach, Florida	Rosalie Franks	E
Winnik, Eugene	2746	Warsaw, Poland, 1935	May 21, 1995	Los Angeles, California	Jacob Pinger	E
Wunderman, Max	24625	Antwerp, Belgium, 1930	January 10, 1997	Beverly Hills, California	Marie Kaufman	E
Yezerskaya, Fira	15232	Gomel', USSR, 1925	May 16, 1996	West Hollywood, California	Anna Feldman	R
Zuckerman, Abraham	3190	Cracow, Poland, 1924	June 14, 1995	Hillside, New Jersey	Shelly Schore	E
Zylberszac-Junger, Goldy	38333	Etterbeek, Belgium, 1928	January 28, 1998	Flushing, New York	Charlotte Rettinger	E

NOTES

Citations from VHA interviews, when first given, provide the interviewee's full name, Interview Code (IC) number, and indexing segment (seg.) number(s); subsequent citations within the same chapter provide the interviewee's full name and indexing segment number(s) but not the IC number. For those interviews that were not indexed when this research was undertaken, the tape number and time codes for the cited passage are given instead of segment numbers. Additional information on VHA interviews (place and year of interviewee's birth, date and place of interview, name of interviewer, language[s] of interview) is listed in the Appendix.

Introduction

1. See Richard Chalfen, *Snapshot Versions of Life* (Bowling Green, OH: Bowling Green State University Popular Press, 1987), 8.

2. For information on survivor oral history videotaping projects, see US Holocaust Memorial Museum, "International Database of Oral History Testimonies," http://www.ushmm.org/online/oral-history/ (accessed September 17, 2015).

Chapter 1

1. Thomas Keneally's novel was originally published as *Schindler's Ark* (London: Hodder and Stoughton, 1982).

2. USC Shoah Foundation, *Testimony: The Legacy of "Schindler's List" and the USC Shoah Foundation* (New York: Newmarket Press/HarperCollins, 2014), 128, 135.

3. Visual History Archive (hereafter VHA) Online, "About Us: The Archive," http://vhaonline.usc.edu/about/archive.aspx (accessed August 1, 2016).

4. USC Shoah Foundation, *Testimony*, 151.

5. "The United States Holocaust Memorial Museum, in partnership with the Fortunoff Video Archive for Holocaust Testimonies at Yale University, produced six interviews with Orthodox Jewish Holocaust survivors in 2011" and continues to record interviews with this population of survivors. US Holocaust Memorial Museum, "Oral History Interviews of the Orthodox Jewish Holocaust Survivors Collection," http://collections.ushmm.org/search/catalog/irn44091 (accessed July 28, 2016).

6. The number of VHA interviews for these categories are as follows: Sinti and Roma (407), political prisoners (263), Jehovah's Witnesses (83), homosexuals (6), survivors of eu-

genics policies (13), non-Jewish survivors of forced labor (11), rescuers and aid providers (1,147), liberators (384), and participants in war crimes trials (62). VHA Online, "Experience Groups Search," http://vha.usc.edu/biosearch/bioSearch.aspx (accessed August 2, 2016).

7. For example, in contrast to the VHA's practice, "many of the interviewers" for the Fortunoff Video Archive "were either analysts or those in training." Leah Wolfson, "'Is There Anything Else You Would Like to Add?': Visual Testimony Encounters the Lyric Author(s)," *South Atlantic Review* 73, no. 3 (Summer 2008): 88.

8. USC Shoah Foundation, *Testimony*, 186, 190.

9. Shoah Foundation Institute, *Interviewer Guidelines* (Los Angeles: University of Southern California, 2007); both this and the VHA's "Pre-interview Questionnaire" are available at USC Shoah Foundation, "Collecting Testimonies," http://sfi.usc.edu/explore /collecting_testimonies (accessed September 17, 2015). See also USC Shoah Foundation, *Testimony*, 197.

10. Shoah Foundation Institute, *Interviewer Guidelines*; Shoah Foundation Institute, *Videographer Guidelines* (Los Angeles: University of Southern California, 2007), available at USC Shoah Foundation, "Collecting Testimonies," http://sfi.usc.edu/explore/col lecting_testimonies (accessed September 17, 2015).

11. Shoah Foundation Institute, *Interviewer Guidelines*, 7, 10.

12. See USC Shoah Foundation, *Testimony*, 221.

13. USC Shoah Foundation, 2007, "The Archive," www.usc.edu/schools/college/ vhi/vhf-new/1-TheArchive.htm [no longer accessible], quoted in Jeffrey Shandler, "Ho-locaust Survivors on *Schindler's List*; or, Reading a Digital Archive against the Grain," *American Literature* 85, no. 4 (2013): 5.

14. VHA interview segments were defined, at first, as narrative units of several min-utes' length each, and the duration of each unit was determined by the indexer. When this proved an inefficient method, the length of an indexing segment was set at one min-ute. In effect, this is a shift from indexing according to the equivalent of a chapter—its length variable and determined by narrative cohesiveness—to indexing according to the equivalent of a page, with a standard, if diegetically arbitrary, length.

15. VHA Online, "USC Shoah Foundation, Visual History Archive: Search," http:// vha.usc.edu/keywordsearch/keywordSearch.aspx (accessed September 17, 2015).

16. Jacques Derrida, *Archive Fever: A Freudian Impression*, trans. Eric Prenowitz (Chicago: University of Chicago Press, 1996), 17.

17. USC Shoah Foundation, *Testimony*, 331.

18. Ibid., 280, 219.

19. USC Shoah Foundation, "Technical Aspects of the Project," http://sfi.usc.edu/ preservation/technical.php (accessed April 3, 2013). See also Hriday Balachandran, Sam Gustman, Christopher Ho, and Luke Sheppard, "Shoah Foundation Architecture," Shoah Foundation Institute for Visual History and Education, University of Southern California, September 21, 2009, http://web.stanford.edu/group/dlss/pasig/PASIG_October 2009/Day2/Shoah-Foundation-Architecture-final.pdf (accessed August 26, 2016).

20. See USC Shoah Foundation, *Testimony*, 250.

21. See, e.g., the discussion of the Shoah Foundation's 2004 video *Giving Voice:*

Today's Kids Get Real about Bias, in Jeffrey Shandler, *Jews, God, and Videotape: Religion and Media in America* (New York: New York University Press, 2009), 116–18.

22. USC Shoah Foundation, *Testimony*, 237, 254, 237.

23. Los Angeles Museum of the Holocaust, "Interactive Exhibits," http://www.la moth.org/visitor-information/guide-to-the-museum/interactive-technology-and-the/ (accessed January 11, 2015).

24. "VHA Online," http://vhaonline.usc.edu (accessed September 24, 2015). This site, launched in 2012, enables public access to about 1,600 videos of interviews with Holocaust survivors and witnesses, along with the Archive's search mechanism.

25. USC Shoah Foundation, "About/IWitness," http://iwitness.usc.edu/SFI/About .aspx (accessed January 3, 2015).

26. USC Shoah Foundation, "Testimonies from North Africa and the Middle East," http://sfi.usc.edu/collections/holocaust/name (accessed August 1, 2016).

27. These include 912 interviews conducted by Jewish Family and Children's Services Holocaust Center, based in California, and 1,179 interviews from eight Canadian-based collections. VHA Online, "Search," http://vhaonline.usc.edu/search (accessed August 29, 2016).

28. The VHA includes interviews with 269 survivors of the 1915–23 Armenian genocide, 10 interviews with survivors of the 1978–96 Guatemalan genocide, 30 interviews with survivors of the 1937 Nanjing massacre, and 66 survivors of the 1994 genocide against the Tutsi in Rwanda. VHA Online, "Experience Groups," http://vhaonline.usc .edu/biosearch/bioSearch (accessed August 29, 2016).

29. USC Shoah Foundation, *Testimony*, 328.

30. See the website of the joint project Echoes and Reflections, which provides resources on Holocaust education to American teachers; http://echoesandreflections.org (accessed May 12, 2015).

31. USC Shoah Foundation, *Testimony*, 317.

32. USC Shoah Foundation, "External Advisory Committee Plans Next Phase of Visual History Archive Program," July 22, 2016, https://sfi.usc.edu/news/2016/07/11854 -external-advisory-committee-plans-next-phase-visual-history-archive-program (accessed August 9, 2016).

33. For an English translation of *Bilder fun a provints-rayze* [Scenes from a provincial journey], see *The I. L. Peretz Reader*, ed. Ruth R. Wisse (New Haven, CT: Yale University Press, 2002), 1/–84.

34. On the An-sky expedition, see Gabriella Safran, *Wandering Soul: The Dybbuk's Creator, S. An-sky* (Cambridge, MA: Harvard University Press, 2010), especially chap. 8; Eugene M. Avrutin et al., eds., *Photographing the Jewish Nation: Pictures from S. An-sky's Ethnographic Expeditions* (Waltham, MA: Brandeis University Press, 2009).

35. On YIVO, see Lucy S. Dawidowicz, *From That Place and Time: A Memoir, 1938–1947* (New Brunswick, NJ: Rutgers University Press, 2008); Barbara Kirshenblatt-Gimblett, Marcus Moseley, and Michael Stanislawski, introduction to *Awakening Lives: Autobiographies of Jewish Youth in Poland before the Holocaust*, ed. Jeffrey Shandler (New Haven, CT: Yale University Press, 2002), xi–xliv.

36. On Soviet scholarship, see, e.g., Gennady Estraikh, *Soviet Yiddish: Language Planning and Linguistic Development* (Oxford: Clarendon Press, 1999); Mark Slobin, ed., *Old Jewish Folk Music: The Collections and Writings of Moshe Beregovski* (Philadelphia: University of Pennsylvania Press, 1982).

37. On the Joint Distribution Committee, see Yehuda Bauer, *My Brother's Keeper: A History of the American Jewish Joint Distribution Committee, 1929–1939* (Philadelphia: Jewish Publication Society, 1974).

38. See Samuel D. Kassow, *Who Will Write Our History? Emanuel Ringelblum, the Warsaw Ghetto, and the Oyneg Shabes Archive* (Bloomington: Indiana University Press, 2007); Lucjan Dobroszycki, ed., *The Chronicle of the Łódź Ghetto, 1941–1944* (New Haven, CT: Yale University Press, 1984).

39. On *Life Is with People,* see Barbara Kirshenblatt-Gimblett, introduction to *Life Is with People: The Culture of the Shtetl,* by Mark Zborowski and Elizabeth Herzog (1952; repr., New York: Schocken, 1995), ix–xlviii.

40. On *yizker-bikher,* see Jack Kugelmass and Jonathan Boyarin, eds., *From a Ruined Garden: The Memorial Books of Polish Jewry* (Bloomington: Indiana University Press, 1998).

41. See Marvin Herzog et al., *The Language and Culture Atlas of Ashkenazic Jewry,* vol. 1: *Historical and Theoretical Foundations,* vol. 2: *Research Tools,* and vol. 3: *The Eastern Yiddish–Western Yiddish Continuum* (Tübingen: Max Niemeyer, 1992, 1995, 2000). For the *LCAAJ* online, see Evidence of Yiddish Documented in European Societies (EYDES), http://www.eydes.de/ (accessed September 24, 2015).

42. Barbara Myerhoff, *Number Our Days* (New York: E. P. Dutton, 1978).

43. Tom Brokaw, *The Greatest Generation* (New York: Random House, 1998).

44. See *Time* magazine, December 31, 1999, 4, 8, 13, 18.

45. "America Remembers the Holocaust," *ABC News Nightline* [telecast], December 28, 1993.

46. Jeffrey Shandler, *While America Watches: Televising the Holocaust* (New York: Oxford University Press, 1999), 249.

47. See ibid., 240–52.

48. On countermonuments, see James E. Young, *The Texture of Memory: Holocaust Memorials and Meaning* (New Haven, CT: Yale University Press, 1993), chap. 7.

49. Shandler, *Jews, God, and Videotape,* 126.

50. On Yad Vashem, see Dorit Harel, *Facts and Feelings: Dilemmas in Designing the Yad Vashem Holocaust History Museum,* trans. Diana Rubanenko ([Israel]: D. Harel, 2010).

51. On Anne Frank remembrance, see Barbara Kirshenblatt-Gimblett and Jeffrey Shandler, eds., *Anne Frank Unbound: Media, Imagination, Memory* (Bloomington: Indiana University Press, 2012).

52. New Jersey Department of Education, "New Jersey Commission on Holocaust Education: Mandate Legislation," www.state.nj.us/njded/holocaust/about_us/mandate .html (accessed March 5, 2007).

53. Pierre Nora, "Between Memory and History: Les Lieux de Mémoire," *Representations* 26 (1989): 7–25; Pierre Nora, *Realms of Memory: Rethinking the French Past,* 3 vols. (New York: Columbia University Press, 1996–98).

54. Paul Connerton, *Bodily Practices: How Societies Remember* (Cambridge: Cambridge University Press, 1989).

55. See, e.g., Peter Novick, *The Holocaust in American Life* (New York: Houghton Mifflin, 1999), 3.

56. Young, *Texture of Memory*; Marianne Hirsch, *Family Frames: Photography, Narrative, and Postmemory* (Cambridge, MA: Harvard University Press, 1997).

57. Saul Friedländer, *Memory, History, and the Extermination of the Jews of Europe* (Bloomington: Indiana University Press, 1993); Berel Lang, *The Future of the Holocaust: Between History and Memory* (Ithaca, NY: Cornell University Press, 1999); Pierre Vidal-Naquet, *Les juifs, la mémoire et le present*, 3 vols. (Paris: Editions La Découverte, 1991–95), published in English as *The Jews: History, Memory, and the Present* (New York: Columbia University Press, 1996).

58. Dan Diner, *Beyond the Conceivable: Studies on Germany, Nazism, and the Holocaust* (Berkeley: University of California Press, 2000); Andreas Huyssen, *Twilight Memories: Marking Time in a Culture of Amnesia* (New York: Routledge, 1995); Tom Segev, *The Seventh Million: The Israelis and the Holocaust*, trans. Haim Watzman (New York: Hill and Wang, 1993); Yael Zerubavel, *Recovered Roots: Collective Memory and the Making of Israeli National Tradition* (Chicago: University of Chicago Press, 1995); Iwona Irwin-Zarecka, *Neutralizing Memory: The Jew in Contemporary Poland* (New Brunswick, NJ: Transaction, 1989); Michael Steinlauf, *Bondage to the Dead: Poland and the Memory of the Holocaust* (Syracuse, NY: Syracuse University Press, 1997); Novick, *Holocaust in American Life*.

59. Geoffrey Hartman, *The Longest Shadow: In the Aftermath of the Holocaust* (Bloomington: Indiana University Press, 1996), chap. 9; Lawrence L. Langer, *Holocaust Testimonies: The Ruins of Memory* (New Haven, CT: Yale University Press, 1991).

60. Dominick LaCapra, *History and Memory after Auschwitz* (Ithaca, NY: Cornell University Press, 1998), 8.

61. Saul Friedländer, ed., *Probing the Limits of Representation: Nazism and the "Final Solution"* (Cambridge, MA: Harvard University Press, 1992).

62. See, e.g., Deborah R. Geis, ed., *Considering "Maus": Approaches to Art Spiegelman's "Survivor's Tale" of the Holocaust* (Tuscaloosa: University of Alabama Press, 2003).

63. See, e.g., Sidra DeKoven Ezrahi, "After Such Knowledge, What Laughter?" *Yale Journal of Criticism* 14, no. 1 (2001): 287–313; Sander L. Gilman, "Is Life Beautiful? Can the Shoah Be Funny? Some Thoughts on Recent and Older Films," *Critical Inquiry* 26, no. 2 (2000): 279–308.

64. See Yosefa Loshitzky, ed., *Spielberg's Holocaust: Critical Perspectives on "Schindler's List"* (Bloomington: Indiana University Press, 1997).

65. Dotson Rader, "We Can't Just Sit Back and Hope," *Parade*, March 27, 1994, 7.

66. UNESCO, "Why Teach about the Holocaust?" (Paris: UNESCO, 2013), http://unesdoc.unesco.org/images/0021/002186/218631E.pdf (accessed December 10, 2014).

67. See Novick, *Holocaust in American Life*; Simone Schweber, *Making Sense of the Holocaust: Lessons from Classroom Practice* (New York: Teachers College Press, 2004); Shandler, *While America Watches*, chap. 8; Shandler, *Jews, God, and Videotape*, chap. 3;

Oren Baruch Stier, *Committed to Memory: Cultural Mediations of the Holocaust* (Amherst: University of Massachusetts Press, 2003).

68. Plato, "Phaedrus," trans. Alexander Nehamas and Paul Woodruff, in *Plato: Complete Works*, ed. John M. Cooper (Indianapolis: Hackett, 1997), 551–52.

69. Roland Barthes, *Camera Lucida: Reflections on Photography*, trans. Richard Howard (1981; repr., New York: Hill and Wang, 2010), 91.

70. Betsy Sparrow, Jenny Liu, and Daniel M. Wegner, "Google Effects on Memory: Cognitive Consequences of Having Information at Our Fingertips," *Science* 333 (August 5, 2011): 776, 778.

71. Alan Rosen, *The Wonder of Their Voices: The 1946 Holocaust Interviews of David Boder* (New York: Oxford University Press, 2010), 20.

72. See *Filmer la guerre, 1941–1946: Les Soviétiques face à la Shoah* (Paris: Mémorial de la Shoah, 2015).

73. See, e.g., Laura Jockusch, *Collect and Record! Jewish Holocaust Documentation in Early Postwar Europe* (New York: Oxford University Press, 2012).

74. See Edward R. Murrow, "Broadcast from Buchenwald," in US Holocaust Memorial Museum, *1945: The Year of Liberation* (Washington, DC: US Holocaust Memorial Museum, 1995), 114–15.

75. See Shandler, *While America Watches*, chap. 1.

76. See Rosen, *Wonder of Their Voices*.

77. See "Voices of the Holocaust," http://voices.iit.edu (accessed September 24, 2015).

78. For the script and audio recording of *The Battle of the Warsaw Ghetto*, see "AJC Radio, Audio Recordings and Scripts: Jewish Holiday Broadcasts, Yom Kippur," http://www.ajcarchives.org/main.php?GroupingId=4140 (accessed September 17, 2015).

79. On this episode of *Reunion*, see "Yiddish Radio Project: Siegbert Freiberg's Story," 2002, http://www.yiddishradioproject.org/exhibits/reunion/ (accessed September 17, 2015).

80. See Shandler, *While America Watches*, chap. 2.

81. See, e.g., Annette Wieviorka, *The Era of the Witness*, trans. Jared Stark (Ithaca, NY: Cornell University Press, 2006).

82. Shandler, *While America Watches*, 91.

83. See "About the Yad Vashem Archives," www1.yadvashem.org/yv/en/about/archive/about_archive_whats_in_archive.asp; Yad Vashem Collection of Testimonies, "Listing of the Record Groups in the Yad Vashem Archives," www1.yadvashem.org/yv/en/about/archive/pdf/list_of_record_groups.pdf (both accessed November 20, 2012).

84. Fewer than one hundred of these interviews were videotaped. The collections of the Center for Holocaust Studies, Documentation, and Research, including these interviews, were moved from Brooklyn to the Museum of Jewish Heritage (MJH) in 1989. The MJH undertook its own project of videotaping interviews with Holocaust survivors from 1989 to 1994. E-mails to author from Bonnie Gurewitsch, archivist/curator, Museum of Jewish Heritage—A Living Memorial to the Holocaust, New York, November 26 and 27, 2012.

85. Michele Langfield and Pam Maclean, "Multiple Framings: Survivor and Non-survivor Interviews in Holocaust Testimony," in *Memories of Mass Repression: Narrating Life Stories in the Aftermath of Atrocity*, ed. Nanci Adler, Selma Leydesdorff, Mary Chamberlain, and Leyla Neyzi (New Brunswick, NJ: Transaction, 2011), 202.

86. Amit Pinchevski, "The Audio Visual Unconscious: Media and Trauma in the Video Archive for Holocaust Testimonies, *Critical Inquiry* 39, no. 1 (Autumn 2012): 144.

87. See Joanne Weiner Rudof, "A Yale University and New Haven Community Project: From Local to Global," Fortunoff Video Archive for Holocaust Testimonies, Yale University, 2012, http://web.library.yale.edu/sites/default/files/files/local_to_global.pdf (accessed September 17, 2015).

88. Judith Miller, *One, by One, by One: The Landmark Exploration of the Holocaust and the Uses of Memory* (New York: Simon and Schuster, 1990), 273.

89. See Shandler, *While America Watches*, 184–99.

90. J. Hoberman, *Film after Film: Or, What Became of 21st Century Cinema?* (London: Verso, 2012), 4.

91. Fred Ritchin, *After Photography* (New York: W. W. Norton, 2009), 19.

92. Barbara Kirshenblatt-Gimblett, "The Electronic Vernacular," in *Connected: Engagements with Media*, ed. George E. Marcus (Chicago: University of Chicago Press, 1996), 45.

93. Daniel L. Schacter, *Searching for Memory: The Brain, the Mind, and the Past* (New York: Basic Books, 1996), 16, 34, 40–41.

Chapter 2

1. Shoshana Felman and Dori Laub, *Testimony: Crises of Witnessing in Literature, Psychoanalysis, and History* (New York: Routledge, 1992), 42.

2. Lenore Blum et al., "Tellers and Listeners: The Impact of Holocaust Narratives," in *Lessons and Legacies: The Meaning of the Holocaust in a Changing World*, ed. Peter Hayes (Evanston, IL: Northwestern University Press, 1991), 316–17.

3. Alexandra Garbarini, "Power in Truth Telling: Jewish Testimonial Strategies before the Shoah," in *Kinship, Community, and Self: Essays in Honor of David Warren Sabean*, ed. Jason Coy, Benjamin Marschke, Jared Poley, and Claudia Verhoeven (New York: Berghahn, 2014), 175.

4. See, e.g., Laura Jockusch, *Collect and Record! Jewish Holocaust Documentation in Early Postwar Europe* (New York: Oxford University Press, 2012).

5. Annette Wieviorka, *The Era of the Witness*, trans. Jared Stark (Ithaca, NY: Cornell University Press, 2006), 51, 57.

6. See, e.g., David G. Roskies, ed., *The Literature of Destruction: Jewish Responses to Catastrophe* (Philadelphia: Jewish Publication Society, 1989).

7. Barbara Kirshenblatt-Gimblett, "The Concept and Varieties of Narrative in East European Jewish Culture," in *Explorations in the Ethnography of Speaking*, ed. Richard Bauman and Joel Sherzer (Cambridge: Cambridge University Press, 1974), 284.

8. Aleida Assmann, "History, Memory, and the Genre of Testimony," *Poetics Today* 27, no. 2 (Summer 2006): 270.

9. Barbara Myerhoff, *Remembered Lives: The Work of Ritual, Storytelling, and Growing Older*, ed. Marc Kaminsky (Ann Arbor: University of Michigan Press, 1990), 233.

10. "Fortunoff Video Archive for Holocaust Testimonies: About," http://web.library .yale.edu/testimonies/about (accessed February 22, 2015).

11. Shoah Foundation Institute, *Interviewer Guidelines* (Los Angeles: University of Southern California, 2007), 10, available at "Collecting Testimonies," http://sfi.usc.edu/ explore/collecting_testimonies (accessed September 17, 2015).

12. James E. Young, *Writing and Rewriting the Holocaust: Narrative and the Consequences of Interpretation* (Bloomington: Indiana University Press, 1988), 159, 171.

13. Barbara Myerhoff, *Stories as Equipment for Living: Last Talks and Tales of Barbara Myerhoff*, ed. Marc Kaminsky and Mark Weiss (Ann Arbor: University of Michigan Press, 2007).

14. On the interrelation of video and television, see James M. Moran, *There's No Place Like Home Video* (Minneapolis: University of Minnesota Press, 2003), especially chap. 4.

15. Fortunoff Video Archive, "About the Archive: Our Concept," http://www.library .yale.edu/testimonies/about/concept.html (accessed February 22, 2015).

16. Michael Rothberg and Jared Stark, "After the Witness: A Report from the Twentieth Anniversary Conference of the Fortunoff Video Archive for Holocaust Testimonies at Yale," *History and Memory* 15, no. 1 (2003): 88.

17. Consider, e.g., the fallout in advance of the exhibition *Mirroring Evil: Nazi Imagery/Recent Art* at The Jewish Museum in New York in 2002. See, e.g., Jeanne Pearlman, "Mirroring Evil: Nazi Imagery/Recent Art Case Study: The Jewish Museum, New York City," http://animatingdemocracy.org/publications/case-studies/visual-arts#jewish museum (accessed September 18, 2015).

18. The VHA index also identifies nineteen interviews that reference *Der Führer schenkt den Juden eine Stadt* [Hitler gives a city to the Jews], a 1944 German propaganda film presenting a falsely positive image of the Terezín concentration camp.

19. Other interviewees may discuss *Schindler's List*, but their references are not listed in the index, e.g., Leopold Page, IC 293, the *Schindlerjude* who inspired Thomas Keneally's book, and Moshe Bejski, IC 23848, another *Schindlerjude*, whose interview is the longest in the VHA at almost sixteen hours.

20. In addition, twelve interviews are in Hebrew, seven in Russian, six in Spanish, five in Hungarian, four in Polish, two in German, and one each in Dutch and Greek.

21. See Jeffrey Shandler, "*Schindler's* Discourse: America Discusses the Holocaust and Its Mediation, from NBC's Miniseries to Spielberg's Film," in *Spielberg's Holocaust: Critical Perspectives on "Schindler's List*," ed. Yosefa Loshitzky (Bloomington: Indiana University Press, 1997), 153–68.

22. USC Shoah Foundation, *Testimony: The Legacy of "Schindler's List" and the USC Shoah Foundation* (New York: Newmarket Press/HarperCollins, 2014), 140.

23. See Jeffrey Shandler, *Jews, God, and Videotape: Religion and Media in America* (New York: New York University Press, 2009), 108–10.

24. "Religious Right Responds to 'Schindler's List,'" *Freedom Writer*, June 1994, http://www.publiceye.org/ifas/fw/9406/schindler.html.

25. See Shandler, "*Schindler's* Discourse," 163.

26. See Michael Janofsky, "Increasingly, Political War of Words Is Fought with Nazi Imagery," *New York Times*, October 23, 1995, A12; CNN.com, "After Rebuke, Congressman Apologizes for 'Schindler's List' Remarks," February 26, 1997, http://web.archive.org /web/20010710041119/http://www.cnn.com/US/9702/26/schindler.debate/.

27. See Stuart Elliott, "Ford Will Travel High Road with Adless 'Schindler's List,'" *New York Times*, February 21, 1997, D1, D4.

28. See, e.g., Liliane Weissberg, "The Tale of a Good German: Reflections on the German Reception of *Schindler's List*," in Loshitzky, *Spielberg's Holocaust*, 171–92.

29. See Haim Bresheeth, "The Great Taboo Broken: Reflections on the Israeli Reception of *Schindler's List* in Israel," in Loshitzky, *Spielberg's Holocaust*, 193–212.

30. Bernard Weinraub, "Islamic Nations Move to Keep Out 'Schindler's List,'" *New York Times*, April 7, 1997, www.nytimes.com/1994/04/07/movies/ islamic-nations-move -to-keep-out-schindler-s-list.html.

31. See Shandler, *Jews, God, and Videotape*, 125–27.

32. This episode of *Seinfeld*, titled "The Raincoats," first aired on NBC on April 28, 1994.

33. Eyal Zandberg, "Critical Laughter: Humor, Popular Culture and Israeli Holocaust Commemoration," *Media, Culture and Society* 28, no. 4 (2006): 572–73.

34. J. Hoberman, "Invisible Cities," *Village Voice*, September 3, 2002, http://www .villagevoice.com/film/invisible-cities-6412722.

35. Shoah Foundation Institute, *Interviewer Guidelines*, 6, 8.

36. Sia Hertsberg, IC 14139, seg. 54.

37. Ritta Silberstein, IC 24365, seg. 73.

38. Marianne Rosner, IC 24958, seg. 61.

39. Marianne Rosner, segs. 99–100. The original Hungarian lyrics to this 1933 song, "Szomorú vasárnap," also known as "Gloomy Sunday," are by László Jávor, set to a melody composed by Rezső Seress. The song was purported to induce a suicidal melancholia in some listeners.

40. See Thomas Keneally, *Schindler's List* (New York: Simon and Schuster, 1982), 240–41.

41. Roman Ferber, IC 43707, segs. 70–71.

42. John Armer, IC 3638, segs. 75–77.

43. Leon Leyson, IC 8916, seg. 159.

44. Helena Jonas Rosenzweig, IC 23626, segs. 168–69.

45. Keneally, *Schindler's List*, 7.

46. Victor Dortheimer, IC 22469, segs. 167–68.

47. Maryla Susser, IC 26484, segs. 22–23.

48. Benek Geizhals, IC 11349, seg. 62.

49. Quoted in Curt Schleier, "Steven Spielberg's New Direction," *Jewish Monthly* 108, no. 4 (1994): 12.

50. Chaskel Schlesinger, IC 1680, seg. 90.

51. Leopold Rosner, IC 17372, seg. 91.

52. Abraham Zuckerman, IC 3190, seg. 109.

53. Esther Fiszman, IC 1350, segs. 62–63.

54. Laura Hillman, IC 1208, seg. 74.

55. David Halpern, IC 34094, seg. 98.

56. George Hartman, IC 10110, seg. 57.

57. Lore Smith, IC 40685, seg. 223.

58. Harriet Solz, IC 1491, seg. 123.

59. Israel Arbeiter, IC 18588, segs. 174–76.

60. Karol Saks, IC 11374, seg. 92.

61. Zoltan Gluck, IC 12812, seg. 48.

62. Goldy Zylberszac-Junger, IC 38333, seg. 135.

63. Horst Senger, IC 9557, seg. 87.

64. Rothberg and Stark, "After the Witness," 89.

65. Noah Shenker, *Reframing Holocaust Testimony* (Bloomington: Indiana University Press, 2015), 112, 119, 125.

66. Dorit Whiteman, IC 34738, seg. 151.

67. Harriet Solz, seg. 123.

68. Something of an exception to this is Israel Arbeiter, who discusses the impossibility of providing a full account of even a single day of his wartime experience (segs. 174–76).

69. Robert Clary, IC 95; Esther Jungreis, IC 518; Tom Lantos, IC 25591; Ruth Westheimer, IC 43928. Clary and Westheimer are included in a 2015 online feature by the *Hollywood Reporter* of eleven Holocaust survivors who have worked in the entertainment industry. See "Hollywood's Last Survivors," http://www.hollywoodreporter.com/features/holocaust-survivors/ (accessed December 18, 2015). This online feature includes information about the Shoah Foundation.

70. Abraham Bomba, IC 18061; Leopold Page, IC 293; Binjamin Wilkomirski, IC 29545. On Wilkomirski, see Stefan Maechle, *The Wilkomirski Affair: A Study in Biographical Truth*, trans. John E. Woods (New York: Schocken Books, 2001).

71. Benjamin Meed, IC 50584; Simon Wiesenthal, IC 35104; Gerda Weissmann Klein, IC 9725. Klein's memoir is *All but My Life* (New York: Hill and Wang, 1957); on Citizenship Counts, see http://citizenshipcounts.org (accessed March 17, 2014).

72. The VHA index identifies 1,489 interviewees who discuss "Holocaust education," of whom 1,389 are Jewish Holocaust survivors.

73. *One Day in Auschwitz,* dir. Steve Purcell, https://www.youtube.comwatch?v=mZYgzW2fS00 (accessed December 12, 2015).

74. The documentary was aired on PBS in February 4, 1981, followed by an edited version shown on *ABC News Closeup* on July 28, 1981.

75. Imperial War Museums, "Hart-Moxon, Kitty (IWM Interview)," http://www.iwm.org.uk/collections/item/object/80016100 (accessed September 18, 2015).

76. Nadine Wojakovski, "Holocaust Memorial Day: Who Will Teach Them When We Are Gone?" *Jewish Chronicle,* January 29, 2016, http://www.thejc.com/lifestyle/lifestyle-features/152911/holocaust-memorial-day-who-will-teach-them-when-we-are-gone.

77. Kitty Hart, *I Am Alive* (London: Abelard-Schuman, 1961), 8–9.

78. Primo Levi's *Se questo è un uomo,* first published in Italian in 1947, was reissued in 1957; the first English-language edition is *If This Is a Man,* trans. Stuart Woolf (New York: Orion Press, 1959). Elie Wiesel's *La nuit,* a reworking of his Yiddish memoir *Un di velt hot geshvign* [And the world was silent] (Buenos Aires: Tsentral-farband fun poylishe yidn in Argentine, 1956), was first published in French in 1958; the first English-language edition is *Night,* trans. Stella Rodway (New York: Hill and Wang, 1960).

79. Hart, *I Am Alive,* 13, 33.

80. Ibid., 20, 10, 120.

81. Peter Morley, *A Life Rewound: Memoirs of a Freelance Producer and Director* (New Romney, UK: Bank House Books, 2010), 225.

82. Ibid., 226–27.

83. Ibid., 228.

84. Ibid., 231, 233, 234.

85. Kitty Hart, *Return to Auschwitz: The Remarkable Life of a Girl Who Survived the Holocaust* (London: Sidgwick and Jackson, 1981), back dust jacket, 14.

86. Ibid., 11–12, 20.

87. Ibid., 9.

88. Kitty Hart-Moxon, IC 45132, segs. 427, 428, 452–53.

89. Kitty Hart-Moxon, segs. 474, 512–13, 475.

90. Kitty Hart-Moxon, segs. 485, 489.

91. Hart, *I Am Alive,* 57–59.

92. *Kitty: Return to Auschwitz,* dir. Peter Morley [documentary film], Yorkshire Television, 1979. My transcription.

93. Hart, *Return to Auschwitz,* 66–67.

94. Ibid., 71–72.

95. *Kitty: Return to Auschwitz.* My transcription.

96. Kitty Hart-Moxon, segs. 158–60.

97. Deborah Schiffrin, "We Knew That's It: Retelling the Turning Point of a Narrative," *Discourse Studies* 5, no. 4 (2003): 541.

98. Kitty Hart-Moxon, segs. 507, 515.

99. Lawrence L. Langer, *Holocaust Testimonies: The Ruins of Memory* (New Haven, CT: Yale University Press, 1991), 41.

Chapter 3

1. Judith Miller, *One, by One, by One: The Landmark Exploration of the Holocaust and the Uses of Memory* (New York: Simon and Schuster, 1990), 268.

2. Flora Benveniste, IC 47902, segs. 1–2.

3. Alan Rosen, *The Wonder of Their Voices: The 1946 Holocaust Interviews of David Boder* (New York: Oxford University Press, 2010), 202, 203.

4. As cited in ibid., 209, incorporating Rosen's emendations to Boder's original transcription. The interview, which took place in Paris on August 4, 1946, can be heard at Voices of the Holocaust, http://voices.iit.edu/interviewee?doc=zgnilekB (accessed July 28, 2016).

5. Rosen, *Wonder of Their Voices,* 208–9, 202–3.

6. Boder self-published his translated transcripts over a period of years in sixteen volumes, under the collective title *Topical Autobiographies of Displaced Persons*; see Rosen, *Wonder of Their Voices*. The Zgnilek interview also testifies to Boder's own multilingualism. Like Zgnilek, Boder was not a native speaker of English. The decision to conduct the interview in this language is likely due to his lack of knowledge of Polish and Zgnilek's limited knowledge of other languages, including German, in which she could perhaps do little more than quote song lyrics, or French, though she was interviewed in Paris, where she had settled after the war.

7. Toby Blum-Dobkin, "Videotaping Holocaust Interviews: Questions and Answers from an Interviewer," *Jewish Folklore and Ethnology Review* 16, no. 1 (1994): 49.

8. Michael Silverstein, "Monoglot 'Standard' in America: Standardization and Metaphors of Linguistic Hegemony," *Working Papers and Proceedings of the Center for Psychosocial Studies* 13 (1987): 1–24.

9. After English, the numbers of Jewish Holocaust survivors who are interviewed in another language in the VHA are considerably smaller; the next largest are Russian (6,618) and Hebrew (6,278), including interviews partially in those languages.

10. See David Crystal, *English as a Global Language* (New York: Cambridge University Press, 1997).

11. See, e.g., Solomon A. Birnbaum, *Yiddish: A Survey and a Grammar* (Toronto: University of Toronto Press, 1979), 40–42.

12. Jeffrey Shandler, ed., *Awakening Lives: Autobiographies of Jewish Youth in Poland before the Holocaust* (New Haven, CT: Yale University Press, 2002), xv–xvi. Though contestants were instructed to write in their language of choice, YIVO's scholars assumed each autobiography would be written in a single language.

13. Jeffrey Shandler, *Adventures in Yiddishland: Postvernacular Language and Culture* (Berkeley: University of California Press, 2005), 18.

14. The VHA also includes ten interviews conducted in Ladino, the traditional vernacular of Sephardic Jews, and one interview in Greek and Ladino. Here, too, one may find a conceptualization of the language as emblematic of demographic and cultural loss. The much smaller number of interviews in Ladino reflects both the relative size of its speech community and the more localized extent of the Holocaust's impact on Sephardim, compared to Yiddish-speaking Jews.

15. Shandler, *Adventures in Yiddishland*, 203n1.

16. Blum-Dobkin, "Videotaping Holocaust Interviews," 49.

17. "The Stonehill Jewish Song Collection," http://www.ctmd.org/stonehill.htm (accessed July 9, 2015).

18. Avraham Novershtern, "Between Town and Gown: The Institutionalization of Yiddish at Israeli Universities," in *Yiddish in the Contemporary World: Papers of the First Mendel Friedman International Conference on Yiddish*, ed. Gennady Estraich and Mikhail Krutikov (Oxford: Legenda, 1999), 16.

19. "About AHEYM," http://www.indiana.edu/aheym/aheym-project.html (accessed August 23, 2011).

20. Dov Lewanoni, IC 19085, seg. 2.

21. Lusia Puterman, IC 12897, segs. 17, 18.

22. Cecilia de Haan, IC 32721, segs. 123–24; Blanka Nas, IC 6051, seg. 109; Ruth Sokolecki, IC 8420, seg. 52.

23. Shandler, *Adventures in Yiddishland,* 22.

24. Anne Szulmejster-Celnikier, "Code-Switching in Yiddish: A Typology," *Linguistique: Revue de la Société internationale de linguistique fonctionnelle / Journal of the International Society for Functional Linguistics* (*Linguistique*) 41, no. 2 (2005): 87.

25. Shmuel Niger, *Bilingualism in the History of Jewish Literature,* trans. Joshua A. Fogel (Lanham, MD: University Press of America, 1990), 11.

26. According to the VHA database, the languages used with Yiddish in the Archive's other bilingual interviews are Russian (in 6 interviews), Spanish (6), Hebrew (5), German (4), French (2), Polish (2), and Portuguese (1).

27. With the exception of twenty-four interviews in both Russian and Ukrainian, the numbers for all other bilingual interviews in the VHA are in the single digits for each of thirty-three different combinations, most of which include three or fewer interviews.

28. Chil Rajchman, IC 5.

29. Eva Guttman, IC 14192.

30. Chaim Bornstein, IC 18510, seg. 18.

31. Kalman Rubner, IC 7899, segs. 91–92.

32. Naomi Seidman, *Faithful Renderings: Jewish-Christian Difference and the Politics of Translation* (Chicago: University of Chicago Press, 2006), 230.

33. Jacob Meller, IC 8879, segs. 4–9, 11.

34. Masha Loen, herself a Holocaust survivor, was interviewed for the VHA (IC 42186). The language of the interview is English.

35. Shoah Foundation Institute, *Interviewer Guidelines* (Los Angeles: University of Southern California, 2007), 11, available at "Collecting Testimonies," http://sfi.usc.edu/explore/collecting_testimonies (accessed September 17, 2015).

36. Jacob Meller, seg. 84. Note Loen's use of *dir,* the familiar form of "you" (in the dative case), whereas interviews conducted in Yiddish by interviewers unacquainted with the survivor generally use the formal form (*ir/aykh*).

37. Lilly Goldstein, IC 45022, segs. 17–18.

38. Ayala Fader, *Mitzvah Girls: Bringing Up the Next Generation of Hasidic Jews in Brooklyn* (Princeton, NJ: Princeton University Press, 2009), 98–99.

39. Susa Marcusohn, IC 23098, seg. 20ff (indexing incomplete).

40. Michael Wenger, IC 16162, seg. 8.

41. Michael Wenger, tape 3, time code 26:17–26:54 (indexing incomplete). Bricha (Hebrew: "flight") was an underground organization that helped Jewish Holocaust survivors leave Europe after World War II and enter Palestine illegally.

42. Michael Wenger, tape 4, time code 10:20–10:40.

43. Leon Welbel, IC 1770, segs. 2, 5.

44. Bela Gelbard, IC 5450. Gilda Hurwitz appears on camera with other family members at the end of the interview.

45. Arlene Katz, IC 1531, segs. 106–12.

46. Barbara Kirshenblatt-Gimblett, "Traditional Storytelling in the Toronto Jewish Community: A Study in Performance and Creativity in an Immigrant Culture" (PhD diss., Indiana University, 1972), 337.

47. Sarah Bunin Benor, "Towards a New Understanding of Jewish Language in the Twenty-First Century," *Religion Compass* 2, no. 6 (2008): 1068.

48. The VHA lists thirty-seven different languages as indexing terms. Only "German language," mentioned in 347 VHA interviews, outnumbers "Yiddish language"; "Hebrew language" is mentioned in 135 interviews and Ladino in 39 interviews. The index also identifies 853 interviews as discussing "language skills" (under the larger category of "covert activities"), defined as follows: "Role that a person's knowledge of a given language or languages played in their ability to adapt to new, unfamiliar, and/or life endangering situations." In addition to "Yiddish culture," the index lists only "Ladino culture" (24 interviews) and "Roma culture" (77 interviews).

49. Alex Reifer, IC 16792, seg. 32.

50. Sidney Glucksman, IC 26276, seg. 10.

51. See, e.g., Sofia Kurtsfeld, IC 35119, seg. 22; Rozaliia Krichevskaia, IC 35800, seg. 23; Moisei Oikerman, IC 49664, seg. 70.

52. See, e.g., Miron Aleksandrovskii, IC 37388, seg. 28; Lev Bakal, IC 34759, seg. 89; Anna Frenkel, IC 38848, seg. 10; Iakov Koifman, IC 16648, seg. 17.

53. Max Wunderman, IC 24625, seg. 2.

54. Suzanne Gross, IC 22180, segs. 4–5.

55. Danielle Levy, IC 38941, seg. 17.

56. Peter Glaser, IC 21449, seg. 3.

57. Arno Cronheim, IC 21483, seg. 12.

58. Ben Zion Schuster, IC 35883, seg. 53.

59. Rose Schwartz, IC 10119, segs. 26–32.

60. Helga Alcone, IC 18663, seg. 76.

61. Esra Jurmann, IC 36824, segs. 155–56.

62. Gunter Faerber, IC 41847, seg. 35.

63. Gilbert Metz, IC 45926, seg. 45.

64. Renee Grobart, IC 3921, segs. 15–16.

65. The lyrics of this song appear in Moyshe Rikhter, *Reb Hertsele meyukhes, oder, Yekele balegole* (Lvov: Dovid Roth, 1907), 48–49.

66. Cecilia Einhorn, IC 49619, seg. 17.

67. David Faber, IC 10416, seg. 14.

68. Bronislava Fuks, IC 30401, seg. 170.

69. Fira Yezerskaya, IC 15232, segs. 41–44; translation from the Russian by Valerie Mayzelshteyn.

70. Esther Brunstein, IC 20838, seg. 35.

71. Georges Cojuc, IC 15904, seg. 88.

72. Ruth Bernard, IC 13786, seg. 22.

73. Gilbert Metz, seg. 45.

74. Stella Engel, IC 7402, seg. 73.

75. Kurt Schloss, IC 2057, seg. 38.

76. Allen Feig, IC 16852, seg. 31.

77. Lea Kronenberg, IC 32760, seg. 42.

78. Sara Fershko, IC 10825, seg. 15.

79. Masha Leon, IC 9071, seg. 21.

80. Doba Apelowicz, IC 29753, segs. 48, 49.

81. Doba Apelowicz, segs. 50–51.

82. The VHA index lists the following categories and quantities for interviews conducted entirely or partly in Yiddish: "creative works" (1), "interviewee original works" (12), "family member original works" (1), "literary recitals" (15), "musical recitals" (29). Several of these interviewees perform in more than one segment of their interviews.

83. Rywka Braun, IC 3624, segs. 127 ff.; Rut Kaplan, IC 9104, seg. 131.

84. Claude Lanzmann, *Shoah: An Oral History of the Holocaust* (New York: Pantheon, 1985), 117. Bomba was also interviewed on video by the US Holocaust Memorial Museum in 1990; see https://www.ushmm.org/wlc/search/?langcode=en&query=bomba&group= (accessed July 21, 2016).

85. Abraham Bomba, IC 18061, seg. 40.

86. Leah Wolfson, "'Is There Anything Else You Would Like to Add?': Visual Testimony Encounters the Lyric Author(s)," *South Atlantic Review* 73, no. 3 (Summer 2008): 86.

87. Abraham Bomba, seg. 40; Emil Goldbarten, IC 7722, seg. 112 ; Sophia Elbaum, IC 7914, segs. 50–53.

88. David Gutman, IC 20037, segs. 10, 12. "In a litvish derfl vayt" is also known by the title "A yidish kind" [A Jewish child]. The lyrics are by Khane Kheytin, not Szmerke Kaczerginski, as Gutman says in the video. See Yad Vashem, "A Yidish Kind—A Jewish Child," http://www.yadvashem.org/yv/en/exhibitions/music/shavli_and_kovno_a_yidish_kind.asp (accessed December 24, 2016).

89. Wolf Scheinberg, IC 14495, segs. 155–82.

90. Rywka Braun, segs. 126–29.

91. Michael Deutsch, IC 1358, seg. 133–36. There are multiple versions of this song, also known as "Kadish fun R. Levi-Yitskhok Berditshever," and several composers have set the words to music. See Ruth Rubin, *Voices of a People: The Story of Yiddish Folksong*, 2nd ed. (New York: McGraw-Hill, 1973), 234.

92. Harold Weiss, IC 22039, seg. 2.

93. Bronislavah Rabinovits, IC 19762, seg. 92.

94. Joseph Blitz, IC 15985, seg. 6.

95. Abraham Blumenthal, IC 16640, segs. 12–13.

96. Minna Grand, IC 7853, seg. 22.

97. Eva Guttman, seg. 82.

98. Eva Guttman, segs. 98–99. "Shikt a har a poyerl in vald arayn" is a cumulative song, similar to the traditional Passover song "Khad gadyo" (Aramaic: "One kid"). See also Ruth Rubin and Mark Slobin, *Yiddish Folksongs from the Ruth Rubin Archive*, ed. Chana Mlotek and Mark Slobin (Detroit, MI: Wayne State University Press, 2007), 127.

99. On Hirsh Glik's "Zog nit keyn mol," see Rubin, *Voices of a People*, 454–55.

100. Adam Brandys, IC 14457, segs. 81–82, 87. The music to "Bay mir bistu sheyn" is by Sholom Secunda. The original Yiddish lyrics are by Jacob Jacobs; the lyrics to the English version, which retains the Yiddish title, are by Sammy Cahn and Saul Chaplin.

101. Rachela Braude, IC 33567, seg. 141.

102. Sol Glaser, IC 32704, segs. 8–9.

103. Chaim Sztajer, IC 5184, segs. 221–55. The VHA adds this sequence to the interview with Adek Stein, IC 3169, segs. 291–323.

104. E-mail to author from Ena Burstin, August 31, 2014. On the museum, see Stan Marks, "Melbourne's Jewish Holocaust Museum and Research Centre, Beginnings and Evolution," *Australian Jewish Historical Society Journal* 16, no. 3 (2002): 341–50.

105. Chaim Sztajer, seg. 227.

106. Chaim Sztajer, seg. 255.

107. Chaim Sztajer, seg. 249.

108. Barbara Myerhoff, *Number Our Days* (New York: Touchstone, 1978), 144.

109. Charlotte Delbo, *Days and Memory*, trans. Rosette Lamont (Evanston, IL: Marlboro Press/Northwestern University Press, 1990), 2.

110. J. L. Austin, *How to Do Things with Words*, 2nd ed., ed. J. O. Urmson and Marina Sbisa (Cambridge, MA: Harvard University Press, 1975), 6–7.

111. Doris Sommer, ed., *Bilingual Games: Some Literary Investigations* (New York: Palgrave Macmillan, 2003), 5–6.

Chapter 4

1. Toby Blum-Dobkin, "Videotaping Holocaust Interviews: Questions and Answers from an Interviewer," *Jewish Folklore and Ethnology Review* 16, no. 1 (1994): 47.

2. Fortunoff Video Archive, "About the Archive: History," http://www.library.yale .edu/testimonies/about/history.html (accessed July 12, 2013).

3. Jeu de Paume, *Esther Shalev-Gerz* (Paris: FAGE, 2010), 90. See also "Esther Shalev-Gerz: Between Listening and Telling," http://www.shalev-gerz.net/?portfolio=between -listening-and-telling (accessed August 2, 2016).

4. I thank Dan Leshem for this observation.

5. Jeffrey A. Wolin, *Written in Memory: Portraits of the Holocaust* (San Francisco: Chronicle Books, 1997).

6. Shoah Foundation Institute, *Videographer Guidelines* (Los Angeles: University of Southern California, 2007), 4, 5, available at "Collecting Testimonies," http://sfi.usc.edu/ explore/collecting_testimonies (accessed September 17, 2015).

7. Ibid., 5, 6, 7.

8. David P. Boder, "The Displaced People of Europe: Preliminary Notes on a Psychological and Anthropological Study," *Illinois Tech Engineer* 12 (1947): 3.

9. Shoah Foundation Institute, *Videographer Guidelines*, 7.

10. Ibid.

11. Geoffrey Hartman, "Tele-suffering and Testimony in the Dot Com Era," in *Visual Culture and the Holocaust*, ed. Barbie Zelizer (New Brunswick, NJ: Rutgers University Press, 2001), 117.

12. *Nazi Concentration Camps*, National Archives and Records Administration, Washington, DC, RG 238 (National Archives Collection of World War II War Crimes Records), inventory no. 238.2. For a discussion of this film, see Jeffrey Shandler, *While America Watches: Televising the Holocaust* (New York: Oxford University Press, 1999), 20–22.

13. Wolfgang Ernst, *Digital Memory and the Archive*, ed. Jussi Parikka (Minneapolis: University of Minnesota Press, 2013), 46.

14. US Holocaust Memorial Museum videos include both a preponderance of interviews filmed against a neutral background and a smaller number of interviews filmed in homes or offices; these backgrounds are sometimes filmed in extreme soft focus. See "Browse All Oral Histories," http://www.ushmm.org/wlc/en/media_list.php ?MediaType=oh (accessed February 5, 2014).

15. Anne Rothe, *Popular Trauma Culture: Selling the Pain of Others in the Mass Media* (New Brunswick, NJ: Rutgers University Press, 2011), 36.

16. Leizer Portnoy, IC 11225, seg. 1.

17. Mayer Tremblinski, IC 40446, segs. 53–56. My translation from the Yiddish.

18. See, e.g., Sofia Abrashkevitch, IC 12345, seg. 116 (injury on arm); Anna Fishman, IC 89, seg. 55 (injury on face and head).

19. Frieda Jakubowicz, IC 31253, seg. 156.

20. Frank Burstin, IC 37151, segs. 97–98.

21. Michael Deutsch, IC 1358, seg. 90.

22. Michael Deutsch, segs. 135–38.

23. Geoffrey Hartman, "The Ethics of Witness," in *Lost in the Archives*, ed. Rebecca Comay (Cambridge, MA: Alphabet City, 2002), 494.

24. Tamara Andriushina, IC 47415, seg. 118.

25. Leon Schmetterling, IC 2659, segs. 41–43.

26. Simon Friedman, IC 11175, segs. 128–30.

27. David McNeill, Liesbet Quaeghebeur, and Susan Duncan, "IW: The Man Who Lost His Body," in *Handbook of Phenomenology and Cognitive Science*, ed. Daniel Schmicking and Shaun Gallagher (Dordrecht, the Netherlands: Springer, 2010), 539.

28. Paul Connerton, *How Societies Remember* (Cambridge: Cambridge University Press, 1989), 72.

29. Maria Berger, IC 32398, seg. 103.

30. Maria Berger, segs. 230, 231.

31. Elizabeth A. Castelli, "Persecution and Spectacle: Cultural Appropriation in the Christian Commemoration of Martyrdom," *Archiv für Religionsgeschichte* 7 (2010): 121, 123.

32. Frieda Jakubowicz, segs. 100–109.

33. Frieda Jakubowicz, seg. 113.

34. See, e.g., US Holocaust Memorial Museum photographs 59963 ("A survivor of the Buchenwald concentration camp displays his tattooed arm") and 66201 ("Jewish women liberated from a factory in Mehlteuer display their tattoos"), http://digitalassets .ushmm.org/photoarchives/ (accessed September 18, 2015).

35. See, e.g., *Marked: Holocaust Survivors and Their Tattoos*, a photographic exhibition by Andrew Harris, Jewish Holocaust Centre, Melbourne, October 14–December 22, 2010, http://www.jhc.org.au/gallery/marked/ (accessed February 22, 2015).

36. Aharon Feldberg, IC 7165, seg. 112.

37. See, e.g., Martha Becher, IC 11877, seg. 75.

38. Adela Becher IC 37975, segs. 45, 157–58.

39. Carl Willner, IC 1899, seg. 141.

40. Joseph Carver, IC 9262, segs. 169–70. The photograph of the number that Carver mentions in the interview does not appear among the photographs and documents at the conclusion of his interview.

41. Kate Arnon, IC 4835, segs. 58, 77.

42. Kitty Hart-Moxon, IC 45132, seg. 150.

43. Kitty Hart-Moxon, segs. 470–71.

44. Kitty Hart-Moxon, seg. 476.

45. Kitty Hart-Moxon, seg. 520.

46. A photograph in which Kitty appears, taken in a displaced persons camp in 1946, shows her left forearm is bandaged, where, according to the caption, "she tried to remove her Auschwitz tattoo." Louette Harding, "Kitty Hart-Moxon: One Woman Shares Her Extraordinary Story as a Concentration Camp Survivor," *Daily Mail Online*, January 24, 2012, http://www.dailymail.co.uk/home/you/article-2087826/Kitty-Hart -Moxon-woman-shares-extraordinary-story-concentration-camp-survivor.html.

47. Voices of the Holocaust, "David P. Boder Interviews Nelly Bondy: August 22, 1946; Paris, France," http://voices.iit.edu/interview?doc+bondyN&display=bondyN_en (accessed February 25, 2015). Ellipses per the original.

48. See Ken Johnson, "An Artist Turns People into His Marionettes," *New York Times*, November 29, 2009, http://www.nytimes.com/2009/11/30/arts/design/30zmijewski.html (accessed December 15, 2016).

49. E-mail to author from Yishay Garbasz, June 19, 2011.

50. David G. Roskies, compiler, *Nightwords: A Liturgy on the Holocaust* (New York: CLAL, 2000), 51.

51. Jodi Rudoren, "Proudly Bearing Elders' Scars, Their Skin Says 'Never Forget,'" *New York Times*, September 30, 2012, http://www.nytimes.com/2012/10/01/world/middle east/with-tattoos-young-israelis-bear-holocaust-scars-of-relatives.html?pagewanted =all&_r=0 (accessed September 18, 2015).

52. Jeffrey Shandler, review of *The Holocaust Object in Polish and Polish-Jewish Culture*, by Bożena Shallcross (Bloomington: Indiana University Press, 2011), *AJS Review* 36, no. 1 (April 2012): 176–77.

53. Shoah Foundation Institute, *Videographer Guidelines*, 8, emphases in original.

54. Leszek Allerhand, IC 27779, segs. 233–42.

55. Lucy Smith, IC 10744, segs. 113–18.

56. Leizer Portnoy, segs. 74–89. These items are also filmed according to the VHA protocols at the end of the video.

57. This is in keeping with instructions to interviewers; see Shoah Foundation Insti-

tute, *Interviewer Guidelines* (Los Angeles: University of Southern California, 2007), 14, available at "Collecting Testimonies," http://sfi.usc.edu/explore/collecting_testimonies (accessed September 17, 2015).

58. Abraham Slucki, IC 723, segs. 234–35.

59. Shoah Foundation Institute, *Videographer Guidelines*, 6. In some interviews, the filming of objects precedes the interview with the survivor's family members.

60. The VHA also indexes under a separate search term seventy-six interviews in which survivors display baptismal certificates.

61. Sophie Billys, IC 10850, seg. 112; Eugene Winnik, IC 2746, seg. 100; Susanne Cohn, IC 52043, seg. 262; Esther Rosman, IC 14218, seg. 165.

62. Maurice Elbaum, IC 9317, seg. 108.

63. Sara Kaye, IC 23573, seg. 112; John Koenigsberg, IC 29548, seg. 70; Eugene Winnik, seg. 100.

64. Maurice Baron, IC 32481, seg. 103.

65. Daisy Shapiro-Rieke, IC 48028, seg. 18.

66. Edith Simblist-Polak, IC 5215, seg. 134.

67. Sonia Liberman, IC 2530, seg. 176.

68. Irene Barkan, IC 2039, seg. 112; Maurice Baron, seg. 103; Eugene Winnik, segs. 45–46.

69. Edith Simblist-Polak, seg. 134; Irma Grundland, IC 5502, seg. 80; Teresa Gericke IC 32466, seg. 119.

70. Leo Turkell, IC 41507, segs. 16–19.

71. Leo Turkell, seg. 31.

72. Leo Turkell, seg. 161.

73. Leo Turkell, seg. 162.

74. I have altered the spelling of both Sokolecki's and Sędzikowa's surnames from their listing in the VHA, after conferring with Crispin Brooks, curator of the USC Shoah Foundation's Visual History Archive.

75. Ruth Sokolecki, IC 8420, segs. 53–57.

76. Ruth Sokolecki, segs. 57–60.

77. Ruth Sokolecki, seg. 67.

78. Ruth Sokolecki, segs. 96–102.

79. Ruth Sokolecki, seg. 118.

80. See Ruth Sokolecki, seg. 114.

81. On folk religion, see Don Yoder, "Toward a Definition of Folk Religion," *Western Folklore* 33, no. 1 (January 1974): 1–15.

82. Joshua Trachtenberg, *Jewish Magic and Superstition: A Study in Folk Religion* (1939; repr., New York: Atheneum, 1979), viii.

83. Ruth Sokolecki, seg. 8. The Czortkower Rebbe at the time was either Rabbi Yisroel Friedman, who led this Hasidic community from 1903 until his death in 1934, or one of his two sons, who succeeded him.

84. See, e.g., the documentary film *Keep the Connection*, dir. Anat Meskanes (DVD), Raab Holocaust Education Center, Michlalah Jerusalem College, n.d. According to its

promotional website, "The film presents fascinating and moving testimony of Jews who, even in the shadow of death—in the ghettoes, in the concentration camps, and on the death marches—continued to don tefillin [Hebrew: 'phylacteries'] as part of their courageous and tenacious spiritual struggle." http://zachor.michlalah.edu/english/produc tions/movies-2.asp (accessed March 30, 2014).

85. Ruth Sokolecki, segs. 108–9. She presumably sent her letter to Pope John Paul II, whose papacy ran from 1978 to 2005.

86. Ruth Sokolecki, seg. 61.

87. Ruth Sokolecki, seg. 95.

88. Ruth Sokolecki, seg. 62.

89. Chaim Potok, *My Name Is Asher Lev* (New York: Knopf, 1972).

90. See Neta Stahl, *Other and Brother: Jesus in the 20th-Century Jewish Literary Landscape* (Oxford: Oxford University Press, 2012); Susan Tumarkin Goodman, *Chagall: Love, War, and Exile* (New Haven, CT: Yale University Press, 2013).

91. Roland Barthes, *Camera Lucida: Reflections on Photography*, trans. Richard Howard (1981; repr., New York: Hill and Wang, 2010), 26. I thank Louis Kaplan and Melissa Shiff for this insight.

92. Günther Thomas, "Witness as a Cultural Form of Communication: Historical Roots, Structural Dynamics, and Current Appearances," in *Media Witnessing: Testimony in the Age of Mass Communication*, ed. Paul Frosh and Amit Pinchevski (New York: Palgrave Macmillan, 2011), 92.

Conclusion

1. Primo Levi, *Il sistema periodico* (Turin: Einaudi, 1975), published in English as *The Periodic Table*, trans. Raymond Rosenthal (New York: Schocken, 1984); Georges Perec, *W ou Le souvenir d'enfance* (Paris: Denoël, 1975), published in English as *W, or the Memory of Childhood*, trans. David Bellos (London: Harvill, 1988).

2. Paul C. Adams, "Television as a Gathering Place," *Annals of the Association of American Geographers* 82, no. 1 (1992): 117–35.

3. Rachel N. Baum, "Remediating the Body of the Witness: Holocaust Testimonies in New Media," paper presented at the International Conference on Bearing Witness More Than Once, Humboldt-Universität, Berlin, March 16, 2016, n.p. Cited with permission.

4. Wulf Kansteiner, "Genocide Memory, Digital Cultures, and the Aestheticization of Violence," *Memory Studies* 7, no. 4 (October 2014): 403–8.

5. *Antoinette Burton*, "'An Assemblage/Before Me': Autobiography as Archive," *Journal of Women's History* 25, no. 2 (Summer 2013): 185.

6. Wolfgang Ernst, *Digital Memory and the Archive*, ed. Jussi Parikka (Minneapolis: University of Minnesota Press, 2013), 84.

7. Todd Presner, "The Ethics of the Algorithm: Close and Distant Listening to the Shoah Foundation Visual History Archive," in *History Unlimited: Probing the Ethics of Holocaust Culture*, ed. Todd Presner, Claudio Fogu, and Wulf Kansteiner (Cambridge, MA: Harvard University Press, 2016), 200–201.

8. When the Shoah Foundation announced in 2016 its five-year plan to implement a new platform and interface for the VHA, the Foundation also explained that it was considering how "user-generated content . . . will be integrated into the VHA over the next several years," including "what kinds of content will be allowed into the VHA, how it will be vetted, and the ethics of permitting members of the public to contribute to the VHA." USC Shoah Foundation, "External Advisory Committee Plans Next Phase of Visual History Archive Program," July 22, 2016, https://sfi.usc.edu/news/2016/07/11854 -external-advisory-committee-plans-next-phase-visual-history-archive-program (accessed August 9, 2016).

9. USC Shoah Foundation, "Partnership with ProQuest to Increase Access to Visual History Archive," March 9, 2016, https://sfi.usc.edu/news/2016/03/11051-partnership -proquest-increase-access-visual-history-archive.

10. José van Dijck, *Mediated Memories in the Digital Age* (Stanford, CA: Stanford University Press, 2007), 2.

INDEX

Number Our Days (Myerhoff), 24, 47
The Number Project (Garbasz), 147–148, 149f
Numbered (Doron), 147

objects, in videos: Christian, 154–165, 156f, 159f, 201n60; as evidence of history, 166; Jewish, 163–164, 201–202n84; photographs, 12, 130, 142, 150–156, 172; and survivor narratives, 104–105, 151–153; as talismans, 156–157, 160–165; VHA format for, 150–154, 156; yellow star badges, 153, 155, 156f
Oirich, Alan, 100
One Day in Auschwitz (film), 68, 69f
One Survivor Remembers (film), 67
online access to VHA. *See* VHA online access

Page, Leopold (Poldek Pfefferberg), 57–58, 67, 190n19
paper "slates," in VHA videos, 98, 99f
Partisan Song, 119
Perec, Georges, 168z
Peretz, Yitskhok, 21
performances, in recordings. *See* recitals
Pfefferberg, Poldek (Leopold Page), 57–58, 67, 190n19
photography: of injuries, 139; memory and, 30–31, 34, 39–40; of objects, 12, 130, 150, 153, 154–156, 172; in survivor interviews, 12, 130, 142, 150–156, 172; of tattoos, 142–144, 143f, 146; VHA protocols for, 12, 150–152, 153
Pinchevski, Amit, 38
Pinger, Jacob, 157
Portnoy, Debbi, 133
Portnoy, Leizer, 130, 152
postvernacular language, 95; Yiddish as, 117, 123, 124
Potok, Chaim, 165
Presner, Todd, 173

Puszczynska, Kasia, 157
Puterman, Lusia, 94

Quaeghebeur, Liesbet , 137

Rabinovits, Bronislavah, 117
radio dramas, 37
Rajchman, Chil, 96, 101
Rappaport, Naomi, 97
Rappoport, Shloyme-Zanvl (An-sky, S.), 21–22, 22f
Realms of Memory (Nora), 30
recitals in interviews, 113–122; bar mitzvah speech, 117; index categories for, 113, 131, 197n82; with model of Treblinka camp, 120–121, 120f; musical performances, 114–115, 117–119, 197n88, 197n91, 197n98, 198n100; as performative speech, 122; placement of, 116–118; poetry, 113–114, 116–118, 116f, 122; prompted by interviewers, 119; of written texts, 113–116; Yiddish in, 113–115, 117–122, 124
recording practices: in Boder's audio inteviews, 88–89, 128; by Fortunoff Archive, 128, 130, 184n7; by US Holocaust Memorial Museum, 130, 199n14. *See also* VHA videotaping protocols
Reich, Walter, 63–64
Reifer, Alex, 106–107
retold narratives: significance of, 48–49, 83–84; in VHA interviews, 70–71, 77–84, 160
return travel: to Auschwitz, 70, 72–74, 78–82; to survivors' hometowns, 160
Return to Auschwitz (Hart), 70, 74–76, 80–81
Reunion (radio program), 37
Ritchin, Fred, 39
Robisa, Mr., 143f
Roma, 11. *See also* "gypsy"
Rosen, Alan, 35, 89

STANFORD STUDIES IN JEWISH HISTORY AND CULTURE

Edited by David Biale and Sarah Abrevaya Stein

This series features novel approaches to examining the Jewish past in the form of innovative work that brings the field into productive dialogue with the newest scholarly concepts and methods. Open to a range of disiplinary and interdisciplinary approaches from history to cultural studies, this series publishes exceptional scholarship balanced by an accessible tone that illustrates histories of difference and addresses issues of current urgency. Books in this list push the boundaries of Jewish Studies and speak compellingly to a wide audience of scholars and students.

For a complete listing of titles in this series,
visit the Stanford University Press website, www.sup.org.

Printed in the USA
CPSIA information can be obtained
at www.ICGtesting.com
LVHW051332300823
756741LV00005B/46

9 781503 602892